KETOGENIC SLOW COOKER COOKBOOK

525 Easy & Delicious Low-carb Keto Recipes
to Lose Weight Fast and Feel Great
by Mastering the Healthy Tastes of slow cooking

Joaquine Jouvessac

© **Copyright 2021 - All rights reserved.**

The content contained within this book may not be reproduced, duplicated or transmitted without direct writ- ten permission from the author or the publisher. Under no circumstances will any blame or legal responsibility be held against the publisher, or author, for any damages, reparation, or monetary loss due to the information contained within this book. Either directly or indirectly.

Legal Notice:

This book is copyright protected. This book is only for personal use. You cannot amend, distribute, sell, use, quote or paraphrase any part, or the content within this book, without the consent of the author or publisher.

Disclaimer Notice:

Please note the information contained within this document is for educational and entertainment purposes only. All effort has been executed to present accurate, up to date, and reliable, complete information. No warranties of any kind are declared or implied. Readers acknowledge that the author is not engaging in the rendering of legal, financial, medical or professional advice. The content within this book has been derived from various sources. Please consult a licensed professional before attempting any techniques outlined in this book. By reading this document, the reader agrees that under no circumstances is the author responsible for any losses, direct or indirect, which are incurred as a result of the use of information contained within this document, including, but not limited to, errors, omissions, or inaccuracies.

TABLE OF CONTENTS

INTRODUCTION 10
BREAKFAST 16

1. Cherry Tomatoes Thyme Asparagus Frittata 16
2. Healthy Low Carb Walnut Zucchini Bread....16
3. Savory Creamy Breakfast Casserole 17
4. Low-Carb Cauliflower Breakfast Casserole ..17
6. Onion Broccoli Cream Cheese Quiche.........18
7. Delicious Thyme Sausage Squash 18
8. Scrambled Eggs with Smoked Salmon 18
9. Garlic-Parmesan Asparagus Slow cooker.....19
10. Persian Omelet Slow cooker 19
11. Broccoli and Cheese Stuffed Squash............19
12. Garlic Butter Keto Spinach 20
13. Keto Slow cooker Tasty Onions 20
14. Slow cooker Benedict Casserole 20
15. Crustless Slow cooker Spinach Quiche 21
16. Broccoli Gratin with Parmesan and Cheese..21
17. Slow cooker Cream Cheese French Toast....21
18. Keto Slow cooker Turkey Stuffed Peppers ..22
19. Cheesy Garlic Brussels Sprouts 22
20. Blueberry Pancake 22
21. Sausage and Peppers..................................23
24. Breakfast Sausage Casserole......................24
25. Stuffed Breakfast Peppers..........................24
26. Cheese and Sausage Breakfast....................25
27. Mushrooms, Cauliflower, and Zucchini Toast ... 25
28. Keto Egg Muffin 25
29. Cauliflower Casserole with Goat Cheese......26
30. Greek Eggs Breakfast Casserole..................26
31. Slow cooker Turkish Breakfast Eggs 26
32. Mexican Style Breakfast Casserole 27
33. Almond Lemon Blueberry Muffins 27
34. Healthy Veggie Omelet 27
35. Pesto Scrambled Eggs 28
36. Kale and Cheese Omelet 28
37. Egg Casserole with Cheeses, Sun-Dried Tomatoes, and Herbs 28
38. Kale, Mushrooms, And Caramelized Onions 29
39. Egg and Cheese Casserole with Chayote Squash 29
40. Sausage and Kale Strata 29
41. Egg Cake with Peppers, Kale, and Cheddar .29
42. Feta Cheese and Kale Breakfast Casserole ..30
43. Cauliflower and Ham Casserole 30
44. Sausage-Stuffed Eggplants..........................30
45. Zucchini Sausage Breakfast "Bake" 30
46. Cheddar Jalapeno Breakfast Sausages 31
47. Chocolate Peanut Butter Breakfast Bars 31
48. Arugula Cheese Herb Frittata.....................31
49. Yummy Cauliflower Crust Breakfast Pizza....32
50. Parmesan Zucchini Paprika & Ricotta Frittata .. 32
51. Cauliflower Slow Breakfast Casserole..........32
52. Breakfast Casserole...................................33
53. Bacon-Mushroom Breakfast 33
54. Keto Sausage & Egg Casserole....................34
55. Egg & Mushroom Breakfast 34
56. Egg, Spinach, and Ham Breakfast Casserole 34
57. Keto Soup with Miso 35
58. Slow cooker Pumpkin Coconut Breakfast Bars. 35
59. Overnight Eggs Benedict Casserole 36
60. Vanilla Pumpkin Bread...............................36
61. Almond Banana Bread 36
62. Sage Cauliflower Casserole 37
63. Pear and Maple Oatmeal 37
64. Almond & Strawberry Oatmeal....................37
65. Cheddar Sausage Cauliflower 37
66. Coconut Quinoa Mix...................................38
67. Cheddar Cauliflower...................................38
68. Cheddar & Bacon Casserole 38
69. Cream Cheese Banana Breakfast 39
70. Carrots and Zucchini Oatmeal 39
71. Cheesy Tater Tot Casserole 39
72. Banana & Blueberry Oats...........................40
73. Peanut Butter Oatmeal 40
74. Cranberry Apple Oats................................40
75. Coconut Raisins Oatmeal 40

SOUPS 42

76. Creamy Harvest Pumpkin Bisque 42
77. Zesty White Chicken Chili...........................42
78. Tuscan Zucchini Stew 43
79. Melt-In-Your-Mouth Beef Stew 43
80. Mexican Chorizo Enchilada Soup 44

81. Hearty Chicken Soup with Veggie Noodles ... 44
82. Superb Chicken, Bacon, Garlic Thyme Soup 44
83. Delightful Chicken-Chorizo Spicy Soup 45
84. Delectable Spearmint Liver and Lamb Heart Soup 45
85. Lovely Lentil Sausage Soup 46
86. Tasty Corned Beef and Heavy Cream Soup .. 46
87. Beef dijon 46
88. Toscana Soup 47
89. Rabbit Stew 47
90. Beef Stew 47
91. Chicken & Kale Soup 48
92. Chicken Chili Soup 48
93. Creamy Smoked Salmon Soup 48
94. Lamb and Rosemary Stew 48
95. Lamb and Eggplant Stew 49
96. Bacon and Cauliflower Soup 49
97. Pot Roast Soup 49
98. Southern Paleo Slow cooker Chili 50
99. Dairy-Free Chili Chicken Soup 50
100. Low Carbohydrate Slow cooker Soup 50
101. Slow Cooker Cheeseburger Soup 51
102. Delicious Kernel Corn Taco Soup 51
103. Sumptuous Ham and Lentil Consommé 51
104. Beef Barley Vegetable Soup 52
105. Delicious Chicken Soup with Lemongrass 52
106. Slow cooker Pork Stew with Tapioca 52
107. Delicious Bacon Cheese Cauliflower Soup ... 53
108. Tasty Tomato Soup with Parmesan and Basil ... 53
109. Luscious Carrot Beef Stew with Cauliflower . 53
110. Delicious Lasagna Consommé 54
111. Cheese Broccoli Bouillabaisse 54
112. Chicken Thigh & Breast Low Carb Soup ... 54
113. Beef & Pumpkin Stew 55
114. Pepper Jalapeno Low Carb Soup 55
115. Lean Beef & Mixed Veggies Soup 56
116. Chicken & Tortilla Soup 56
117. Chicken Chile Verde 56
118. Cauliflower & Ham Cauliflower Stew 57
119. Minestrone Ground Beef Soup 57
120. Vegetable Stew 57
121. Delicious Beef Meatball and Sour Cream Soup 58
122. Veggie Soup with Minty Balls 58
123. Chicken Cordon Bleu Soup 58
124. Ginger Pumpkin Soup 59
125. Pumpkin Soup 59
126. SPINACH Soup 59
127. Mexican Chicken Soup 60
128. Butternut Squash Soup 60
129. Cabbage, Kielbasa, and Onion Soup 60
130. Broccoli Cheddar Soup 60
131. Cream of Zucchini Soup 61
132. Tomato Soup 61
133. Mexican Corn and Shrimp Soup 61
134. Tuscan Fish Soup 62
135. Seafood Stir-Fry Soup 62
136. Chicken Kale Soup 62
137. Pork Ramen 63
138. Shrimp Fajita Soup 63
139. Chinese Oyster Soup 63
140. Vegan Cream of Mushroom Soup 63
141. Veggie-Noodle Soup 64

VEGETABLES 65

142. Keto Spinach-Feta Quiche 65
143. Cheesy Zucchini-Asparagus Frittata 65
144. Slow-Cooked Yellow Squash Zucchini 66
145. Parmesan Mushrooms 66
146. Mashed Garlic Cauliflower 66
147. Elbows Casserole 66
148. Cheesy Beer Dip Salsa 67
149. Brussels Sprout Dip 67
150. Braised Cabbage 67
151. Homemade Vegetable Stock 68
152. Vegetable Korma 68
153. Stuffed Eggplant 68
154. Bacon Cheddar Broccoli Salad 68
155. Cracked-Out Keto Slaw 69
156. Zucchini Pasta 69
157. Twice Baked Spaghetti Squash 69
158. Mushroom Risotto 70
159. Vegan Bibimbap 70
160. Avocado Pesto Kelp Noodles 70
161. Creamy Curry Sauce Noodle Bowl 70
162. Spinach Artichoke Casserole 71
163. Asparagus with Lemon 71
164. Zucchini and Yellow Squash 71

165. Gluten-Free Zucchini Bread 72
166. Eggplant Parmesan 72
167. Zucchini Lasagna 72
168. Cauliflower Bolognese on Zucchini Noodles 72
169. Garlic Tomato, Zucchini, and Yellow Squash ... 73
170. Parmesan Zucchini and Tomato Gratin 73
171. Slow-Cooked Summer Vegetables 73
172. Cheesy Cauliflower Garlic Bread 73
173. Cheesy Cauliflower Gratin 74
174. Creamy Ricotta Spaghetti Squash 74
175. Creamy Keto Mash 74
176. Garlic Ranch Mushrooms 75
177. Easy Creamed Spinach 75
178. Zoodles with Cauliflower-Tomato Sauce 75
179. Spaghetti Squash Carbonara 75
180. Summery Bell Pepper + Eggplant Salad 76
181. Zucchini Pasta 76
182. Chinese Broccoli 76
183. Slow Cooker Spaghetti Squash 76
184. Mushroom Stew 77
185. Cabbage Steaks 77
186. Mashed Cauliflower 77
187. Bacon-Wrapped Cauliflower 78
188. Cauliflower Casserole 78
189. Cauliflower Rice 78
190. Curry Cauliflower 79
191. Garlic Cauliflower Steaks 79
192. Zucchini Gratin 79
193. Eggplant Gratin 79
194. Moroccan Eggplant Mash 80
195. Sautéed Bell Peppers 80
196. Garlic Artichoke 80
197. Spinach Portobello 81
198. Kale Quiche 81

FISH & SHELLFISH 82

199. Butterfly Tilapia 82
200. Tuna and Olive-Orange Tapenade 82
201. Heart and Tuna Stuffed Mushroom 83
202. Etouffee 83
203. Poached Salmon 84
204. Cod And Vegetables 84
205. Mahi-Mahi Taco Wraps 84
206. Shrimp Scampi 85
207. Shrimp Tacos 85
208. Fish Curry 85
209. Salmon with Creamy Lemon Sauce 86
210. Salmon with Lemon-Caper Sauce 86
211. Spicy Barbecue Shrimp 87
212. Lemon Dill Halibut 87
213. Coconut Cilantro Curry Shrimp 87
214. Shrimp in Marinara Sauce 88
215. Garlic Shrimp 88
216. Salmon Poached in White Wine and Lemon .88
217. Lemon Pepper Tilapia 89
218. Poached Salmon in Court-Bouillon Recipe ...89
219. Braised Squid with Tomatoes and Fennel 89
220. Fish and Tomatoes 89
221. Hot Crab Dip 90
222. Cod and Zoodles Stew 90
223. Slow-Cooked Tilapia 90
224. Salmon Lemon and Dill 90
225. Creamy Crab Zucchini Casserole 91
226. Lobster Bisque 91
227. Clam Chowder 91
228. Soy-Ginger Steamed Pompano 91
229. Vietnamese Braised Catfish 92
230. Chili Shrimps 92
231. Fennel Scented Fish Stew 92
232. Spicy Shrimp Fra Diavolo 93
233. Shrimp Scampi with Spaghetti Squash 93
234. Tuna and White Beans 93
235. Slow cooker Swordfish Steaks 93
236. Sweet and Sour Shrimp 94
237. Lazy Man's Seafood Stew 94
238. Halibut Vinaigrette 94
239. Slow cooker Crab Legs 95
240. Asian-Inspired Ginger Tuna Steaks 95
241. Rustic Buttered Mussels 95
242. Boiled Lobster Tails 95
243. Creamy Shrimp Chowder 96
244. Hearty White Fish Stew 96
245. Catfish Creole 96
246. Cod with Fennel and Tomatoes 97
247. Thai Shrimp Rice 97
248. Caribbean Shrimp 97
249. Herb Lemon Cod 98
250. White Fish Fillet with Tomatoes 98

#	Recipe	Page
251.	Coconut Fish Curry	98
252.	Louisiana Shrimp	99
253.	Cajun Corn Shrimp Chowder	99
254.	BBQ Shrimp	99
255.	Delicious Shrimp Fajitas	99
256.	Spicy Shrimp	100
257.	Healthy Lime Salmon	100
258.	Shrimp Pasta	100
259.	Tasty Shrimp Curry	101
263.	Capers Salmon	102
264.	Easy Cilantro Lime Salmon	102
265.	Creamy Curried Shrimp	102
266.	Herb Flounder Fillet	102
267.	Onion White Fish Fillet	103
268.	Lemon Halibut	103
269.	Garlicky Shrimp	103
270.	Hot Shrimp	104
271.	Easy Lemon Dill Salmon	104
272.	Salmon and Asparagus	104

POULTRY 106

#	Recipe	Page
273.	Amazing Sour Cream Chicken	106
274.	Fantastic Lemon Thyme Chicken	106
275.	Delightful Balsamic Oregano Chicken	107
276.	Tantalizing Chicken Breast with Artichoke Stuffing	107
277.	Chipotle Barbecue Chicken	107
278.	Colombian Chicken	107
279.	Spicy Shredded Chicken Lettuce Wraps	108
280.	Slow cooker Ranch Chicken	108
281.	Coconut Cilantro Shrimp Curry	108
282.	Slow Teriyaki Chicken	109
283.	Slow cooker Butter Masala Chicken	109
284.	Chicken with Bacon Gravy	109
285.	Garlic Butter Chicken with Cream Cheese	110
286.	Cheesy Adobo Chicken	110
287.	Lemongrass coco-chicken	110
288.	Ketogenic Chicken Tikka Masala	110
289.	Balsamic Chicken Thighs	111
290.	Garlic Dill Chicken Thighs	111
291.	Chicken Lo Mein	111
292.	Ethiopian Doro Watt Chicken	112
293.	Delicious Southwest Chicken	112
294.	Flavors Peanut Butter Chicken	112
295.	Easy Salsa Chicken	113
296.	Greek Lemon Chicken	113
297.	Easy Chicken Noodles	113
298.	Orange Chicken	114
299.	Delicious BBQ Chicken	114
300.	Parmesan Chicken Rice	114
301.	Queso Chicken Tacos	114
302.	Easy Mexican Chicken	115
303.	Mustard Mushroom Chicken	115
304.	Herb Chicken Breasts	115
305.	Balsamic Chicken	115
306.	Creamy Chicken Penne	116
307.	Tasty Chicken Fajita Pasta	116
308.	Moist & Juicy Chicken Breast	116
309.	Asian Chicken	117
310.	Flavorful Chicken Casserole	117
311.	Chicken Orzo	117
312.	Garlic Herb Roasted Pepper Chicken	118
313.	Slow Cook Turkey Breast	118
314.	Simple Chicken & Mushrooms	118
315.	Lemon Herb Chicken	119
316.	Creamy Chicken Curry	119
317.	Taco Chicken	119
318.	Cider-braised Chicken	120
319.	Butter Chicken	120
320.	Spicy Chili Chicken	120
321.	Pesto Chicken	121
322.	Rosemary Turkey Breast	121
323.	Garlic Olive Chicken	121
324.	Delicious Chickpea Chicken	121
325.	Creamy Italian Chicken	122
326.	Chicken and Vegetables	122
327.	Chicken Gyros	122
328.	Slow cooker Creamy Salsa Chicken	122
329.	Pizza Casserole	123
330.	Moist and Spicy Pulled Chicken Breast	123
331.	Whole Roasted Chicken	123
332.	Simple Chicken Chili	124
333.	Chicken in Salsa Verde	124
334.	Duck in sauce	124
335.	CHILI GROUND DUCK	124
336.	SPICY HEALTHY CHICKEN	125
337.	GINGERY CHICKEN	125

PORK & LAMB 126

338. Mouth-Watering Minced Pork Zucchini Lasagna 126
339. Beautiful BBQ Ribs 127
340. Gorgeous Coconut Turmeric Pork Curry ...127
341. Kalua Pork 127
342. Tasty Cuban Mojo Pork 127
343. Slow Cooker Pork Loin 128
344. Green Chili Pork 128
345. Thai Curried Pork 128
346. Chinese 5-Spice Pork Ribs 129
347. Pork Stew with Oyster Mushrooms 129
348. Paprika Pork Tenderloin 129
349. Pork Carnitas 130
350. Lemongrass Coconut Pulled Pork 130
351. Pork Loin Roast with Onion Gravy 130
352. Lime Pork Chops 131
353. Chili Pulled Pork 131
354. Ranch Pork Chops 131
355. Delicious Coconut Pork 132
356. Spicy Adobo Pulled Pork 132
357. Tasty Pork Tacos 132
358. Stuffed peppers 132
359. Onion Pork Chops 133
360. Creamy Pork Chops 133
361. Scrumptious Bay Leaf Pork Roast Shoulder 133
362. Dressed Pork Leg Roast 134
363. Seriously Delicious Lamb Roast 134
364. Kashmiri Lamb Curry 134
365. Tasty Lamb Shoulders 135
366. Thyme Lamb Chops 135
367. Garlic Herbed Lamb Chops 135
368. Barbacoa Lamb 136
369. Lamb Provençal 136
370. Greek Style Lamb Shanks 136
371. Lamb with Mint & Green Beans 137
372. Delicious Balsamic Lamb Chops 137
373. Succulent Lamb 137
374. Tarragon Lamb & Beans 138
375. Apricot Pulled Pork 138
376. Pork Chops with Cumin Butter and Garlic .138
377. New Mexico Carne Adovada 138
378. Smoky Pork with Cabbage 139
379. Simple Roasted Pork Shoulder 139

380. Flavors Pork Chops 139
381. Pork Loin with Peanut Sauce 140
382. Creamy Herbed Tenderloin 140
383. Classic Sausage and Peppers 140
384. Ribs with a Kick 141
385. Salsa Pork Chops 141
386. Curried Pork Chops 142
387. Poultry Seasoned Pork Chops 142
388. No Stick Ribs 142
389. Macadamia Crusted Pork Steaks 142
390. Feta Meatballs 143
391. Lemon Lamb and Asparagus 143
392. Lamb of Italy with Brussels Sprouts 144
393. Asian Lamb 144
394. Moroccan Lamb 145
395. Moroccan Lamb Stew 145

BEEF 146

396. Slow cooker Beef Roast 146
397. Beef and Cabbage Roast 146
398. Coffee- Braised Brisket 147
399. Beef Shoulder in BBQ Sauce 147
400. Homemade Meatballs and Spaghetti Squash ...147
401. Bacon Cheeseburger Casserole 148
402. BBQ Beef Burritos 148
403. Beef Ribs 149
404. Braised Oxtails 149
405. Brisket & Onions 149
406. Italian Ragu 150
407. Pot Roast Beef Brisket 150
408. Amazing Spiced Beef Eye SLOW COOKED 150
409. Beef Stroganoff 151
410. Chili Lime Beef 151
411. Beef in Sauce 151
412. Beef with Greens 151
413. Beef and Scallions Bowl 152
414. Balsamic Beef 152
415. Balsamic Beef ROAST 152
416. Onion Beef 153
417. Cilantro Beef 153
418. Beef and Artichokes Bowls 153
419. Mustard Beef 153
420. Beef Masala 154
421. Beef Sauté with Endives 154

422. Sweet Beef	154
423. Thyme Beef	155
424. Hot Beef	155
425. Beef Chops with Sprouts	155
426. Beef Ragout with Beans	156
427. Braised Beef	156
428. Coconut Beef	156
430. Beef Roast	157
431. Lunch Beef	157
432. Braised Beef Strips	157
433. Beef Dip	158
436. Beef and Sauerkraut Bowl	158
437. Easy Meatball Slow cooker	159
438. Beef & Broccoli	159
439. Chili Colorado	159
440. Mississippi Roast	160
441. Peppers & Onion Steak	160
442. Beef Chimichangas	160
443. Artichoke Pepper Beef	160
444. Italian Beef Roast	161
445. Olive Feta Beef	161
446. Olive Artichokes Beef	161
447. Sriracha Beef	162
448. Garlic Tomatoes Chuck Roast	162
449. Stuffed Bell Peppers	162
450. Butter Beef	162

DESSERTS 164

451. Hot Fudge Cake	164
452. Fudgy Secret Brownies	164
453. Black and Blue Cobbler	165
454. Baked Custard	165
455. Maple Pot de Crème	165
456. Slow-Cooker Pumpkin Pie Pudding	166
457. Tasty Apple and Cranberry Dessert	166
458. Caramel Pecan Pudding	166
459. Mouth-Watering Chocolate Cake	166
460. Fabulous Peanut Vanilla Chocolate Cake	167
461. Poppy Seed Butter Cake	167
462. Lemon Cake	167
463. Raspberry & Coconut Cake	168
464. Chocolate Cheesecake	168
465. Crème Brule	169
466. Peanut Butter & Chocolate Cake	169
467. Keto Coconut Hot Chocolate	169
468. Ambrosia	169
469. Dark Chocolate and Peppermint Pots	170
470. Creamy Vanilla Custard	170
471. Coconut, Chocolate, Almond Truffle Bake	170
472. Peanut Butter, Chocolate, And Pecan Cupcakes	171
473. Vanilla and Strawberry Cheesecake	171
474. Coffee Creams with Toasted Seed Crumble Topping	171
475. Lemon Cheesecake	172
476. Apple, Avocado, and Mango Bowls	172
477. Ricotta Cream	172
478. Tomato Jam	173
479. Green Tea Pudding	173
480. Coconut Jam	173
481. Banana Bread	173
482. Bread and Berries Pudding	174
483. Candied Lemon	174
484. Tapioca and Chia Pudding	174
485. Chocolate and Liquor Cream	174
486. Dates and Rice Pudding	175
487. Butternut Squash Sweet Mix	175
488. Almonds, Walnuts, and Mango Bowls	175
489. Tapioca Pudding	175
490. Berries Salad	176
491. Fresh Cream Mix	176
492. Pears and Apples Bowls	176
493. Macadamia Fudge Truffles	176
494. Chocolate Covered Bacon Cupcakes	177
495. Chocolate & Berry Layered Jars	177
496. Choco-peanut Cake	177
497. Slow cooker Apple Pudding Cake	178
498. Slow cooker Brownie Cookies	178
499. Slow cooker Chocolate Caramel Monkey Bread	179
500. Slow Cooker Coffee Cake	179
501. Slow Cooker Apple Pear Crisp	179
502. Key Lime Dump Cake Recipe	180
503. Slow cooker Cherry Dump Cake Recipe	180
504. Slow cooker Pumpkin Spice Cake Recipe	180
505. Slow cooker Blueberry Dump Cake Recipe	181
506. Slow cooker Strawberry Dump Cake Recipe	181
507. Sugar-Free Chocolate Molten Lava Cake	181

508. Blueberry Lemon Custard Cake 182
509. Slow-Cooked Pumpkin Custard 182
510. Almond Flour Mocha Fudge Cake 182
512. Slow Cooker Bread Pudding 183
513. Tiramisu Bread Pudding 183
514. Slow Cooker Sugar-Free Dairy-Free Fudge .....
    183
515. Poppy Seed-Lemon Bread 184
516. Nutmeg-Infused Pumpkin Bread 184
517. Slow cooker Baked Apples Recipe 185
518. Salty-Sweet Almond Butter and Chocolate 185
519. Coconut Squares with Blueberry Glaze 185
520. Chocolate and Blackberry Cheesecake Sauce .
    185
521. Berry & Coconut Cake 186
522. Cocoa Pudding Cake 186
523. Wonderful Raspberry Almond Cake 186
524. Scrumptious Chocolate Cocoa Cake 187
525. Chocolate and strawberries Cupcakes 187

INTRODUCTION

Welcome to The Ketogenic Slow Cooker Cookbook! You're soon going to discover many recipes that will allow you to follow a ketogenic diet keeping you healthy and freeing your time. Just put the ingredients in the slow cooker in the morning and it'll take care of your diet with some juicy meals for the night!

Keto diet, in its simplest definition, is a diet that has low carbohydrate content and, in contrast, a much higher content of fat. It is also commonly referred to as the LCHF diet - low carb, high fat.

In the keto diet, the dietary expectation of you is to make sure your intake of protein-rich foods is appropriate, as this is the very foundation of the diet. There was a time when it was used as a treatment method for many types of ailments and diseases, whereas currently, it has garnered vast amounts of popularity for its effectiveness in weight loss, especially for those who are taking up the keto diet specifically to lose weight.

All around the world, it is being hailed by experts and specialists as the diet that can change your life with the smallest of alterations made in your dietary habits and lifestyle.

Normally, what happens in your body is that it burns carbohydrates to generate energy for you to function on. While on the keto diet, fats do the job of being the primary source of energy. Any person with a normal diet ends up consuming enormous quantities of carbohydrates, be it as a choice or something they consider to be the general approach to diets. But it is important to note that when carbohydrates are converted into glucose, the vast amounts of carbs turn into outrageous amounts of glucose that are released into your bloodstream, which in turn leads to weight gain.

This is where the ketogenic diet steps in. The replacement of carbohydrates with fats turns them into ketones. And in turn – ketones become the principal energy source.

Keto and its Types

There isn't just one - there are many types of ketogenic diets. Some of the common forms are:
- High-Protein Ketogenic Diet: In this diet, the protein quantity dominates the rest of the components of the diet.
- Targeted Ketogenic Diet (TKD): Here, you are permitted to include carbohydrates in the diet with the condition that you engage in an intense and regular workout regime.
- Standard Ketogenic Diet (SKD): This diet's standard meal is supposed to consist of 5% carbs, 75% fat, and 20% proteins.
- Cyclical Ketogenic Diet (CKD): Intake days that are high in carbohydrates are allowed.

Benefits
- A ketogenic diet is a powerful tool for people who wish to lose weight due to the reduction in carbohydrate intake that forces the body to burn fat rather than carbohydrates for energy.
- There is even science-based speculation a keto diet can increase wellbeing and help treat or decrease the probability of cancer.
- Mental clarity and raised cognition
- Increased energy amounts
- Less appetite
- Steady blood sugar levels from small to no ingestion of carbohydrates
- Improved skin particularly for anyone who has acne
- Enriched cholesterol and cholesterol levels
- Hormone regulation and not as severe PMS symptoms

What is Ketosis?

Ketosis is a metabolic condition where your body utilizes fat and ketones instead of sugar (glucose) as its principal fuel source.

Glucose is stored on your liver and published as necessary for energy. But after carb ingestion has been exceptionally low for one or two days, these sugar stores become depleted. Your liver can earn some sugar from amino acids from the protein that you consume using a process called gluconeogenesis, but not nearly sufficient to fulfill the requirements of your mind, which demands a continuous fuel source.

SLOW COOKING: YOUR WAY TO HEALTH

Having a slow cooker is an effortless, fast, and most flexible cooking method at any home. It didn't require you any cooking skills; it saves your time as the slow cooker does all the working time for you, truly safe and can even be used in any places like a hotel room or even student dorm as they possess a kettle like-shape, making it more portable than a stove. So, in the following guides, we will be talking about some of the helpful basic ways to guarantee that you get the best out of your slow cooker.

What Is It?

The slow cooker appeared in 1970 and was marketed as a bean cooker. But as it was modified, people started to use it to heat food and keep it warm for prolonged periods. And look how far we've come; people are cooking delicious healthy meals in it. It is a perfect small kitchen appliance that consists of a glass lid, porcelain, or a ceramic pot (it is inside of the heating unit) and, of course, a heating element. The modern Slow Cooker could be of an oval or round shape and various sizes, from small to large. All the Slow Cookers have two settings: LOW (it corresponds to the temperature of 200°F mostly) and HIGH (up to 300°F). The WARM selection that is among the majority of the Slow cookers' options nowadays allows keeping the prepared dishes warm for a long time. Some of the Slow Cooker models have a timer that will enable you to control cooking time if you are busy.

Why Slow Cook?

Some of the reasons to use a slow cooker include:

•Enhances flavor: Cooking ingredients over several hours with spices, herbs, and other seasonings creates vegetables and proteins that burst with delicious flavors. This slow process allows the flavors to mellow and deepens for an enhanced eating experience.

•Saves time: Cooking at home takes a great deal of time: prepping, sautéing, stirring, turning the heat up and down, and watching the meal so that it does not over-or undercook. If you're unable to invest the time, you might find yourself reaching for convenience foods instead of healthy choices. Slow cookers allow you to do other activities while the meal cooks. You can put your ingredients in the slow cooker in the morning and come home to a perfectly cooked meal.

•Convenient: Besides the time-saving aspect, using a slow cooker can free up the stove and oven for other dishes. This can be very convenient for large holiday meals or when you want to serve a side dish and entrée as well as a delectable dessert. Clean-up is simple when you use the slow cooker for messy meals because most inserts are nonstick or are easily cleaned with a little soapy water, and each meal is prepared in either just the machine or using one additional vessel to sauté ingredients. There is no wide assortment of pots, pans, and baking dishes to contend with at the end of the day.

•Low heat production: If you have ever cooked dinner on a scorching summer afternoon, you will appreciate the low amount of heat produced by a slow cooker. Even after eight hours of operation, slow cookers do not heat your kitchen and you will not be sweating over the hot stovetop. Slow cookers use about a third of the energy of conventional cooking methods, just a little more energy than a traditional light bulb.

•Supports healthy eating: Cooking your food at high heat can reduce the nutrition profile of your foods, breaking down and removing the majority of vitamins, minerals, and antioxidants while producing unhealthy chemical compounds that can contribute to disease. Low-heat cooking retains all the goodness that you want for your diet.

•Saves Money: Slow cookers save you money because of the low amount of electricity they use and because the best ingredients for slow cooking are the less expensive cuts of beef and heartier inexpensive vegetables. Tougher cuts of meat—brisket, chuck, shanks—break down beautifully to fork-tender goodness. Another cost-saving benefit is that most 6-quart slow cookers will produce enough of a recipe to stretch your meals over at least two days. Leftovers are one of the best methods for saving money.

The Right Cooker for You

Slow cookers have changed a lot over the years. These days you can purchase models that range from very simple models to ones that look like they should be on a space station. When buying the right model for your needs, you have to consider what you are cooking, how many portions, and if you will be home during the cooking process. All these factors are important when deciding on the size, shape, and features of your slow cooker.

Size and Shape

Slow cookers come in a multitude of sizes and shapes, so it is important to consider your needs and what will work best for the type of food prepared on the keto diet. Some models range from ½-quart to large 8-quart models and everything in-between.

The small slow cookers (½-quart to 2-quart) are usually used for dips or sauces, as well as recipes designed for one person. Medium-sized slow cookers (3-quart to 4-quart) are great for baking or for meals that create food for two to three people. The slow cooker recommended for most of the recipes in this book is the 5-quart to 6-quart model because it is perfect for the large cuts of meat on the keto diet and can prepare food for four people, including leftovers. The enormous 7-quart to 8-quart appliance is meant for very large meals. If you have money in your budget, owning both a 3-quart and 6-quart model would be the best of both worlds.

When it comes to shapes, you will have to decide between round, oval, and rectangular. Round slow cookers are fine for stews and chili but do not work well for large pieces of meat. These should probably not be your choice. Oval and rectangular slow cookers both allow for the ingredients you will regularly use that are large, like roasts, ribs, and chops, and have the added advantage of fitting loaf pans, ramekins, and casserole dishes, as well. Some desserts and bread are best cooked in another container placed in the slow cooker, and you will see several recipes in this book that use that technique.

Features

Now that you know the size and shape of the recommended slow cooker, it is time to consider what you want this appliance to do for you. Depending on your budget, at a minimum, you want a slow cooker with temperature controls that cover warm, low, and high, as well as a removable insert. These are the primary features of the bare-bones models that will get the job done. However, if you want to truly experience a set-it-and-forget-it appliance that creates the best meals possible in this cooking environment, you might want to consider the following features:

- Digital programmable controls: You can program temperature, when the slow cooker starts, how long it cooks, and when the slow cooker switches to warm.
- Glass lid: These are heavier and allow you to look into the slow cooker without removing them, so there is little heat loss. Opt for a lid with clamps, and you can transport your cooked meal easily to parties and gatherings if needed.
- Temperature probe: Once you have a slow cooker with this feature, you will wonder how you cooked previously without it. The temperature probe allows you to cook your meat, poultry, and egg dishes to an exact temperature and then switches to warm when completed.
- Precooking feature: Some models have a precooking feature that allows you to brown your meat and poultry right in the insert. You will still have to take the time to do this step, but you won't have a skillet to clean afterward.

1. Slow Cooking Tips & Tricks

Slow cookers are simple to use, but you can increase your success with a few tips and techniques. In the following list, some tips are suggestions and some should be considered more seriously for safety or health reasons. The intent is to provide the best information possible so that your meals are delicious and easy.

Always read the user manual and any other literature. You will find an assortment of instructions included in the slow-cooker box so take the time to sit down and read everything completely before using a new device. You might think you know how everything works, but each model is a little different and it is best to be informed about all of the things your slow cooker can do.

Grease the insert of the slow cooker before cooking. Cleaning a slow cooker insert can be a challenge, so grease the insert, even for soups and stews. You don't want to scrub the insert with abrasive brushes or scraping bits of cooked-on food off because you will wreck its nonstick surface.

Add dairy and herbs at the end of the cooking process. Dairy and fresh herbs do not hold up well during long cooking times. Dairy splits and creates a grainy, unpleasant texture, and herbs lose their flavor, color, and texture. Always add these ingredients at the end.

Always cut your ingredients into similar-sized pieces. Slow cookers are not meant to be used for staggered cooking recipes such as stir-fries where the more delicate ingredients are added last to avoid overcooking. Evenly sized pieces mean your ingredients will be ready at the same time and your meals will be cooked evenly.

Adjust your seasonings. Slow cookers can have an unexpected effect on herbs and spices so it is important to taste and adjust at the end of the process. Some spices, such as curry or cayenne, can get more intense, while the long cooking time can reduce the impact of dried herbs. It is best to hold off on too much salt until the very end as well because it will get stronger.

Never use frozen meats or poultry. The ingredients in slow cookers need to reach 140°F within 4 hours for food safety, so large cuts of meat or poultry should be fully thawed. You can add small frozen items like meatballs to a slow cooker because these can come to temperature within this time range.

Place your insert right from the refrigerator into the slow cooker. When you remove your previously prepared meal from the refrigerator, let the insert sit out at room temperature for 30 minutes or so to avoid cracking it with extreme temperature changes. Also, never remove the hot insert from your slow cooker and place it on a cold surface.

Resume cooking after a power outage of over two hours. Power outages can happen in any season, and for food-safety reasons, you have to err on the side of caution. If an outage lasts for more than two hours, especially during the first few hours of the cooking time, you need to discard the food because the amount of time spent in the food danger zone (40°F to 140°F) will have been too long. If the outage is less than two hours and it occurs after your food has been cooking for at least four hours, then you can resume cooking until the end of the original time or transfer the food to a pot or casserole dish and finish it on the stove or in the oven. When in doubt, throw the food out.

Use the recommended cooking times in high altitudes. As with most other cooking methods, slow cookers need more cooking time if you live above an altitude of 3,000 feet. The liquid in the slow cooker will simmer at a lower temperature so high-heat settings are recommended, or if you can program the slow cooker, then set it to maintain the food at 200°F or higher. You can also use a temperature probe set to 165°F internal temperature if your slow cooker has this feature.

2. Ketogenic Diet Tips and Tricks

In this part, we are going to be giving you tips and tricks to make this diet work better for you and help you get an idea of routines that you can put in place for yourself.

Tip number one that is so important is DRINK WATER! This is vital for any diet that you're on, and you need it if not on one as well. However, this vital tip is crucial on a keto diet because when you are eating fewer carbs, you are storing less water, meaning that you are going to get dehydrated very easily. You should aim for more than the daily amount of water; however, remember that drinking too much water can be fatal as your kidneys can only handle so much at once. While this has mostly happened to soldiers in the military, it does happen to dieters as well, so it is something to be aware of.

Along with that same tip is to keep your electrolytes. You have three major electrolytes in your body. When you are on a keto diet, your body is reducing the amount of water that you store. It can be flushing out the electrolytes that your body needs as well, and this can make you sick. Some of the ways that you can battle this is by either salting your food or drinking bone broth. You can also eat pickled vegetables.

Eat when you're hungry instead of snacking or eating constantly. This is also going to help, and when you focus on natural foods and healthy foods, this will help you even more. Eating foods that are processed is the worst thing you can do for fighting cravings, so you should get into the routine of trying to eat whole foods instead.

Another routine that you can get into is setting a note somewhere that you can see it that will remind you of why you're doing this in the first place and why it's important to you. Dieting is hard, and you will have moments of weakness where you're wondering why you are doing this. Having a reminder will help you feel better, and it can help with your perspective.

Tracking progress is something that straddles the fence. A lot of people say that this helps many individuals and you can celebrate your wins; however, as everyone is different and they have different goals, progress can be slower in some than others. This can cause others to be frustrated and sad, as well as wanting to give up. One of the very most important things to remember is that while progress takes time, and you shouldn't get discouraged if you don't see results right away. With most diets, it takes at least a month to see any results. So, don't get discouraged and keep trying if your body is saying that you can. If you can't, then you will need to talk to your doctor and see if something else is for you.

You should make it a daily or everyday routine to try and lower your stress. Stress will not allow you to get into ketosis, which states that keto wants to put you in. The reason for this being that stress increases the hormone known as cortisol in your blood, and it will prevent your body from being able to burn fats for energy. This is because your body has too much sugar in your blood. If you're going through a really high period of stress right now in your life, then this diet is not a great idea. Some great ideas for this would be getting into the habit or routine of taking the time to do something relaxing, like walking and making sure that you're getting enough sleep, which leads to the following routine that you need to do.

You need to get enough sleep. This is so important not just for your diet but also for your mind and body as well. Poor sleep also raises those stress hormones that can cause issues for you, so you need to get into the routine of getting seven hours of sleep at night on the minimum and nine hours if you can. If you're getting less than this, you need to change the routine you have in place right now and make sure that you establish a new routine where you are getting more sleep. As a result, your health and diet will be better.

3. Conversion Tables

Oven Temperatures

FAHRENHEIT	CELSIUS (C)
250°F	120°C
300°F	150°C
325°F	165°C
350°F	180°C
375°F	190°C
400°F	200°C
425°F	220°C
450°F	230°C

Volume Equivalents (Liquid)

US STANDARD	METRIC (APPROXIMATE)
1/8 TSP	0.5 ML
¼ TSP	1 ML
½ TSP	2 ML
¾ TSP	4 ML
1 TSP	5 ML
1 TBSP	15 ML
¼ CUP	59 ML
⅓ CUP	79 ML
½ CUP	118 ML
⅔ CUP	156 ML
¾ CUP	177 ML
1 CUP	235 ML
2 CUPS OR 1 PINT	475 ML
3 CUPS	700 ML
4 CUPS OR 1 QUART	1 L
½ GALLON	2 L
1 GALLON	4 L

Weight Equivalents

US STANDARD	METRIC (APPROXIMATE)
½ OUNCE	15 GRAMS
1 OUNCE	30 GRAMS
2 OUNCES	60 GRAMS
4 OUNCES	115 GRAMS
8 OUNCES	225 GRAMS
12 OUNCES	340 GRAMS
16 OUNCES OR 1 POUND	455 GRAMS

Volume Equivalents (Dry)

US STANDARD	US STANDARD (OUNCES)	METRIC (APPROXIMATE)
2 TBSP	1 FL. OZ.	30 ML
¼ CUP	2 FL. OZ.	60 ML
½ CUP	4 FL. OZ.	120 ML
1 CUP	8 FL. OZ.	240 ML
1½ CUPS	12 FL. OZ.	355 ML
2 CUPS OR 1 PINT	16 FL. OZ.	475 ML
4 CUPS OR 1 QUART	32 FL. OZ.	1 L
1 GALLON	128 FL. OZ.	4 L

BREAKFAST

1. **CHERRY TOMATOES THYME ASPARAGUS FRITTATA**

Preparation Time: 15 minutes

Cooking Time: 6 hours

Servings: 6

Ingredients:
- 2 tbsp unsalted butter, ghee, or extra-virgin olive oil
- 12 large eggs
- ¼ cup heavy (whipping) cream
- 1 tbsp minced fresh thyme
- ½ tsp kosher salt
- ¼ tsp freshly ground black pepper
- 1½ cups shredded sharp white Cheddar cheese, divided
- ½ cup grated Parmesan cheese
- 16 cherry tomatoes
- 16 asparagus spears

Directions:

Glaze the inside of the slow cooker with butter.

In the slow cooker, beat the eggs, then whisk in the heavy cream, thyme, salt, and pepper.

Add ¾ cup of Cheddar cheese and the Parmesan cheese and stir to mix.

Sprinkle the remaining ¾ cup of Cheddar cheese over the top. Scatter the cherry tomatoes over the frittata.

Arrange the asparagus spears decoratively over the top. Cook within 6 hours on low or 3 hours on soaring. Serve.

Nutrition:

Calories: 370

Fat: 29g

Carbs: 4g

Protein: 24g

2. **HEALTHY LOW CARB WALNUT ZUCCHINI BREAD**

Preparation Time: 15 minutes

Cooking Time: 3 hours & 10 minutes

Servings: 12

Ingredients:
- 3 eggs
- 1/2 cup walnuts, chopped
- 2 cups zucchini, shredded
- 2 tsp vanilla
- 1/2 cup pure all-purpose sweetener
- 1/3 cup coconut oil, softened
- 1/2 tsp baking soda
- 1 1/2 tsp baking powder

- 2 tsp cinnamon
- 1/3 cup coconut flour
- 1 cup almond flour
- 1/2 Tsp salt

Directions:

Mix the almond flour, baking powder, cinnamon, baking soda, coconut flour, and salt in a bowl. Set aside.

Whisk eggs, vanilla, sweetener, and oil in another bowl.

Put dry batter to the wet and fold well. Add walnut and zucchini and fold well.

Pour batter into the silicone bread pan. Place the bread pan into the slow cooker on the rack.

Cook on high within 3 hours. Cut the bread loaf into slices and serve.

Nutrition:

Calories: 174

Fat: 15.4g

Carb: 5.8g

Protein: 5.3g

3. SAVORY CREAMY BREAKFAST CASSEROLE

Preparation Time: 15 minutes

Cooking Time: 6 hours

Servings: 8

Ingredients:

- 1 tbsp unsalted butter, Ghee
- 10 large eggs, beaten
- 1 cup heavy (whipping) cream
- 1½ cups shredded sharp Cheddar cheese, divided
- ½ cup grated Romano cheese
- ½ tsp kosher salt
- ¼ tsp freshly ground black pepper
- 8 ounces thick-cut ham, diced
- ¾ head broccoli, cut into small florets
- ½ onion, diced

Directions:

Grease the slow cooker with butter.

Whisk the eggs, heavy cream, ½ cup of Cheddar cheese, the Romano cheese, salt, and pepper inside the slow cooker.

Stir in the ham, broccoli, and onion. Put the remaining 1 cup of Cheddar cheese over the top.

Cook within 6 hours on low or 3 hours on high. Serve hot.

Nutrition:

Calories: 465

Fat: 36g

Carbs: 7g

Protein: 28g

4. LOW-CARB CAULIFLOWER BREAKFAST CASSEROLE

Preparation Time: 15 minutes

Cooking Time: 6 hours

Servings: 6

Ingredients:

- 1 tbsp unsalted butter, Ghee
- 12 large eggs
- ½ cup heavy cream
- 1 tsp kosher salt
- ½ tsp ground black pepper
- ½ tsp ground mustard
- 1 head cauliflower, shredded or minced
- 1 onion, diced
- 10 ounces cooked sausage links, sliced
- 2 cups shredded Cheddar cheese, divided

Directions:

Grease the slow cooker with butter.

Beat the eggs, then whisk in heavy cream, 1 tsp of salt, ½ tsp of pepper, and the ground mustard in a large bowl.

Spread about one-third of the cauliflower in an even layer at the bottom of the cooker.

Layer one-third of the onions over the cauliflower, then one-third of the sausage, and top with ½ cup of Cheddar cheese. Season with salt and pepper. Repeat twice.

Pour the egg batter evenly over the layered ingredients, then sprinkle the remaining ½ cup Cheddar cheese on top—Cook within 6 hours on low. Serve hot.

Nutrition:

Calories: 523

Fat: 40g

Carbs: 7g

Protein: 33g

5. WALNUT RASPBERRY MUFFINS

Preparation Time: 15 minutes

Cooking Time: 3 hours

Servings: 3

Ingredients:

- 1 cup almond flour
- 1 cup walnuts, chopped
- 1 egg
- 3 drops of natural sweetener
- ¼ cup fresh raspberries
- ¼ tsp lemon zest, grated
- 2 tbsp butter, melted
- ½ tsp baking powder

Directions:
Whisk the egg into a bowl. Add the rest of the fixing, and mix.

Pour batter into lined or greased muffin molds. Pour up to ¾ of the cup.

Pour 6 ounces of water into the slow cooker. Place an aluminum foil at the bottom, and the muffin molds inside.

Set the slow cooker on 'High' within 2-3 hours. Let it cool in the cooker for a while.

Remove from the cooker. Loosen the edges of the muffins. Invert on to a plate and serve.

Nutrition:
Calories: 223
Fat: 21g
Carb: 5g
Protein: 6 g

6. ONION BROCCOLI CREAM CHEESE QUICHE

Preparation Time: 15 minutes
Cooking Time: 2 hours & 25 minutes
Servings: 8

Ingredients:
- 9 eggs
- 2 cups cheese, shredded and divided
- 8 oz cream cheese
- 1/4 tsp onion powder
- 3 cups broccoli, cut into florets
- 1/4 tsp pepper
- 3/4 tsp salt

Directions:
Add broccoli into the boiling water and cook for 3 minutes. Drain well and set aside to cool.

Add eggs, cream cheese, onion powder, pepper, and salt in a mixing bowl and beat until well combined.

Spray slow cooker from inside using cooking spray.

Add cooked broccoli into the slow cooker then sprinkle half a cup cheese.

Pour egg mixture over broccoli and cheese mixture.

Cook on high within 2 hours and 15 minutes.

Once it is done, then sprinkle the remaining cheese and cover for 10 minutes or until cheese melted. Serve.

Nutrition:
Calories 296
Fat 24.3g
Carb 3.9g
Protein 16.4g

7. DELICIOUS THYME SAUSAGE SQUASH

Preparation Time: 15 minutes
Cooking Time: 6 hours
Servings: 4

Ingredients:
- 2 tbsp extra-virgin olive oil
- 14 ounces smoked chicken sausage, thinly sliced
- ¼ cup chicken broth
- 1 onion, halved and sliced
- ½ medium butternut squash, peeled, diced
- 1 small green bell pepper, strips
- ½ small red bell pepper, strips
- ½ small yellow bell pepper, strips
- 2 tsp snipped fresh thyme or ½ tsp dried thyme, crushed
- ½ tsp kosher salt
- ½ tsp freshly ground black pepper
- 1 cup shredded Swiss cheese

Directions:
Combine the olive oil, sausage, broth, onion, butternut squash, bell peppers, thyme, salt, and pepper in the slow cooker. Toss to mix. Cook within 6 hours on low.

Before serving, sprinkle the Swiss cheese over the top, cover, and cook for about 3 minutes more to melt the cheese.

Nutrition:
Calories: 502
Fat: 38g
Carbs: 12g
Protein: 27g

8. SCRAMBLED EGGS WITH SMOKED SALMON

Preparation Time: 15 minutes
Cooking Time: 2 hours
Servings: 6

Ingredients:
- Smoked salmon ¼ lb.
- Eggs12 pcs fresh
- Heavy cream½ cup
- Almond flour¼ cup
- Salt and black pepper at will
- Butter2 tbsp
- Fresh chives at will

Directions:
Cut the slices of salmon. Set aside for garnish. Chop the rest of the salmon into small pieces.

Take a medium bowl, whisk the eggs, and cream together. Add half of the chopped chives, season eggs with salt and pepper. Add flour.

Dissolve the butter over medium heat, then pour into the mixture. Grease the Slow Cooker with oil or cooking spray.

Add salmon pieces to the mixture, pour it into the Slow Cooker. Set to cook on low within 2 hours.

Garnish the dish with remaining salmon, chives. Serve warm and enjoy!

Nutrition:

Calories: 263

Carbs: 0g

Fat: 0g

Protein: 0g

9. GARLIC-PARMESAN ASPARAGUS SLOW COOKER

Preparation Time: 15 minutes

Cooking Time: 1 hour

Servings: 6

Ingredients:

- Olive oil extra virgin 2 tbsp
- Minced garlic 2 tsp
- Egg 1 pcs fresh
- Garlic salt 1/2 tsp
- Fresh asparagus 12 ounces
- Parmesan cheese 1/3 cup
- Pepper at will

Directions:

Peel the garlic and mince it. Wash the asparagus. Shred the Parmesan cheese.

Take a medium-sized bowl combine oil, garlic, cracked egg, and salt together. Whisk everything well.

Cover the green beans and coat them well.

Spread the cooking spray over the Slow Cooker's bottom, put the coated asparagus, season with the shredded cheese. Toss.

Cook on high within 1 hour. Once the time is over, you may also season with the rest of the cheese. Serve.

Nutrition:

Calories: 88

Carbs: 7g

Fat: 9g

Protein: 7g

10. PERSIAN OMELET SLOW COOKER

Preparation Time: 15 minutes

Cooking Time: 3 hours

Servings: 14

Ingredients:

- Olive oil 2 tbsp
- Butter 1 tbsp
- Red onion 1 large
- Green onions 4 pcs
- Garlic 2 cloves
- Spinach 2 oz
- Fresh chives ¼ cup
- Cilantro leaves ¼ cup
- Parsley leaves ¼ cup
- Fresh dill 2 tbsp
- Kosher salt and black pepper at will
- Pine nuts ¼ cup
- Eggs 9 large
- Whole milk ¼ cup
- Greek yogurt 1 cup

Directions:

Take a saucepan to melt the butter. Add red onion, stirring occasionally; it takes about 8-9 minutes.

Add green onions, garlic, continue cooking for 4 minutes. Put the spinach, chives, parsley, cilantro, add salt and pepper at will. Remove the skillet, add the pine nuts.

Take a bowl, crack the eggs, add milk, and a little pepper, and whisk. Mix the eggs with a veggie mixture.

Open the Slow Cooker and spread the cooking spray over the bottom and sides. Pour the mix into the Slow Cooker. Cook on low for 3 hours. Serve with Greek yogurt. Bon Appetite!

Nutrition:

Calories: 220

Carbs: 9g

Fat: 16g

Protein: 12g

11. BROCCOLI AND CHEESE STUFFED SQUASH

Preparation Time: 15 minutes

Cooking Time: 3 hours

Servings: 7

Ingredients:

- Squash 1 pcs, halves
- Broccoli florets 2 cups
- Garlic 3 pcs
- Red pepper flakes 1 tsp
- Italian season 1 tsp
- Mozzarella cheese 1/2 cup
- Parmesan cheese 1/3 cup
- Cooking spray
- Salt and pepper at will

Directions:

Grease the Slow Cooker. Put the squash halves in the Slow Cooker.

Add a little bit of water at room temperature to the bottom of the Slow Cooker.

Put on low within 2 hours, until squash is mild. Take off the squash and let it cool for about 15 minutes.

Take a medium skillet, add pepper flakes and a little bit of oil and cook for 20 seconds, stir it continuously.

Add broccoli, minced garlic to the skillet, continue to stir thoroughly, until the broccoli is tender.

Take the squash and using a fork; take off the flesh of the squash. Add it to the medium bowl and conjoin with the broccoli mixture.

Shred the Parmesan cheese carefully, put salt and pepper at will, add seasoning to the mixture. Mix well and fill the squash.

Put the filled squash again in the Slow Cooker, dress with mozzarella cheese each squash half.

Cover and cook on low within 1 hour. Remove the dish and serve.

Nutrition:
Calories: 230
Carbs: 22g
Fat: 6g
Protein: 21g

12. GARLIC BUTTER KETO SPINACH

Preparation Time: 15 minutes
Cooking Time: 1 hour
Servings: 4

Ingredients:
- Salted butter 2 tbsp
- Garlic, minced 4 cloves
- Baby spinach 8 oz
- Pinch of salt
- Lemon juice 1 tsp

Directions:
Heat-up a little skillet, add the butter, melt. Sautee the garlic until a bit tender.

Spray the cooking spray over the bottom of the Slow Cooker.

Put the spinach into the Slow Cooker, season with salt and lemon juice, tender garlic, butter.

Put to cook on low within 1 hour. Garnish with fresh lemon wedges. Serve hot.

Nutrition:
Calories: 38
Carbs: 2g
Fat: 3g
Protein: 2g

13. KETO SLOW COOKER TASTY ONIONS

Preparation Time: 15 minutes
Cooking Time: 6 hours
Servings: 4

Ingredients:
- Onions 4 (or 5) large pcs, sliced
- Butter or coconut oil 4 tbsp
- Coconut aminos 1/4 cup
- Splenda (optional)
- Salt and pepper to taste

Directions:
Place the onion slices into the Slow Cooker. Top the onion slices with coconut amino and butter; you might add Splenda at will.

Cook it on low during 6-7 hours. Serve over the grilled vegetables.

Nutrition:
Calories: 38
Carbs: 9g
Fat: 0g
Protein: 0g

14. SLOW COOKER BENEDICT CASSEROLE

Preparation Time: 15 minutes
Cooking Time: 4 hours
Servings: 7

Ingredients:
- For the Casserole
- Muffin 1 large, cut into portions
- Canadian bacon 1 lb. Thick-cut
- Eggs 10 large
- Milk 1 cup
- Salt and pepper to taste
- For garnish
- For the Sauce
- Egg 6 yolks
- Lemon juice 1 1/2 tbsp
- Unsalted butter, melted 1 1/2 sticks
- Pinch of cayenne

Directions:
For the muffin: Using a medium-sized skillet, melt the butter. Add coconut and almond flour, egg, salt, and stir everything well. Add baking soda. Grease the Slow Cooker with cooking spray. Pour the mixture, put it on low for 2 hours. Remove once done.

Grease again the Slow Cooker with cooking spray, cut the muffin into equal pieces, put it on the bottom.

Slice the bacon, sprinkle half of it over top of the muffin pieces.

Whisk milk, eggs, season with salt and black pepper in a large bowl.

Pour the egg batter evenly over the muffin pieces and top with the rest of the bacon.

Cook on low within 2 hours in the slow cooker. Remove, and keep the muffins covered before serving.

To make the sauce, set up a double boiler, put the egg yolks, squeeze lemon juice in a bowl, and mix.

Put your bowl over the double boiler, continue whisking carefully; the bowl mustn't get too hot.

Put in the melted butter while continuing to whisk.

Season with salt and pepper. You may also add a little bit more lemon juice or cayenne.

Serve and enjoy.

Nutrition:

Calories: 286

Carbs: 16g

Fat: 19g

Protein: 14g

15. CRUSTLESS SLOW COOKER SPINACH QUICHE

Preparation Time: 15 minutes

Cooking Time: 2 hours

Servings: 11

Ingredients:

- Frozen spinach 10 oz package
- Butter or ghee 1 tbsp
- Red bell pepper 1 medium
- Cheddar cheese 1 1/2 cups
- Eggs 8 pcs
- Homemade sour cream 1 cup
- Fresh chives 2 tbsp
- Sea salt 1/2 tsp
- Ground black pepper 1/4 tsp
- Ground almond flour 1/2 cup
- Baking soda 1/4 tsp

Directions:

Let the frozen spinach thaw and drain it well. Chop finely. Wash the pepper and slice it. Remove the seeds.

Grate the cheddar cheese and set it aside. Chop the fresh chives finely.

Grease the slow cooker with cooking spray.

Take a little skillet, heat the butter over high heat on the stove, sauté the pepper until tender, for about 6 minutes. Mix the eggs, sour cream, salt, plus pepper in a large bowl.

Add grated cheese and chives and continue to mix. In another medium-sized bowl, combine almond flour with baking soda.

Pour into the egg mixture, add peppers to the egg's mixture, pour gently into the slow cooker.

Set to cook on high within 2 hours then Serve.

Nutrition:

Calories: 153

Carbs: 19g

Fat: 3g

Protein: 9g

16. BROCCOLI GRATIN WITH PARMESAN AND CHEESE

Preparation Time: 15 minutes

Cooking Time: 1 hour

Servings: 7

Ingredients:

- Bite-size broccoli flowerets 8 cups
- Swiss cheese 1 1/2 cups
- Mayo 8 tsp
- Lemon juice 1 1/2 tbsp
- Dijon mustard 3/4 tsp
- Green onions 3 tbsp
- Parmesan cheese 1/4 cup
- Black pepper and salt to taste

Directions:

Wash broccoli and cut into small florets. Grate both parmesan and Swiss cheese into a bowl. Set aside.

Squeeze the juice of a lemon into a cup. Wash and chop the green onions.

Grease with cooking spray or olive oil (optional) over the bottom of the slow cooker.

Put broccoli florets in a single layer. Mix in a separate bowl lemon juice, mustard, mayo, black pepper, add to the mixture green onion and grated cheese.

Put the mixture over the broccoli, cover, and cook on low for 1 hour. Serve hot.

Nutrition:

Calories: 210

Carbs: 44g

Fat: 2g

Protein: 5g

17. SLOW COOKER CREAM CHEESE FRENCH TOAST

Preparation Time: 15 minutes

Cooking Time: 2 hours

Servings: 9

Ingredients:

- Cream cheese 1 (8-oz) package
- Slivered almonds ¼ cup
- Keto bread 1 loaf

- Eggs 4 pcs
- Almond extract 1 tsp
- Sweetener 1 tbsp
- Milk 1 cup
- Butter 2 tbsp
- Cheddar cheese ½ cup
- Stevia, at will, for dressing

Directions:

Mix cream cheese with almonds in a large bowl. Slice the keto bread into 2-inch slices. Try to make a 1/2-inch slit (horizontal) at the bottom of every piece to make a pocket.

Fill all the slices with a cream mixture. Set aside. In a little bowl, mix eggs, extract the sweetener in milk. Coat the keto slices into the mix.

Grease with cooking spray the slow cooker over the bottom and sides, then put the coated keto slices on the slow cooker's base. Put on the top of each separate piece additional shredded cheese.

Cook on low for 2 hours. Serve hot.

Nutrition:

Calories: 280

Carbs: 34g

Fat: 8g

Protein: 19g

18. KETO SLOW COOKER TURKEY STUFFED PEPPERS

Preparation Time: 15 minutes

Cooking Time: 6 hours

Servings: 7

Ingredients:

- Olive oil 1 tbsp
- Ground turkey 1 lb.
- Onion 1 pcs
- Garlic 1 clove
- Green bell peppers 4 pcs
- Tomato sauce/pasta sauce (low carb) 24 oz jar
- Water 1/2 cup

Directions:

Peel and cut the small onion, peel the garlic, and press or mince it.

Wash the bell peppers, cut off the tops and clean them accurately.

Take a medium bowl, put their ground turkey, cut onion, pressed or minced garlic, and add pasta sauce.

Separate the compound into four equal parts, place the mixtures into the prepared cleaned peppers.

Spread the olive oil over the slow cooker bottom, and sides put the peppers inside, and top them with sauce.

Add a little water into the slow cooker, cook on low for 6-7 hours.

Serve with remaining sauce and enjoy.

Nutrition:

Calories: 245

Carbs: 26g

Fat: 7g

Protein: 19g

19. CHEESY GARLIC BRUSSELS SPROUTS

Preparation Time: 15 minutes

Cooking Time: 3 hours

Servings: 6

Ingredients:

- 1 tbsp unsalted butter
- 2½ pounds brussels sprouts, trimmed and halved
- ¾ cup grated parmesan cheese
- 2 tbsp heavy cream
- 1/8 tsp freshly grated nutmeg
- 4 cloves garlic, thinly sliced
- 4 ounces cream cheese, cubed
- ½ tsp kosher salt
- ¼ tsp ground black pepper

Directions:

Coat the insert of a 4- to - 6-quart slow cooker with the butter. Add the garlic, cream cheese, Brussels sprouts, pepper, and salt.

Toss to mix very well—cover and cook on the low, about 2 to 3 hours.

Turn off the slow cooker. Stir in cream, parmesan, and nutmeg until the cheeses thaw and the Brussels sprouts are coated in a creamy sauce.

Taste, season with more pepper if required. Serve.

Nutrition:

Calories: 159

Fat: 9.5g

Saturated fat: 5.5g

Carbs: 14.1g

Fiber: 5.4g

Sugars: 3.7 g

Protein: 7.7g

Sodium: 279.8 mg

20. BLUEBERRY PANCAKE

Preparation Time: 15 minutes

Cooking Time: 40 minutes

Servings: 8

Ingredients:

- 1½ cups milk
- 2 large eggs
- 1 tsp vanilla
- 2 cups almond flour
- 2½ tsp baking powder
- 2 tbsp Stevia or other Keto-approved sugar
- ¼ cup fresh blueberries

Directions:

Toss the eggs, vanilla, and milk together in a small bowl. Stir flour, Stevia, and baking powder together in a large bowl until well-mixed.

Add the wet fixings to the dry and stir just until mixed.

Pour the batter into the slow cooker. Add the blueberries.

Set the timer at 40 minutes on low.

Check to confirm if the pancake is cooked through by pressing the top. Serve and enjoy with syrup, fruit, or whipped cream.

Nutrition:

Calories: 174
Carbs: 30g
Protein: 6g
Fat: 2g
Cholesterol: 45mg
Sodium: 37mg
Potassium: 266mg

21. SAUSAGE AND PEPPERS

Preparation Time: 15 minutes
Cooking Time: 6 hours
Servings: 8

Ingredients:

- 6 medium cloves garlic
- 2 large yellow onions
- 4 green bell peppers, cleaned and thinly sliced
- 28 ounces canned unsalted crushed tomatoes
- ¼ cup of cold water
- 1 bay leaf
- 2 pounds uncooked Italian Sausage Links, mild or spicy
- 1 tbsp kosher salt
- 1 tsp Italian seasoning
- ¼ tsp dried oregano
- ½ tsp crushed red pepper flakes

Directions:

Thinly slice the garlic. Peel the onions and halve, then cut.

Add the chopped garlic and sliced onion into the slow cooker.

Remember to spray the slow cooker with oil. Cut the bell peppers in half.

Remove the ribs and any seeds in them. Then slice thinly.

Add the sliced bell peppers, Italian seasoning, salt, crushed red pepper flakes, dried oregano, 1 can of crushed tomatoes, and ¼ cup of water to the slow cooker.

Toss to coat and liquid is uniformly distributed. Take out almost half of the peppers and the onion mixture to a bowl.

Immerse the uncooked sausage in the middle and then add the peppers and the onions back to the slow cooker.

Put the bay leaf, then cover, set to low, and cook for 6 hours. Serve hot.

Nutrition:

Calories: 456
Fat: 36g
Cholesterol: 86mg
Sodium: 1838mg
Potassium: 746mg
Carbs: 15g
Fiber: 4g
Sugars: 7g
Protein: 19g

22. TOMATO SCRAMBLED EGGS

Preparation Time: 5 minutes
Cooking Time: 4 hours
Servings: 3

Ingredients:

- 3 eggs, beaten
- 1 tbsp butter
- 1 tbsp marinara sauce
- 2 tbsp sour cream, full-fat
- Paprika, oregano and salt to taste

Directions:

In a mixing bowl, combine all fixings.

Cook in the slow cooker on high within 2 hours or on low for 4 hours.

Halfway before the cooking time, use a fork to break the eggs into small pieces. Continue cooking until eggs are well done. Serve.

Nutrition:

Calories: 167
Carbohydrates: 3.3g
Protein: 20.4g
Fat: 41.5g
Sugars: 0 g

Sodium: 721mg
Fiber: 0.7g

23. CHEESY CAULIFLOWERS GRATIN

Preparation Time: 15 minutes
Cooking Time: 1 hour
Servings: 7

Ingredients:

- Cauliflower, chopped 8 cups
- Cheddar cheese 1 1/2 cups
- Parmesan cheese 1/4 cup
- Lime juice 1 1/2 tbsp
- Dijon mustard 3/4 tsp
- Red onions 3 tbsp
- Paprika and salt to taste

Directions:

Wash cauliflowers and cut into small florets. Grate both parmesan and cheddar cheese into a bowl. Set aside.

Squeeze the juice of a lime into a cup. Wash and chop the onions.

Grease with cooking spray or olive oil (optional) over the bottom of the slow cooker.

Put broccoli florets in a single layer. Mix in a separate bowl lime juice, mustard, paprika, add to the red onion and grated cheese.

Put the mixture over the cauliflowers, cover, and cook on low for 1 hour. Serve hot.

Nutrition:

Calories: 210
Carbs: 44g
Fat: 2g
Protein: 5g

24. BREAKFAST SAUSAGE CASSEROLE

Preparation Time: 15 minutes
Cooking Time: 3 hours
Servings: 6

Ingredients:

- 1 lb. pork sausage
- ½ cup chopped green bell pepper
- ½ cup chopped red bell pepper
- 1 tbsp ghee
- 12 large eggs
- ½ cup of coconut milk
- 1 tbsp nutritional yeast
- 1 tsp dry rubbed sage
- 1 tsp dried thyme
- ½ tsp garlic powder
- ½ tsp ground black pepper
- ½ tsp salt
- ½ cup sliced red onion

Directions:

Heat-up a medium cast-iron skillet over medium heat for 2 minutes. Add the pork sausage, then break it into small crumbles.

Cook for 3 minutes. Stir in the black pepper, sea salt, thyme, sage, and garlic powder.

Cook for an additional 5 minutes. Turn the heat off.

Stir in the bell peppers and the chopped onion. Coat the bowl of the slow cooker with ghee.

Add the pork and vegetable mixture to the bottom of the slow cooker.

Whisk the coconut milk, nutritional yeast, and eggs until the eggs are well incorporated together in a large bowl. Pour it into the slow cooker on top of the pork mixture.

Cook on low for 2 to 3 hours. Chop into 6 servings.

Nutrition:

Calories: 77
Carbs: 2g
Fat: 5g
Protein: 5g

25. STUFFED BREAKFAST PEPPERS

Preparation Time: 15 minutes
Cooking Time: 45 minutes
Servings: 6

Ingredients:

- 3 bell peppers halved and seeded
- 4 eggs
- ½ cup milk
- ¾ tsp salt
- 2 tbsp chopped green onion
- ¼ cup chopped frozen spinach thawed, squeezed dry
- ¾ cup shredded cheddar cheese divided
- ½ cup finely chopped ham

Directions:

Line slow cooker with tin foil. Arrange the peppers in the slow cooker and fill with the remaining fixings. Cook on low within 3-4 hours. Serve.

Nutrition:

Calories: 180
Carbs: 3g
Protein: 8g
Fat: 15g
Cholesterol: 205mg
Sodium: 430mg
Fiber: 1g

Sugars: 2g

26. CHEESE AND SAUSAGE BREAKFAST

Preparation Time: 15 minutes
Cooking Time: 2 hours
Servings: 8

Ingredients:
- 2 tbsp butter, softened
- 8 oz. breakfast sausage
- 1 lb. cauliflower
- 12 eggs
- 1 cup milk
- ¾ tsp salt
- ¼ tsp black pepper
- 4 oz. shredded mild cheddar cheese

Directions:

Coat the slow cooker and inside of the foil collar using softened butter.

Sauté in a large skillet over medium heat, the breakfast sausage until cooked through and browned, about 5 to 8 minutes.

Put the cauliflower into a microwave-safe bowl. Add 1 tbsp water and cover bowl with a damp paper towel—microwave on high within 3 to 4 minutes.

Arrange the sausage and cauliflower in the bottom of the slow cooker.

Toss eggs, black pepper, milk, and salt to combine. Add the cheese; stir to mix very well.

Pour the egg/cheese mixture over sausage and cauliflower.

Then put 2 layers of paper towels below the slow cooker lid before.

Cook on high for 2 hours. Slice and serve.

Nutrition:

Calories: 326
Carbs: 14g
Protein: 18g
Fat: 22g
Cholesterol: 291mg
Sodium: 650mg
Potassium: 408mg
Fiber: 2g
Sugars: 4g

27. MUSHROOMS, CAULIFLOWER, AND ZUCCHINI TOAST

Preparation Time: 15 minutes
Cooking Time: 7 hours
Servings: 8

Ingredients:
- 3-pound boneless beef chuck roast
- 2 cups keto compliant beef broth
- 5-7 radishes, cut into halves
- 1½ cups cauliflower florets
- ½ cup chopped celery
- 1/3 cup zucchini rounds
- ¼ cup chopped orange bell pepper
- 1 tsp xanthan gum (optional to thicken the gravy)
- 2 sprigs of fresh rosemary
- Fresh parsley (for garnish)
- 1 tsp Himalayan sea salt
- ½ tsp freshly ground black pepper
- 1 tsp garlic powder
- ½ tsp dried Italian seasoning
- 1 tbsp avocado oil or ghee
- 1 small onion chopped
- ½ cup sliced mushrooms
- 1 tbsp tomato paste
- 1 tsp keto compliant Worcestershire sauce
- 2 tsp coconut aminos

Directions:

Season the roast with Italian seasoning, black pepper, garlic powder, and salt. Let it stand alone for about 27 to 30 minutes.

Add oil to a large skillet on medium-high heat. Add the roast; sear until brown, about 4 minutes on all sides.

Add the diced mushrooms and onions; let them cook for about 1 to 2 minutes until sweet-smelling.

Transfer the roast and the onions to the bottom of a slow cooker, then pour in the broth; then cook on high for 4 hours or low for 7 hours.

Add the vegetables: zucchini, celery, turnips, bell peppers, and cauliflower. Set it again for about 1 hour.

Transfer then shred into chunks with 2 forks.

Sprinkle with diced parsley if preferred. Serve hot with gravy.

Nutrition:

Calories: 345
Total Fat: 21g
Carbs: 4g
Fiber: 1g
Protein: 34g

28. KETO EGG MUFFIN

Preparation Time: 15 minutes
Cooking Time: 2 hours
Servings: 6

Ingredients:

- 2 (1 oz.) scallions, finely chopped
- 5 oz. cooked bacon or salami, chopped
- 12 eggs
- 2 tbsp red pesto or green pesto (optional)
- Salt and pepper, to taste
- 1½ cups (6 oz.) shredded cheddar cheese

Directions:

Preheat the oven to 175 °C (350 °F).

Line a muffin tin with an insertable baking cup or grease a silicone muffin tin with butter or use a non-stick muffin tin (two muffins per serving).

Add the scallions and the bacon or salami cooked to the bottom of the tin.

Whisk together the eggs, pesto, salt, and pepper until blended.

Pour the egg mixture over the scallions and the meat. Sprinkle with the cheese on top.

Bake for 15-20 minutes depending on the size of the muffin tin.

Nutrition:

kcal: 335

Net carbs: 2 % (2 g)

Fiber: 0 g

Fat: 73 % (27 g)

Protein: 25 % (21 g)

29. CAULIFLOWER CASSEROLE WITH GOAT CHEESE

Preparation Time: 15 minutes

Cooking Time: 3 hours

Servings: 12

Ingredients:

- Cauliflower florets 6 cups
- Olive oil 4 tsp
- Dried oregano 1 tsp
- Salt 1/2 tsp
- Ground pepper 1/2 tsp
- Goat cheese crumbled 2 oz.
- The sauce:
- Olive oil 1 tsp
- Garlic 3 cloves
- Crushed tomatoes 1 (28 oz.) Can
- Bay leaves 2 pcs
- Salt 1/4 tsp
- Minced flat-leaf parsley 1/4 cup

Directions:

Grease the slow cooker with cooking spray, put the cauliflower on its bottom, add olive oil, oregano, and pepper. Salt if desired.

Cook on the low setting within 2 hours until the cauliflower florets get tender and a little bit brown.

For making the sauce: Take a medium-sized skillet, heat the olive oil, add garlic and cook for 1 minute, stir it thoroughly all the time.

Add the crushed tomatoes and bay leaves; let it simmer for some minutes. Remove the bay leaves, dress with pepper and salt.

Put the sauce over the cauliflower florets in the slow cooker once the time is over.

Spread the Goat cheese over the dish, cover the slow cooker, and continue cooking for 1 hour on low. Serve warm!

Nutrition:

Calories: 170

Carbs: 10g

Fat: 13g

Protein: 7g

30. GREEK EGGS BREAKFAST CASSEROLE

Preparation Time: 15 minutes

Cooking Time: 6 hours

Servings: 9

Ingredients:

- Eggs (whisked) 12 pcs
- Milk ½ cup
- Salt ½ tsp
- Black pepper 1 tsp
- Red onion 1 tbsp
- Garlic 1 tsp
- Sun-dried tomatoes ½ cup
- Spinach 2 cups
- Feta cheese ½ cup crushed
- Pepper at will

Directions:

Whisk the eggs in a bowl.

Add to the mixture milk, pepper, salt, and stir to combine. Add the minced onion and garlic.

Add dried tomatoes and spinach. Pour all the batter into the slow cooker, add Feta cheese.

Set to cook on the low setting within 5-6 hours. Serve.

Nutrition:

Calories: 253

Carbs: 1g

Fat: 17g

Protein: 22g

31. SLOW COOKER TURKISH BREAKFAST EGGS

Preparation Time: 15 minutes

Cooking Time: 4 hours

Servings: 9

Ingredients:
- Olive oil 1 tbsp
- Onions 2 pcs, chopped
- Red bell pepper 1 pcs, sliced
- Red chili 1 small
- Cherry tomatoes 8 pcs
- Keto bread 1 slice
- Eggs 4
- Milk 2 tbsp
- Small bunch of parsley, chopped
- Natural yogurt 4 tbsp
- Pepper at will

Directions:

Grease the slow cooker using oil.

Heat-up, the oil, add the onions, pepper, and chili in a large skillet, then stir. Cook until the veggies begin to soften.

Transfer it to the Slow Cooker, then add the cherry tomatoes and bread, stir everything well.

Cook on low for 4 hours—season with fresh parsley and yogurt.

Nutrition:

Calories: 123

Carbs: 17g

Fat: 5g

Protein: 1g

32. MEXICAN STYLE BREAKFAST CASSEROLE

Preparation Time: 15 minutes

Cooking Time: 5 hours

Servings: 5

Ingredients:
- 5 eggs
- 6 ounces pork sausage, cooked, drained
- ½ cup 1% milk
- ½ tsp garlic powder
- 2 jalapeños, deseeded, finely chopped
- ½ tsp ground cumin
- ½ tsp ground coriander
- 1 ½ cups chunky salsa
- 1 ½ cup pepper Jack cheese, shredded
- Salt to taste
- Pepper to taste
- ¼ cup fresh cilantro

Directions:

Coat the slow cooker with cooking spray. Mix the eggs, salt, pepper, plus milk in a bowl.

Add garlic powder, cumin, coriander, and sausage and mix well.

Pour the mixture into the slow cooker. Set the slow cooker on 'Low' within 4-5 hours or on 'High' for 2-3 hours. Place toppings of your choice and serve.

Nutrition:

Calories: 320

Fat: 24.1 g

Carb: 5.2 g

Protein: 17.9 g

33. ALMOND LEMON BLUEBERRY MUFFINS

Preparation Time: 15 minutes

Cooking Time: 3 hours

Servings: 3

Ingredients:
- 1 cup almond flour
- 1 large egg
- 3 drops stevia
- ¼ cup fresh blueberries
- ¼ tsp lemon zest, grated
- ¼ tsp pure lemon extract
- ½ cup heavy whipping cream
- 2 tbsp butter, melted
- ½ tsp baking powder

Directions:

Whisk the egg into a bowl. Add the rest of the fixing, and mix.

Pour batter into lined or greased muffin molds. Pour up to ¾ of the cup.

Pour 6 ounces of water into the slow cooker. Place an aluminum foil at the bottom, and the muffin molds inside.

Set the slow cooker on 'High' within 2-3 hours. Let it cool in the cooker for a while.

Remove from the cooker. Loosen the edges of the muffins. Invert on to a plate and serve.

Nutrition:

Calories: 223

Fat: 21g

Carb: 5g

Protein: 6 g

34. HEALTHY VEGGIE OMELET

Preparation Time: 15 minutes

Cooking Time: 1 hour & 40 minutes

Servings: 4

Ingredients:
- 6 eggs
- 1 tsp parsley, dried
- 1 tsp garlic powder
- 1 bell pepper, diced
- 1/2 cup onion, sliced
- 1 cup spinach
- 1/2 cup almond milk, unsweetened
- 4 egg whites
- Pepper and Salt to taste

Directions:
Grease the slow cooker from inside using cooking spray.
Whisk egg whites, eggs, parsley, garlic powder, almond milk, pepper, and salt in a large bowl.
Stir in bell peppers, spinach, and onion. Pour egg batter into the slow cooker.
Cook on high within 90 minutes or until egg sets. Cut into the slices and serve.

Nutrition:
Calories: 200
Fat: 13.9 g
Carb: 5.8 g
Protein 13.4 g

35. PESTO SCRAMBLED EGGS

Preparation Time: 5 minutes
Cooking Time: 4 hours
Servings: 3

Ingredients:
- 3 large eggs, beaten
- 1 tbsp butter
- 1 tbsp organic green pesto sauce
- 2 tbsp sour cream, full-fat
- Salt and pepper to taste

Directions:
In a mixing bowl, combine all fixings.
Cook in the slow cooker on high within 2 hours or on low for 4 hours.
Halfway before the cooking time, use a fork to break the eggs into small pieces. Continue cooking until eggs are well done. Serve.

Nutrition:
Calories: 167
Carbohydrates: 3.3g
Protein: 20.4g
Fat: 41.5g
Sugars: 0 g
Sodium: 721mg

Fiber: 0.7g

36. KALE AND CHEESE OMELET

Preparation Time: 5 minutes
Cooking Time: 4 hours
Servings: 2

Ingredients:
- 5 eggs, beaten
- 2 tbsp onion, chopped
- 2 tsp olive oil
- 3 ounces kale, chopped
- 1/3 cup white cheese, grated

Directions:
Mix all fixings in a bowl. Put it in the slow cooker. Cook on high within 2 hours or on low for 3 hours.

Nutrition:
Calories: 372
Carbohydrates: 2.1g
Protein: 24.5g
Fat: 36.2g
Sugars: 0.2g
Sodium: 362mg
Fiber: 1.3g

37. EGG CASSEROLE WITH CHEESES, SUN-DRIED TOMATOES, AND HERBS

Preparation Time: 5 minutes
Cooking Time: 4 hours
Servings: 8

Ingredients:
- 10 eggs
- 2 tbsp milk
- 3 tbsp sun-dried tomatoes, chopped
- 2 tbsp onion, minced
- 2 tbsp basil, chopped
- 1 tbsp thyme leaves
- Salt and pepper to taste
- 1 cup mixed Italian cheese, grated

Directions:
Mix all items in a bowl. Put it inside your slow cooker, and set to cook on high for 2 hours or low for 3 hours.

Nutrition:
Calories: 140
Carbohydrates: 3.87g
Protein: 10.93g
Fat: 8.89g
Sugars: 1.27g
Sodium: 309mg

Fiber: 0.3g

38. KALE, MUSHROOMS, AND CARAMELIZED ONIONS

Preparation Time: 10 minutes
Cooking Time: 4 hours
Servings: 6

Ingredients:
- 2 tsp olive oil
- ½ tbsp onion, caramelized
- 1 red bell pepper, diced
- 1 cup mushrooms, sliced
- 2 cups kale, chopped
- 1 tsp dried thyme
- 10 large eggs, beaten
- ¼ cup milk
- 2 cups cheese, shredded
- Salt and pepper to taste

Directions:
Place all fixings in the slow cooker. Cook on high within 3 hours or on low for 4 hours.

Nutrition:
Calories: 223
Carbohydrates: 4.6g
Protein: 32.1g
Fat: 36.3g
Sugars: 0.8g
Sodium: 471mg
Fiber: 2.1g

39. EGG AND CHEESE CASSEROLE WITH CHAYOTE SQUASH

Preparation Time: 5 minutes
Cooking Time: 4 hours
Servings: 4

Ingredients:
1 tsp olive oil
1 red onion, diced
2 small chayote squash, grated
½ small red bell pepper, diced
10 large eggs, beaten
¼ cup low-fat cottage cheese
2 tbsp milk
½ tsp ground cumin
2 cups grated cheesed
Salt and pepper to taste

Directions:
Combine all fixings in a mixing bowl. Pour into the slow cooker.
Cook on high within 3 hours or on low for 4 hours.

Nutrition:
Calories: 209
Carbohydrates: 6.3g
Protein: 35.2g
Fat: 33.6g
Sugars: 1.5g
Sodium: 362mg
Fiber: 3.2g

40. SAUSAGE AND KALE STRATA

Preparation Time: 5 minutes
Cooking Time: 4 hours
Servings: 12

Ingredients:
- 12 eggs, beaten
- 2 ½ cups milk
- Salt and pepper to taste
- 2 tbsp fresh oregano, minced
- 2 pounds breakfast sausages, sliced
- 1 bunch kale, torn into pieces
- 16 ounces white mushrooms, sliced
- 2 ½ cups Monterey Jack cheese, grated

Directions:
Mix all fixings in a large mixing bowl until well combined. Pour into the slow cooker and close the lid. Set to cook on high within 3 hours or low for 4 hours.

Nutrition:
Calories: 231
Carbohydrates: 4.5g
Protein: 32.3g
Fat: 37.4g
Sugars: 0.6g
Sodium: 525mg
Fiber: 3.2g

41. EGG CAKE WITH PEPPERS, KALE, AND CHEDDAR

Preparation Time: 10 minutes
Cooking Time: 4 hours
Servings: 6

Ingredients:
- 1 dozen eggs, beaten
- ¼ cup milk
- ¼ cup almond flour
- 1 clove of garlic, minced

- Salt and pepper to taste
- 1 cup kale, chopped
- 1 red bell pepper, chopped
- ¾ cup mozzarella cheese, grated
- 1 green onion, chopped

Directions:

In a mixing bowl, combine all fixings.

Pour into the slow cooker. Cook on high within 4 hours or on high for 6 hours. Serve.

Nutrition:

Calories: 527
Carbohydrates: 3.1g
Protein: 42.3g
Fat: 45.6g
Sugars: 0.5g
Sodium: 425mg
Fiber: 2.4g

42. FETA CHEESE AND KALE BREAKFAST CASSEROLE

Preparation Time: 5 minutes
Cooking Time: 4 hours
Servings: 6

Ingredients:

- 10 ounces kale, chopped
- 2 tsp olive oil
- ¾ cup feta cheese, crumbled
- 12 eggs, beaten
- Salt and pepper to taste

Directions:

Mix all fixings in a large mixing bowl until well combined. Put the batter inside the slow cooker, then cook on high for 3 hours or low for 4 hours.

Nutrition:

Calories: 397
Carbohydrates: 4g
Protein: 32.2g
Fat: 29.4g
Sugars: 0.6g
Sodium: 425mg
Fiber: 3.2g

43. CAULIFLOWER AND HAM CASSEROLE

Preparation Time: 5 minutes
Cooking Time: 4 hours
Servings: 6

Ingredients:

- 1 head cauliflower, grated
- 1 cup ham, cubed
- ½ cup mozzarella cheese, grated
- ½ cup cheddar cheese, grated
- 1 onion, chopped
- Salt and pepper to taste
- 10 eggs, beaten

Directions:

Mix all fixings in a bowl. Pour into the slow cooker.

Cook on high within 3 hours or on low for 4 hours.

Nutrition:

Calories: 418
Carbohydrates: 5.2g
Protein: 28.1g
Fat: 42.4g
Sugars: 0.5g
Sodium: 831mg
Fiber: 2.1g

44. SAUSAGE-STUFFED EGGPLANTS

Preparation Time: 10 minutes
Cooking Time: 6 hours
Servings: 6

Ingredients:

- 12 ounces sausage links, chopped
- 2 cloves of garlic, minced
- 2 tbsp rosemary, fresh
- Salt and pepper to taste
- 3 small eggplants, sliced
- 6 slices mozzarella cheese

Directions:

Mix all items in a bowl. Line a foil at the bottom of the slow cooker.

Grease with cooking spray. Pour into the slow cooker and cook on low for 6 hours or on high for 4 hours.

Nutrition:

Calories: 471
Carbohydrates: 6.3g
Protein: 16.83g
Fat: 38.9g
Sugars: 0.4g
Sodium: 1107mg
Fiber: 3.8g

45. ZUCCHINI SAUSAGE BREAKFAST "BAKE"

Preparation Time: 5 minutes
Cooking Time: 4 hours
Servings: 12

Ingredients:
- 1-pound Italian sausages, chopped
- ½ cup coconut flour
- 2 tsp baking powder
- 1 tsp salt
- ½ tsp pepper
- 8 ounces cream cheese
- 10 large eggs
- 2 small zucchinis, grated and excess water squeezed
- 4 cloves of garlic, minced
- 1 cup cheese, shredded

Directions:

Mix all fixings in a bowl. Set in the slow cooker; cook within 3 hours on high or on low for 4 hours.

Nutrition:

Calories: 344
Carbohydrates: 6.3g
Protein: 21g
Fat: 27g
Sugars: 0.4g
Sodium: 736mg
Fiber: 4g

46. CHEDDAR JALAPENO BREAKFAST SAUSAGES

Preparation Time: 5 minutes
Cooking Time: 6 hours
Servings: 12

Ingredients:
- 12 medium-sized breakfast sausages
- 1 jalapeno pepper, chopped
- ½ cup cheddar cheese, grated
- ¼ cup heavy cream
- Salt and pepper to taste

Directions:

Mix all items in a bowl, then put them into the slow cooker.
Set to cook on low for 6 hours or on high for 4 hours.
Garnish with parsley on top.

Nutrition:

Calories: 472
Carbohydrates: 1.2g
Protein: 32.6g
Fat: 42.4g
Sugars: 0g
Sodium: 731mg
Fiber: 0.4g

47. CHOCOLATE PEANUT BUTTER BREAKFAST BARS

Preparation Time: 15 minutes
Cooking Time: 6 hours
Servings: 12

Ingredients:
- 4 ounces cream cheese, softened
- 1 large egg, beaten
- 2 cups almond flour
- ½ cup chunky peanut butter
- ½ cup heavy cream
- 3 tbsp stevia sweetener
- 1 tsp vanilla extract
- ½ cup dark chocolate chips

Directions:

Mix the cream cheese, egg, almond flour, peanut butter, heavy cream, stevia, vanilla extract, and chocolate chips in a large mixing bowl using a hand mixer.

Put the bottom of the slow cooker with foil and grease with cooking spray.

Pour the batter inside the slow cooker and cook for 5 hours or on low or 3 hours on high.

Nutrition:

Calories: 170
Carbohydrates: 4.4g
Protein: 8.1g
Fat: 20.5g
Sugars: 1.2g
Sodium: 732mg
Fiber: 1.7g

48. ARUGULA CHEESE HERB FRITTATA

Preparation Time: 15 minutes
Cooking Time: 3 hours & 10 minutes
Servings: 6

Ingredients:
- 8 eggs
- 3/4 cup goat cheese, crumbled
- 1/2 cup onion, sliced
- 1 1/2 cups red peppers, roasted and chopped
- 4 cups baby arugula
- 1 tsp oregano, dried
- 1/3 cup almond milk
- Pepper and salt to taste

Directions:

Grease the slow cooker using a cooking spray. Whisk eggs, oregano, and almond milk in a mixing bowl.

Put pepper and salt. Arrange red peppers, onion, arugula, and cheese into the slow cooker.

Pour egg batter into the slow cooker over the vegetables. Cook on low within 3 hours. Serve hot and enjoy.

Nutrition:
Calories: 178
Fat: 12.8g
Carb: 6g
Protein: 11.4g

49. YUMMY CAULIFLOWER CRUST BREAKFAST PIZZA

Preparation Time: 15 minutes
Cooking Time: 5 hours
Servings: 4

Ingredients:
- 2 large eggs
- 3 cups riced cauliflower
- 1 cup grated Parmesan cheese
- 8 ounces goat cheese, divided
- ½ tsp kosher salt
- 1 tbsp extra-virgin olive oil
- Grated zest of 1 lemon

Directions:
Beat the eggs, cauliflower, Parmesan cheese, 2 ounces of goat cheese, and the salt until well mixed in a large bowl.

Grease the slow cooker using olive oil. Press the cauliflower batter in an even layer around the cooker's bottom and extend slightly up the sides.

Stir the remaining 6 ounces of goat cheese and the lemon zest in a small bowl. Dollop spoonsful onto the cauliflower crust, distributing it evenly.

Set the lid on the slow cooker, but prop it slightly open with a chopstick or wooden spoon. Cook within 6 hours on low or 3 hours on high, until the edges are slightly browned.

When finished, turn off the cooker but let the pizza sit in it 30 minutes before serving. Serve warm.

Nutrition:
Calories: 389
Fat: 29g
Carbs: 6g
Protein: 24g

50. PARMESAN ZUCCHINI PAPRIKA & RICOTTA FRITTATA

Preparation Time: 15 minutes
Cooking Time: 6 hours
Servings: 6

Ingredients:
- 2 medium zucchinis, shredded
- 1 tsp kosher salt, divided
- 1 tbsp extra-virgin olive oil
- 12 large eggs
- 3 tbsp heavy (whipping) cream
- 3 tbsp finely chopped fresh parsley
- 1 tbsp fresh thyme
- ½ tsp paprika
- ½ tsp freshly ground black pepper
- 6 ounces ricotta cheese
- 12 cherry tomatoes, halved
- ½ cup grated Parmesan cheese

Directions:
Toss the shredded zucchini with ½ tsp of salt in a colander set in the sink. Let the zucchini sit for a few minutes, then squeeze out the excess liquid with your hands.

Grease the slow cooker with olive oil.

Beat the eggs, heavy cream, parsley, thyme, paprika, pepper, and the remaining ½ tsp of salt in a large bowl.

Put the zucchini and stir. Transfer the mixture to the prepared insert.

Using a large spoon, dollop the ricotta cheese into the egg mixture, distributing it evenly.

Top with the tomatoes and sprinkle the Parmesan cheese over the top. Set to cook within 6 hours on low or 3 hours on high. Serve at room temperature.

Nutrition:
Calories: 291
Fat: 22g
Carbs: 4g
Protein: 18g

51. CAULIFLOWER SLOW BREAKFAST CASSEROLE

Preparation Time: 15 minutes
Cooking Time: 5-7 hours
Servings: 10

Ingredients:
- Eggs - 12
- Milk - ½ cup
- Dry mustard - ½ tsp
- Kosher salt - 1 tsp
- Pepper - ½ tsp
- Cauliflower, shredded - 1 head
- Additional salt and pepper to season the layers - as required
- Small onion, diced - 1
- Packaged pre-cooked breakfast sausages, sliced - 5 ounces

- Shredded cheddar cheese – 8 ounces

Directions:

First of all, grease a 6-quart slow cooker properly with cooking spray.

Mix well all the item likes the eggs, milk, dry mustard, salt, and pepper.

From the shredded cauliflower, take one-third portion and layer it in the bottom of the slow slow cooker. After that place one-third of the sliced onion on top.

Use pepper and salt to season and top it with one-third portion of sausage and cheese.

Repeat the same process by maintaining two layers.

Pour the eggs mixture over slow cooker

Cook on low for 5-7 hours and wait until eggs are set properly and the top color is browned.

Nutrition:

Calories 87.7

Calories from Fat 49

Total Fat 5.4 g

Cholesterol 1mg

Total Carbohydrates 2.2g

Dietary Fiber 1.2g

Protein 8g

52. BREAKFAST CASSEROLE

Preparation Time: 15-20 minutes

Cooking Time: 6 hours

Servings: 8

Ingredients:

- Brown jicama hashed or brown daikon radish - 4 cups
- Cooked, crumbled, and drained bacon slices – 12 ounces
- Cooked, drained, and grounded sausage - 1 pound
- Onion, sweet yellow, chopped - 1
- Diced green bell pepper – 1
- Fresh mushroom, sliced - 1 to ½ cups
- Fresh spinach - 1 to ½ cups
- Shredded cheese - 2 cups (Monterrey Jack preferred)
- Feta cheese, shredded - ½ cup
- Eggs - 1 dozen
- Heavy white cream - 1 cup
- Salt - 1 tbsp
- Pepper - 1 tbsp

Directions:

First of all, put a layer of hashed browns in the bottom of the cooker with low flame.

Then put the layer of bacon and sausage over it.

Put all the spices upon the layer.

Now take a bowl and whisk the eggs, cream, salt, and pepper together.

Pour the mixture of eggs into the cooker.

Cover it and let it cook for 6 hours on high flame or 12 hours on low flame.

Nutrition:

Calories 443

Carbohydrates 8g

Fat 38g

Fiber 2g

Protein 18g

53. BACON-MUSHROOM BREAKFAST

Preparation Time: 15 minutes

Cooking Time: 1 hour 45 minutes

Servings: 4

Ingredients:

- Bacon large, sliced – 3½ Ounces
- White mushrooms, chopped – 2½ Ounces
- Eggs – 6 Nos.
- Shallots, chopped – 3 tbsp
- Bell pepper, chopped - ¾ Cup
- Kale leaves large, shredded – 8 Nos.
- Ghee – 1 tbsp.
- Parmesan cheese – 1 Cup
- Avocado and green leaves (Optional)

Directions:

Clean the kale leaves, remove the hard stems and chop them into small pieces.

In a skillet cook the bacon, till it becomes crispy, and add mushrooms, red pepper, and shallot.

Add kale and cut down the flame and let the kale become tender in the skillet.

Now take a medium bowl and beat all eggs, add pepper and salt.

In the slow cooker, add ghee and let it become hot. Spread the ghee on all sides of the cooker.

Put the sautéed vegetable into the base of the cooker.

Spread the cheese over the vegetables.

Then, add the beaten eggs on top.

Just stir it gently.

Set the cooker on low heat and cook for about 6 hours.

Serve hot with sliced avocado and green leaves.

Nutrition:

Calories: 313

Carb: 4g

Protein: 22.9g

Fat: 22.2

Potassium: 503mg

Magnesium: 65mg

54. KETO SAUSAGE & EGG CASSEROLE

Preparation Time: 15-20 minutes

Cooking Time: 4-5 hours

Servings: 6-8

Ingredients:
- Large Eggs - 12
- Pork sausage links, cooked and sliced - 12 ounces
- Broccoli, finely chopped - 1
- Cheddar Shredded - 1 cup
- Whipping cream - ¾ cup
- Garlic cloves, minced - 2
- Salt - to taste (½ tsp)
- Pepper - ½ tbsp

Directions:

Take a 6quart ceramic slow cooker and grease its interior.

Put one layer of broccoli, half portion of the cheese, and half part of sausage into the ceramic cooker. Repeat the layering and put all the ingredients in the cooker.

Take a large bowl, and mix eggs, garlic, whipping cream, pepper, and salt thoroughly.

Transfer the mix over the layered ingredients in the ceramic cooker.

Cover and cooker for about 5 hours.

Make sure the edges are not overcooked.

Check the center and make sure your finger bounces back when touching.

Nutrition:

Calories: 484

Fat: 38.86g

Cholesterol: 399mg

Potassium: 8mg

Carbohydrates: 5.39g

Dietary Fiber: 1.18g

Sodium: 858mg

Protein: 26.13g

55. EGG & MUSHROOM BREAKFAST

Preparation Time: 15 minutes

Cooking Time: 6 hours

Servings: 4

Ingredients:
- Mushrooms, chopped - 1 cup
- Bacon large - 3
- Eggs - 6
- Chopped shallots - 3 tbsp
- Bell pepper, red - ½ cup
- Shredded, kale leaves - 8 large
- Parmesan cheese, shredded - 1 cup
- Butter or ghee - 1 tbsp
- Pepper - ¼ spoon
- Salt to taste
- Spinach - for dressing
- Avocado, sliced - for dressing
- Virgin olive oil - for dressing

Directions:

Wash, clean, and slice the bacon

Wash, clean and remove the stem of the kale and chop it nicely.

Take a pan and cook bacon until it becomes crispy.

Add mushroom, pepper, and shallot and continue heating until it becomes soft.

Now add kale and switch off the stove and let the kale wilt.

Take a small mixing bowl and beat the eggs, with pepper and salt.

Put on the slow cooker and add some butter.

Grease the inside of the cooker properly with butter.

Transfer the sautéed vegetables to the cooker.

Spread the cheese over it.

Add the beaten egg on top of the mixture.

Stir well and slow heat for about 6 hours.

You may occasionally check the food after 4 hours.

Check with your finger to bounce back.

Serve it with sliced avocado, spread with spinach dressed in olive oil.

Nutrition:

Total carbs: 6.1g

Fiber: 2.1g

Net carbs: 4g

Fat: 22.2g

Protein: 22.9g

Saturated fat: 9.8g

Calories: 313kcal

Magnesium: 65mg

Potassium: 503mg

56. EGG, SPINACH, AND HAM BREAKFAST CASSEROLE

Preparation Time: 10 minutes

Cooking Time: 1 hour and 30 minutes

Servings: 6

Ingredients:
- Large eggs - 6

- Salt - ½ tsp
- Black pepper - ¼ tsp
- Milk - ¼ cup
- Greek yogurt - ½ cup
- Thyme - ½ tsp
- Onion powder - ½ tsp
- Garlic powder - ½ tsp
- Diced mushrooms - ⅓ cup
- Baby spinach (packed) - 1 cup
- Shredded pepper jack cheese – 1 cup
- Ham, diced – 1 cup

Directions:

Mix eggs, salt, pepper, milk, yogurt, thyme, onion powder, garlic powder properly in a bowl.

Add mushrooms, spinach, cheese, ham, and stir.

Now take a 6-quart slow cooker and spray with non-stick cooking spray.

Pour egg mixture into the cooker and put on slow.

Cover and cook on high for 90-120 minutes until eggs appropriately set.

Slice and serve for breakfast or dinner.

Nutrition:

Calories: 155.6
Total Fat: 8.7g
Cholesterol: 86.1mg
Sodium: 758.8mg
Total Carbs: 2.5g
Dietary Fiber: 0.3g
Protein: 15.6g

57. KETO SOUP WITH MISO

Preparation Time: 15 minutes
Cooking Time: 8 hours
Servings: 4

Ingredients:

- Chopped onion - 1 medium
- Miso, white good quality - 2 tbsp
- Olive oil - 4 tbsp
- Garlic, minced - 1 tsp
- Broccoli flowerets - 1 cup
- Zucchini, chopped - 1 cup
- Celery stalks, cut into pieces - 2 stalks
- Pumpkin, diced - 1 cup
- Pepper as required
- Salt to taste

Directions:

Take a slow cooker and put 2 tbsp olive oil and keep aside.

Then take a large skillet, put 2 tbsp of oil, and heat it.

Add onion, garlic, pumpkin, celery to the heating skillet by sprinkling a bit of salt.

Sauté for 5 minutes

Transfer this mixture to the slow cooker and put all other ingredients.

Now pour about 4 cups of water and salt to taste.

Stir well.

Take 3 tbsp of water and mix the Miso and add to the slow cooker.

Put it in the slow cooker for about 8 hours.

Serve warm

Nutrition:

Carbohydrate: 6g
Net carbs: 4.86g
Fat: 19g
Fiber: 3g
Protein: 12g

58. SLOW KER PUMPKIN COCONUT BREAKFAST BARS

Preparation Time: 20 minutes
Cooking Time: 3 hours
Servings: 8

Ingredients:

- Canned puree pumpkin
- Swerve sweetener
- A spoon of raw apple cider vinegar
- 3 eggs, beaten
- A c. of coconut flour
- Pumpkin pie spice
- Cinnamon
- Baking soda
- Salt to taste
- 1/3 c. pecan, toasted and chopped

Directions:

Use parchment paper lightly oiled with cooking oil.

Mix the pumpkin puree, sweetener, apple cider vinegar, and eggs.

Differently mix the salt, pumpkin pie spice, coconut flour, baking soda, and cinnamon.

Pour the wet ingredients into the dry ingredients and mix.

Pour the batter into the Slow cooker and sprinkle with pecans.

Cover with lid. Cook for 3 hours on low or until a toothpick inserted in the middle comes out clean.

Nutrition:

Calories: 187.4

Carbohydrates: 8.5g
Fat: 17.2g
Sugars: 2.5g
Sodium: 1 5mg
Fiber: 3g

59. OVERNIGHT EGGS BENEDICT CASSEROLE

Preparation Time: 25 minutes
Cooking Time: 3 hours
Servings: 10

Ingredients:
- Canadian bacon, sliced
- 1 c. milk
- Large eggs, beaten
- 6 egg yolks
- Pepper and salt
- 2 tbsp. chives, chopped
- 1 ½ sticks butter, cubed

Directions:
Spray cooking oil in the Slow cooker's ceramic interior.
Take the bacon slices at the bottom of the Slow cooker.
Mix the eggs and milk. Season with pepper and salt.
Pour over the bacon.
Close the lid and cook for 1 ½ hour.
Open the lid and Take the egg yolks on top. Sprinkle with chopped chives.
Continue cooking for another 1 ½ hours or until the egg mixture is done.
While still warm, keep butter on top.

Nutrition:
Calories per serving: 256
Carbohydrates: 2g
Protein: 16.2g
Fat: 21g
Sugars: 0g
Sodium: 734mg
Fiber: 0.3g

60. VANILLA PUMPKIN BREAD

Preparation Time: 10 minutes
Cooking Time: 2 hours
Servings: 2

Ingredients:
- Cooking spray
- ½ cup white flour
- ½ cup almond flour
- ½ tsp baking soda
- A pinch of cinnamon powder
- 2 tbsp olive oil
- 2 tbsp Stevia
- 1 egg
- ½ tbsp milk
- ½ tsp vanilla extract
- ½ cup pumpkin puree
- 2 tbsp walnuts, chopped
- 2 tbsp chocolate chips

Directions:
In a bowl, mix white flour with almond flour, baking soda, and cinnamon and stir.
Add Stevia, olive oil, egg, milk, vanilla extract, pumpkin puree, walnuts, and chocolate chips, and stir well.
Grease a loaf pan that fits your slow cooker with cooking spray, pour pumpkin bread, transfer to your cooker and cook on High for 2 hours.
Slice bread, divide between plates, and serve.
Enjoy!

Nutrition:
Calories: 200,
Fat: 3g,
Fiber: 5g,
Carbs: 8g,
Protein: 4g.

61. ALMOND BANANA BREAD

Preparation Time: 10 minutes
Cooking Time: 4 hours
Servings: 2

Ingredients:
- 1 egg
- 2 tbsp butter, melted
- 1 cup almond flour
- ½ tsp baking powder
- ¼ tsp baking soda
- A pinch of cinnamon powder
- A pinch of nutmeg, ground
- 2 bananas, mashed
- ¼ cup almonds, sliced
- Cooking spray

Directions:
In a bowl, mix flour, baking powder, baking soda, cinnamon, and nutmeg and stir.
Add egg, butter, almonds, and bananas and stir well.
Grease your slow cooker with cooking spray, pour bread mix, cover, and cook on Low for 4 hours.
Slice bread and serve for breakfast.
Enjoy!

Nutrition:
Calories: 211,
Fat: 3g,
Fiber: 6g,
Carbs: 12g,
Protein: 5g.

62. SAGE CAULIFLOWER CASSEROLE

Preparation Time: 10 minutes
Cooking Time: 3 hours and 30 minutes
Servings: 2

Ingredients:
- 1 tsp onion powder
- 2 eggs, whisked
- ½ tsp garlic powder
- ½ tsp sage, dried
- Salt and black pepper to the taste
- ½ yellow onion, chopped
- 1 tbsp parsley, chopped
- 2 garlic cloves, minced
- A pinch of red pepper flakes
- ½ tbsp olive oil
- 4 cups cauliflower, chopped

Directions:
Grease your slow cooker with the oil, add cauliflower, onion, garlic, parsley, and pepper flakes and toss a bit.
In a bowl, mix eggs with onion powder, garlic powder, sage, salt, and pepper, whisk well, and pour over cauliflower.
Cover, cook on High for 3 hours and 30 minutes, divide into 2 plates and serve for breakfast.
Enjoy!

Nutrition:
Calories: 218,
Fat: 6g,
Fiber: 6g,
Carbs: 14g,
Protein: 5g.

63. PEAR AND MAPLE OATMEAL

Preparation Time: 10 minutes
Cooking Time: 7 hours
Servings: 2

Ingredients:
- 1 and ½ cups milk
- ½ cup steel cut oats
- ½ tsp vanilla extract
- 1 pear, chopped
- ½ tsp maple extract

Directions:
In your slow cooker, combine milk with oats, vanilla, pear, maple extract, stir, cover, and cook on Low for 7 hours.
Divide into bowls and serve for breakfast.
Enjoy!

Nutrition:
Calories 200,
Fat 5g,
Fiber 7g,
Carbs 14g,
Protein 4g.

64. ALMOND & STRAWBERRY OATMEAL

Preparation Time: 10 minutes
Cooking Time: 6 hours
Servings: 2

Ingredients:
- 1 cup steel-cut oats
- 3 cups water
- 1 cup almond milk
- 1 cup strawberries, chopped
- ½ cup Greek yogurt
- ½ tsp cinnamon powder
- ½ tsp vanilla extract

Directions:
In your slow cooker, mix oats with water, milk, strawberries, yogurt, cinnamon, and vanilla, toss, cover, and cook on Low for 6 hours.
Stir your oatmeal one more time, divide into bowls and serve for breakfast.
Enjoy!

Nutrition:
Calories 201,
Fat 3g,
Fiber 6g,
Carbs 12g,
Protein 6g.

65. CHEDDAR SAUSAGE CAULIFLOWER

Preparation Time: 10 minutes
Cooking Time: 4 hours
Servings: 2

Ingredients:
- 1 cauliflower, chopped
- ½ red bell pepper, chopped
- ½ green bell pepper, chopped

- ½ yellow onion, chopped
- 4 ounces smoked Andouille sausage, sliced
- 1 cup cheddar cheese, shredded
- ¼ cup sour cream
- A pinch of oregano, dried
- ¼ tsp basil, dried
- 4 ounces chicken cream
- Salt and black pepper to the taste
- 1 tbsp parsley, chopped

Directions:

Put the cauliflower in your slow cooker, add red bell pepper, green bell pepper, onion, sausage, cheese, sour cream, oregano, basil, salt, pepper, and chicken cream, cover and cook on low for 4 hours.

Add parsley, toss, divide between plates and serve for breakfast.

Enjoy!

Nutrition:

Calories 355,

Fat 14g,

Fiber 4g,

Carbs 20g,

Protein 22g.

66. COCONUT QUINOA MIX

Preparation Time: 10 minutes

Cooking Time: 8 hours

Servings: 2

Ingredients:

- ½ cup quinoa
- 1 cup water
- ½ cup coconut milk
- 1 tbsp Stevia
- A pinch of salt
- 1 tbsp berries

Directions:

In your slow cooker, mix quinoa with water, coconut milk, Stevia, and salt, stir well, cover, and cook on Low for 8 hours.

Divide into 2 bowls, sprinkle berries on top and serve for breakfast.

Enjoy!

Nutrition:

Calories 261,

Fat 5g,

Fiber 7g,

Carbs 12g,

Protein 5g.

67. CHEDDAR CAULIFLOWER

Preparation Time: 10 minutes

Cooking Time: 3 hours

Servings: 2

Ingredients:

- 1 tbsp butter
- 2 tbsp mushrooms, chopped
- 2 tbsp yellow onion, chopped
- ¼ tsp garlic powder
- 1 tbsp almond flour
- ½ cup milk
- ¼ cup sour cream
- 2 cups cauliflower, shredded
- ¼ cup cheddar cheese, shredded
- Salt and black pepper to the taste
- ½ tbsp parsley, chopped
- Cooking spray

Directions:

Heat a pan with the butter over medium heat, add onion and mushroom, garlic powder, and flour, stir, and cook for 1 minute.

Add milk gradually, stir, cook until it thickens and take off the heat.

Grease your slow cooker with cooking spray and add mushrooms mix.

Add cauliflower, sour cream, cheddar cheese, salt and pepper, cover, and cook on High for 3 hours.

Divide between plates and serve right away for breakfast with parsley sprinkled on top

Enjoy!

Nutrition:

Calories 245,

Fat 4g,

Fiber 7g,

Carbs 7g,

Protein 10g.

68. CHEDDAR & BACON CASSEROLE

Preparation Time: 10 minutes

Cooking Time: 3 hours

Servings: 2

Ingredients:

- 5 ounces cauliflower, shredded
- 2 bacon slices, cooked and chopped
- 2 ounces cheddar cheese, shredded
- 3 eggs, whisked
- 1 green onion, chopped
- ¼ cup milk

- Cooking spray
- A pinch of salt and black pepper

Directions:

Grease your slow cooker with cooking spray and add cauliflower, bacon, and cheese.

In a bowl, mix eggs with green onion, milk, salt, and pepper, whisk well and add to slow cooker.

Cover, cook on High for 3 hours, divide between plates and serve.

Enjoy!

Nutrition:

Calories 281g,

Fat 4g,

Fiber 6g,

Carbs 12g,

Protein 11g.

69. CREAM CHEESE BANANA BREAKFAST

Preparation Time: 10 minutes

Cooking Time: 4 hours

Servings: 2

Ingredients:

- ½ French baguette, sliced
- 2 bananas, sliced
- 2 ounces cream cheese
- ¼ cup walnuts, chopped
- 1 egg, whisked
- 3 tbsp skim milk
- 2 tbsp Stevia
- ½ tsp cinnamon powder
- A pinch of nutmeg, ground
- ¼ tsp vanilla extract
- 1 tbsp butter
- Cooking spray

Directions:

Spread cream cheese on all bread slices and grease your slow cooker with cooking spray.

Arrange bread slices in your slow cooker, layer banana slices, and walnuts.

In a bowl, mix eggs with skim milk, Stevia, cinnamon, nutmeg, and vanilla extract, and whisk and add over bread slices.

Add butter, cover, cook on Low for 4 hours, divide between plates and serve for breakfast.

Enjoy!

Nutrition:

Calories 251g,

Fat 5g,

Fiber 7g,

Carbs 12g,

Protein 4g.

70. CARROTS AND ZUCCHINI OATMEAL

Preparation Time: 10 minutes

Cooking Time: 8 hours

Servings: 2

Ingredients:

- ½ cup steel cut oats
- 1 cup coconut milk
- 1 carrot, grated
- ¼ zucchini, grated
- A pinch of nutmeg, ground
- A pinch of cloves, ground
- ½ tsp cinnamon powder
- ¼ cup pecans, chopped
- Cooking spray

Directions:

Grease your slow cooker with cooking spray, add oats, milk, carrot, zucchini, nutmeg, cloves, cinnamon, and toss, cover, and cook on Low for 8 hours.

Divide into 2 bowls, sprinkle pecans on top and serve.

Enjoy!

Nutrition:

Calories 200,

Fat 4g,

Fiber 8g,

Carbs 11g,

Protein 5g

71. CHEESY TATER TOT CASSEROLE

Preparation Time: 10 minutes

Cooking Time: 4 hours

Servings: 2

Ingredients:

- Cooking spray
- 5 ounces tater tots, frozen
- 2 eggs, whisked
- ½ pound turkey sausage, ground
- 1 tbsp heavy cream
- ¼ tsp thyme, dried
- ¼ tsp garlic powder
- A pinch of salt and black pepper
- ½ cup Colby jack cheese, shredded

Directions:

Grease your slow cooker with cooking spray, spread tater tots on the bottom, add sausage, thyme, garlic powder, salt, pepper, and whisked eggs.

Add cheese, cover pot, and cook on Low for 4 hours.
Divide between plates and serve for breakfast.
Enjoy!

Nutrition:
Calories 231,
Fat 5g,
Fiber 9g,
Carbs 15g,
Protein 11g.

72. BANANA & BLUEBERRY OATS

Preparation Time: 10 minutes
Cooking Time: 6 hours
Servings: 2

Ingredients:
- 1/2 cup steel-cut oats
- ¼ cup quinoa
- ½ cup blueberries
- 1 banana, mashed
- A pinch of cinnamon powder
- 2 tbsp Stevia
- 2 cups water
- Cooking spray
- ½ cup coconut milk

Directions:
Grease your slow cooker with cooking spray, add oats, quinoa, blueberries, banana, cinnamon, Stevia, water, and coconut milk, stir, cover, and cook on Low for 6 hours.
Divide into 2 bowls and serve for breakfast.
Enjoy!

Nutrition:
Calories 200,
Fat 4g,
Fiber 5g,
Carbs 8g,
Protein 5g.

73. PEANUT BUTTER OATMEAL

Preparation Time: 10 minutes
Cooking Time: 8 hours
Servings: 2

Ingredients:
- 1 banana, mashed
- 1 and ½ cups almond milk
- ½ cup steel cut oats
- 2 tbsp peanut butter
- ½ tsp vanilla extract
- ½ tsp cinnamon powder
- ½ tbsp chia seeds

Directions:
In your slow cooker, mix almond milk with banana, oats, peanut butter, vanilla extract, cinnamon, and chia, stir, cover, and cook on Low for 8 hours.
Stir oatmeal one more time, divide into 2 bowls and serve.
Enjoy!

Nutrition:
Calories 222,
Fat 5g,
Fiber 6g,
Carbs 9g,
Protein 11g.

74. CRANBERRY APPLE OATS

Preparation Time: 10 minutes
Cooking Time: 3 hours
Servings: 2

Ingredients:
- Cooking spray
- 2 cups water
- 1 cup old fashioned oats
- ¼ cup cranberries, dried
- 1 apple, chopped
- 1 tbsp butter, melted
- ½ tsp cinnamon powder

Directions:
Grease your slow cooker with cooking spray, add water, oats, cranberries, apple, butter, and cinnamon, stir well, cover, and cook on Low for 3 hours.
Stir oatmeal again divides into bowls, and serves for breakfast.
Enjoy!

Nutrition:
Calories 182,
Fat 4g,
Fiber 6g,
Carbs 8g,
Protein 10g.

75. COCONUT RAISINS OATMEAL

Preparation Time: 10 minutes
Cooking Time: 8 hours
Servings: 2

Ingredients:
- ½ cup water

- ½ cup coconut milk
- ½ cup steel cut oats
- ½ cup carrots, grated
- ¼ cup raisins
- A pinch of cinnamon powder
- A pinch of ginger, ground
- A pinch of nutmeg, ground
- ¼ cup coconut flakes, shredded
- 1 tbsp orange zest, grated
- ½ tsp vanilla extract
- ½ tbsp Stevia
- 2 tbsp walnuts, chopped

Directions:

In your slow cooker, mix water with coconut milk, oats, carrots, raisins, cinnamon, ginger, nutmeg, coconut flakes, orange zest, vanilla extract, and Stevia, stir, cover, and cook on Low for 8 hours.

Add walnuts, stir, divide into 2 bowls and serve for breakfast.

Enjoy!

Nutrition:

Calories 200,

Fat 4g,

Fiber 6g,

Carbs 8g,

Protein 8g.

SOUPS

76. CREAMY HARVEST PUMPKIN BISQUE

Preparation Time: 15 minutes

Cooking Time: 5 hours

Servings: 8

Ingredients:
- 1 medium pumpkin (butternut, Stevia, etc.)
- 2 carrots, chopped
- 1 medium yellow onion, chopped
- 2 cups vegetable stock
- 1 tsp curry powder
- ½ tsp ground ginger
- ½ tsp ground nutmeg
- ½ tsp cumin
- 1 cup heavy cream
- Kosher salt
- Freshly ground black pepper

Directions:

Peel pumpkin skin, and remove pulp and seeds. Cube up the pumpkin flesh.

Place pumpkin, carrots, onion, vegetable stock, and spices in the slow cooker.

Cook within 4-5 hours, low or 2-3 hours, high. Make sure vegetables are incredibly tender.

Pulse in a blender, then return it inside the slow cooker and add in the heavy cream, stirring until thoroughly mixed. Season with salt and pepper as desired. Heat back up to desired heat and serve.

Nutrition:

Carbs: 13g

Calories: 125

Fat: 5g

Protein: 2g

77. ZESTY WHITE CHICKEN CHILI

Preparation Time: 15 minutes

Cooking Time: 8 hours

Servings: 6

Ingredients:
- 2 lbs. Boneless, skinless chicken breasts or thighs
- 1 large yellow onion, diced
- 1 medium green bell pepper, chopped
- 1 small jalapeno, minced
- 6 cloves garlic, minced
- 3 tsp. ground cumin (add more to taste)
- 1 tsp. dried oregano
- 2 tsp. chili powder (add more to taste)

- 1 tsp. kosher salt
- ¼ tsp. black pepper
- 6 cups chicken stock
- 1 lime, juiced
- ½ cup fresh cilantro, chopped
- ½ cup chives chopped

Directions:

Throw the peppers, jalapeno, onion, garlic, spices into the slow cooker. Place the chicken on top and fill with all of the broth.

Cook covered on low for 7-8 hours. Check the chicken with a fork to see if it is falling apart.

Add the lime juice and stir, add salt and pepper to taste.

When serving, top off with cilantro and chives.

Nutrition:

Carbs: 6g

Calories: 105

Fat: 0g

Protein: 25 g

78. TUSCAN ZUCCHINI STEW

Preparation Time: 20 minutes

Cooking Time: 6 hours

Servings: 6

Ingredients:

- 1 1/2 pounds Italian-seasoned sausage (spicy or sweet, whatever you prefer)
- 1 cup celery, chopped small
- 3 cups sliced zucchini, sliced into thin rounds
- 1 green bell pepper, chopped small
- 1 red or yellow bell pepper, chopped
- 1 large onion, diced
- 3 cloves garlic, minced
- ½ tsp. fresh ground black pepper
- 2 tsp salt
- 1 (28 oz) can diced tomatoes
- 2 (14 oz) cans of fire-roasted diced tomatoes
- ½ c. water
- 1 tsp Stevia
- 2 tsp Italian seasoning
- 1 tsp dried basil
- ¼ c. asiago cheese, grated
- Red pepper flakes (optional)

Directions:

Fry the sausage on medium heat on the stove. Break up the meat with a spatula and make sure it's fully cooked (5-8 minutes). Drain off the grease.

Add the celery, onions and peppers continue to cook until the vegetables become soft and translucent (7-8 minutes). Add minced garlic and cook and stir continually until fragrant (2 minutes) Add the salt and pepper, stir and remove from the heat.

Pour sausage mixture into the slow cooker. Put the 3 cans of diced tomatoes, the spices, the Stevia, and the water

Cook on low for 4-6 hours. Top with grated asiago, and add a fresh sprig of basil (optional).

Nutrition:

Carbs: 16g

Calories: 280

Fat: 22g

Protein: 23g

79. MELT-IN-YOUR-MOUTH BEEF STEW

Preparation Time: 15 minutes

Cooking Time: 7 hours

Servings: 10

Ingredients:

- 2 lbs. stewing beef, diced into 1-inch cubes
- 2 tbsp. extra virgin olive oil
- 3 large carrots (4-5 medium/small), chopped
- 2 large yellow onions, diced
- 2 large stalks of celery, chopped
- 5 cloves garlic, minced
- 1 tsp kosher salt
- ¼ tsp fresh ground black pepper
- Salt and pepper to taste
- 1/4 cup almond flour (can use 1/8c. cornstarch instead)
- 3 cups beef broth
- ¼ c. Dijon mustard
- 2 tbsp. Worcestershire sauce
- 1 tbsp. Stevia
- 3/4 tbsp. dried rosemary
- 1 tsp. dried thyme

Directions:

Massage the beef with salt plus pepper and coat all sides with flour.

Heat-up the oil in a large skillet over medium heat, then put the onions and garlic and sauté for 1-2 minutes. Add the flower-coated beef to the skillet and sear on all sides for 2-3 minutes.

Place the beef and onions and garlic into the slow cooker and add the carrots.

Put the skillet with the beef drippings back on the burner and add all of the rest of the ingredients to the hot skillet (beef broth, Dijon, Worcestershire, Stevia, rosemary, thyme).

Stir the mixture, and make sure to stir up any beef or garlic remnants at the bottom of the pan. Heat-up, then stir until the Stevia has dissolved the mixture is well-combined.

Pour the broth mixture over the beef and carrots in the slow cooker—Cook within 7-8 hours, low or high for 4 hours. Keep warm until you're ready to serve it. Garnish with fresh parsley if desired

Nutrition:

Carbs: 11g
Calories: 250
Fat: 12g
Protein: 24g

80. MEXICAN CHORIZO ENCHILADA SOUP

Preparation Time: 15 minutes
Cooking Time: 4 hours
Servings: 8

Ingredients:

- 1 lb. ground beef
- 1 lb. chorizo sausage
- 2, (8oz.) packages Neufchâtel (cream) cheese
- 2 cans of roasted tomatoes, dice
- 1 medium jalapeno, chopped finely
- 1 large onion, chopped
- 1 clove of garlic, minced
- 1 green bell pepper, chopped
- 1 (1.25 oz) package taco seasoning (or more to taste)
- 4 cups of chicken stock
- ¼ c. fresh cilantro
- ¼ c. shredded sharp cheddar cheese (optional)
- Regular sour cream(optional)

Directions:

Heat-up a large skillet, and brown the beef and chorizo over medium heat. Break the meat up until crumbly with a spatula. Stir in onion, jalapeno, and bell pepper. Cook until onions start to soften (5-7 minutes). Put the garlic and continue to stir and cook for 2 more minutes.

Sprinkle the taco seasoning packet over the meat mixture and stir.

Put the meat batter inside the slow cooker and add the Neufchâtel cheese and canned tomatoes. Stir until the cheese breaks down and mixes in.

Cook within 4 hours, low or high for 2 hours.

Put the cilantro and cook for another 10-15 minutes.

Garnish with cheddar cheese and sour cream, and serve.

Nutrition:

Carbs: 7g
Calories: 531
Fat: 42 g
Protein: 28g

81. HEARTY CHICKEN SOUP WITH VEGGIE NOODLES

Preparation Time: 15 minutes
Cooking Time: 8 hours
Servings: 8

Ingredients:

- 1 1/2 lbs. boneless chicken breast, cubes
- 2 cups carrots, sliced into thin rounds
- 1 large yellow onion, diced
- 3 stalks celery, chopped
- 4 cloves garlic, minced
- 3 tbsp. extra virgin olive oil
- 1/2 tsp Italian seasoning
- ¼ tsp dried parsley
- 6 cups chicken stock
- 1 cup water
- ½ tsp kosher salt
- ¼ tsp. freshly ground black pepper
- 2 medium-sized zucchinis
- 2 cups chopped Napa cabbage

Directions:

Place all ingredients except cabbage and zucchini into the slow cooker. Stir until evenly mixed

Cook on low for 6-8 hrs.

In the last 2 hours of cooking, take the zucchini, and make Zucchini noodles. If you do not have a veggie noodle machine, peel the zucchini, then use the peeler to shave off thin strips of zucchini.

Take the zucchini noodles and the chopped cabbage and sauté in a large skillet over medium heat with extra virgin olive oil. Stir occasionally as the vegetables soften, and the cabbage starts to caramelize and brown a little bit (about 7-8 minutes). Put the vegetables inside the slow cooker, then continue to cook for the remaining 1-2 hours, then serve.

Nutrition:

Carbs: 7g
Calories: 145
Fat: 6g
Protein: 20g

82. SUPERB CHICKEN, BACON, GARLIC THYME SOUP

Preparation Time: 15 minutes
Cooking Time: 6 hours
Servings: 4

Ingredients:
- 2 tbsp of unsalted butter
- 1 chopped onion
- 1 chopped pepper
- 8 chicken thighs
- 8 slices of bacon
- 1 tbsp of thyme
- 1 tsp of salt
- 1 tsp of pepper
- 1 tbsp of minced garlic
- 1 tbsp of coconut flour
- 3 tbsp of lemon juice
- 1 cup of chicken stock
- ¼ cup of unsweetened coconut milk
- 3 tbsp of tomato paste

Directions:
Spread the butter on the slow cooker base and arrange the peppers and onions on top of it.

Add the chicken thighs and then layer with the bacon. Add the remaining fixing.

Cook within 6 hours, low. Cut the thighs into pieces, arrange in bowls and serve.

Nutrition:
Calories: 396
Fat: 21g
Carbs: 7g
Fiber: 2g
Protein: 41g

83. DELIGHTFUL CHICKEN-CHORIZO SPICY SOUP

Preparation Time: 15 minutes
Cooking Time: 3.5 hours
Servings: 10

Ingredients:
- 4 pounds of skinless, boneless chicken
- 1 pound of chorizo
- 4 cups of chicken stock
- 1 cup of heavy cream
- 1 can of stewed tomatoes
- 2 tbsp of minced garlic
- 2 tbsp of Worcestershire sauce
- 2 tbsp of red sauce
- Parmesan and sour cream for garnish

Directions:
Heat a frying pan and brown the sausage.

Place the chicken into the slow cooker and add the remaining ingredients except for the parmesan and sour cream.

Cook within 3 hours, high. Garnish with parmesan and sour cream.

Nutrition:
Calories: 659
Fat: 37g
Carbs: 6g
Fiber: 1g
Protein: 52g

84. DELECTABLE SPEARMINT LIVER AND LAMB HEART SOUP

Preparation Time: 15 minutes
Cooking Time: 10 hours
Servings: 4

Ingredients:
- 3 cups of livers and lamb hearts
- 1 cup of cubed lamb meat
- 2 cups of broth of your choice
- 2 cups of hot water
- 2 bunches of diced spring onions
- 1 pack of chopped fresh spearmint
- 2 cups of fresh spinach
- 1 tsp of garlic powder
- 1 tsp of dried basil
- 1 tsp of sweet paprika
- 1 tsp of ground pimento
- 4 lightly crushed cloves
- ½ tsp of cinnamon
- 4 tbsp of olive oil
- Salt and pepper to taste
- 1 large egg
- 1 cup of Greek yogurt, full fat

Directions:
Put all of the fixings to the slow cooker except the yogurt and the egg.

Cover and cook for 10 hours on low.

Slice the meat into chunks, then put it back to the slow cooker.

Mix the yogurt and the egg in a bowl. Add some of the cooking liquid from the slow cooker. Mix thoroughly.

Put the batter inside the slow cooker, then stir to combine. Allow to heat through, and serve.

Nutrition:
Carbs: 12g
Protein: 56g
Fat: 38g
Calories: 560

85. LOVELY LENTIL SAUSAGE SOUP

Preparation Time: 15 minutes
Cooking Time: 6 hours
Servings: 4

Ingredients:
- 1 ½ pound of Italian sausage
- 2 tbsp of butter
- 2 tbsp of olive oil
- 5 cups of chicken stock
- 1 ½ cups of lentils
- 1 cup of spinach
- ½ cup of diced carrots
- 4 minced cloves of garlic
- 1 trimmed leek
- 1 diced celery rib
- 1 cup of heavy cream
- ½ cup of shredded Parmesan cheese
- 2 tbsp of Dijon mustard
- 2 tbsp of red wine vinegar
- Salt and pepper to taste

Directions:
Place the stock and the lentils into the slow cooker.
In a saucepan, heat the olive oil and the butter and brown the sausage.
In the same saucepan, sauté the celery, pepper, salt, garlic, leek, spinach, onions, and carrots for 10 minutes.
Pour the mixture into the slow cooker. Cook on low for 6-8 hours. Spoon into bowls and serve.

Nutrition:
Calories: 195
Fat: 14g
Carbs: 4.9g
Protein: 11g

86. TASTY CORNED BEEF AND HEAVY CREAM SOUP

Preparation Time: 15 minutes
Cocking Time: 5 hours and 30 minutes
Servings: 4

Ingredients:
- 1 diced onion
- 2 diced celery ribs
- 2 cloves of minced garlic
- 1 pound of chopped corn beef
- 4 cups of beef stock
- 1 cup of sauerkraut
- 1 tsp of sea salt
- 1 tsp of caraway seeds
- ¾ tsp of black pepper
- 2 cups of heavy cream
- 1 ½ cups of shredded Swiss cheese

Directions:
Heat-up the butter, then sauté the celery, garlic, and onions in a saucepan.
Pour the mixture into the slow cooker.
Put the rest of the items except the cream and the cheese.
Cover and cook on low for 4 hours and 30 minutes.
Add the cream and the cheese and cook for another hour.

Nutrition:
Calories: 225
Fat: 18.5g
Carbs: 4g
Protein: 11.5g

87. BEEF DIJON

Preparation Time: 15 minutes
Cooking Time: 5 hours
Servings: 4

Ingredients:
- 2 tbsp. Steak seasoning - to taste
- 2 tbsp. Avocado oil
- 2 tbsp. Peanut oil
- 2 tbsp. Balsamic vinegar/dry sherry
- 2 tbsp. large chopped green onions/small chopped onions for the garnish - extra
- 1/4 c. whipping cream
- 1 c. fresh crimini mushrooms - sliced
- 1 tbsp. Dijon mustard

Directions:
Warm up the oils using the high heat setting on the stovetop. Flavor each of the steaks with pepper and arrange to a skillet.
Cook two to three minutes per side until done.
Place into the slow cooker. Pour in the skillet drippings, half of the mushrooms, and the onions.
Cook on the low setting for four hours.
When the cooking time is done, scoop out the onions, mushrooms, and steaks to a serving platter.
In a separate dish - whisk together the mustard, balsamic vinegar, whipping cream, and the steak drippings from the slow cooker.
Pour the gravy over the steaks.
Enjoy with some brown rice, riced cauliflower, or potatoes.

Nutrition:
Calories: 535

Fat: 40g
Carbs: 5g
Protein: 39g

88. TOSCANA SOUP

Preparation Time: 15 minutes
Cooking Time: 8 hours
Servings: 5

Ingredients:
- Italian sausage – ½ lb.
- Olive oil 1 tbsp
- Onion – ¼ cup, diced
- Chicken stock – 18 oz.
- Garlic – cloves, minced
- Chopped kale – 1 ½ cups
- Cauliflower – ½ head, diced florets
- Salt – ½ tsp.
- Crushed red pepper flakes – ¼ tsp.
- Heavy cream – ¼ cup
- Pepper – ½ tsp.

Directions:

In a pan, brown the sausage. Transfer the sausage to the Crock-Pot and discard the grease.

Add the oil into the skillet and sauté the onions for 3 to 4 minutes. Add to the Crock-Pot.

Except for the cream, add the rest of the ingredients to the Crock-Pot.

Mix, then cook within 8 hours, low. Add the cream when cooked.

Stir and serve hot.

Nutrition:
Calories: 246
Fat: 19g
Carbs: 7g
Protein: 14g

89. RABBIT STEW

Preparation Time: 15 minutes
Cooking Time: 5 hours
Servings: 6

Ingredients:
- Rabbit 3 lbs., cut into pieces
- Uncured bacon ½ lb., cubed
- Butter 2 tbsp.
- Dry white wine 2 cups
- Large sweet onion 1, chopped
- Bay leaves 2
- Rosemary 1 large sprig
- Salt and pepper to taste

Directions:

Add the cubed bacon and butter to a skillet.

Add the sliced onion and cook for 5 minutes. Then remove the onion and leave the fat in the pan.

Add the rabbit and sauté on high heat until browned. Put in the wine, then simmer for a couple of minutes.

Add everything from the pan to the Crock-Pot. Add bay leaves, rosemary, salt, and pepper.

Cook within 5 hours, low.

Nutrition:
Calories: 517
Fat: 32g
Carbs: 2g
Protein: 36g

90. BEEF STEW

Preparation Time: 15 minutes
Cooking Time: 5 hours
Servings: 5

Ingredients:
- Beef – 2 lbs.
- Coconut oil 3 tbsp
- Beef broth 3 cups
- Medium onion 1, chopped
- Apple cider vinegar 2 tbsp.
- Fresh thyme 1 tbsp.
- Erythritol –2 tsp.
- Ground cinnamon – 2 tsp.
- Minced garlic – 1 ½ tbsp.
- Bay leaves – 2
- Black pepper – 1 ½ tsp.
- Sage, rosemary, salt, fish sauce, soy sauce – 1 tsp. each

Directions:

Cut up the beef into 1-inch cubes, dice the veggies. Season the meat with salt and pepper.

Add oil in a hot skillet and brown the meat in batches. Once done, add the veggies and cook for a couple of minutes.

Add everything except for thyme, rosemary, and sage in the Crock-Pot.

Cook within 3 hours, high. Put the thyme, rosemary plus sage, then cook 1 to 2 hours in the same setting. Serve.

Nutrition:
Calories: 337.6
Fat: 13.8g
Carbs: 5.5g
Protein: 42.1g

91. CHICKEN & KALE SOUP

Preparation Time: 15 minutes
Cooking Time: 6 hours
Servings: 6

Ingredients:

- Chicken breast or thigh meat - 2 lbs., without bone or skin
- Chicken broth - 14 oz.
- Olive oil ½ cup, plus 1 tbsp
- Diced onion - 1/3 cup
- Chicken stock - 32 oz.
- Baby kale leaves - 5 oz.
- Salt and pepper to taste
- Lemon juice - ¼ cup

Directions:

Heat-up the 1 tbsp of olive oil in a pan over medium heat, then massage the chicken with salt and pepper and place it in the pan.

Lower the heat to medium and cover—Cook within 15 minutes. Shred the meat, then put it in the slow cooker.

Mix the rest of the oil, onion, and chicken broth in a bowl. Add it to the slow cooker.

Put the rest of the fixing, then cook on low for 6 hours. Stir a couple of times as it cooks.

Nutrition:

Calories: 261
Fat: 21g
Carbs: 2g
Protein: 14.1g

92. CHICKEN CHILI SOUP

Preparation Time: 15 minutes
Cooking Time: 6 hours
Servings: 4

Ingredients:

- Onion - ½, chopped
- Unsalted butter - 1 tbsp.
- Green pepper - ½, chopped
- Chicken thighs - 4, boneless
- Bacon - 4 slices
- Salt and pepper to taste
- Thyme - ½ tbsp.
- Minced garlic - ½ tbsp.
- Coconut flour - ½ tbsp.
- Lemon juice 1 ½ tbsp
- Chicken stock - ½ cup
- Tomato paste - 1 ½ tbsp.
- Unsweetened coconut milk - 2 tbsp.

Directions:

Add the butter into the Crock-Pot. Add the sliced onion and peppers.

Then add the chicken on top, and sprinkle with sliced bacon. Put all the dry fixing, then lastly add the liquids.

Cook within 6 hours, low. Mix and break apart the chicken. Serve.

Nutrition:

Calories: 396
Fat: 21g
Carbs: 7g
Protein: 41g

93. CREAMY SMOKED SALMON SOUP

Preparation Time: 15 minutes
Cooking Time: 3 hours
Servings: 4

Ingredients:

- Smoked salmon - ½ lb., roughly chopped
- Garlic - 3 cloves, crushed
- Small onion - 1, finely chopped
- Leek - 1, finely chopped
- Heavy cream - 1 ½ cups
- Olive oil - 2 tbsp.
- Salt and pepper to taste
- Fish stock - 1 ½ cups

Directions:

Add oil into the Crock-Pot. Add fish stock, leek, salmon, garlic, and onion into the pot.

Cook within 2 hours, low. Add the cream and stir—Cook for 1 hour more.

Adjust seasoning and serve.

Nutrition:

Calories: 309
Fat: 26.4g
Carbs: 7g
Protein: 12.3g

94. LAMB AND ROSEMARY STEW

Preparation Time: 15 minutes
Cooking Time: 8 hours
Servings: 4

Ingredients:

- Boneless lamb - 1 ½ lb., cut into cubes
- Onion - 1, roughly chopped
- Garlic - 3 cloves, finely chopped
- Dried rosemary - 1 tsp.

- Lamb stock cube – 1
- Olive oil – 3 tbsp. divided
- Water – 2 cups
- Salt and pepper to taste

Directions:

Add olive oil into the Crock-Pot. Brown the lamb in an oiled skillet for 2 minutes.

Add 2 cups of water, stock cube, rosemary, garlic, onion, lamb, salt, and pepper to the pot.

Cook on low within 8 hours. Serve.

Nutrition:

Calories: 427

Fat: 23.3g

Carbs: 3.9g

Protein: 48.6g

95. LAMB AND EGGPLANT STEW

Preparation Time: 15 minutes

Cooking Time: 8 hours & 30 minutes

Servings: 4

Ingredients:

- Minced lamb – 1 ½ lb.
- Onion – 1, finely chopped
- Garlic – 3 cloves, crushed
- Large eggplant ½, cut into small cubes
- Tomatoes 1, chopped
- Lamb stock cube 1
- Dried rosemary 1 tsp
- Grated mozzarella ¾ cup
- Olive oil 2 tbsp
- Water – 2 cups
- Salt and pepper to taste

Directions:

Add olive oil into the Crock-Pot. Add water, lamb, onion, garlic, eggplant, stock cube, tomatoes, rosemary, salt, and pepper to the pot. Stir to mix.

Cook within 8 hours, high. Remove the lid and stir the stew.

Sprinkle the mozzarella on top, cover with the lid, and cook 30 minutes more. Serve.

Nutrition:

Calories: 432

Fat: 21g

Carbs: 8.8g

Protein: 50.9g

96. BACON AND CAULIFLOWER SOUP

Preparation Time: 15 minutes

Cooking Time: 4 hours

Servings: 4

Ingredients:

- Large cauliflower head – ¾, cut into chunks
- Garlic – 3 cloves, crushed
- Onion – ¾, finely chopped
- Bacon – 4 slices, cut into small pieces
- Chicken stock – 2 cups
- Smoked paprika – ½ tsp.
- Chili powder – ½ tsp.
- Heavy cream – ¾ cup
- Olive oil 2 tbsp
- Salt and pepper to taste
- Paprika to taste

Directions:

Add olive oil into the Crock-Pot. Add the garlic, cauliflower, onion, bacon, stock, paprika, chili, salt, and pepper to the pot. Stir to mix.

Cook on high within 4 hours. Open the lid and blend with a hand mixer.

Add the cream and mix. Serve sprinkled with paprika.

Nutrition:

Calories: 265

Fat: 22.3g

Carbs: 6.1g

Protein: 10.4g

97. POT ROAST SOUP

Preparation Time: 15 minutes

Cooking Time: 5-8 hours

Servings: 4

Ingredients:

- 1/2 diced medium butternut squash
- 3/4 cup chicken stock
- 1 diced big onion
- 1 (14 ounces) can diced tomatoes
- 1 1/4 pounds stew meat
- 3 diced big carrots
- 7 1/2 ounces mushrooms, diced
- Dried cumin
- Dried basil
- Dried oregano
- Salt & pepper, as desired
- Splash apple cider vinegar

Directions:

Arrange the vegetables in layers at the bottom of the slow cooker.

Pour in the stew meat, then sprinkle in the spices as desired, then stir to combine.

Cook for 5 hours on low settings and high settings for 8 hours.

Serve and enjoy.

Nutrition:

Calories: 80

Carbs: 10g

Fat: 2g

Protein: 7g

98. SOUTHERN PALEO SLOW COOKER CHILI

Preparation Time: 10 minutes

Cooking Time: 8 hours

Servings: 6

Ingredients:

- 1/2 tsp sea salt
- 1 tsp paprika
- 1 diced big onion
- 1 tsp onion powder
- 1 tsp garlic powder
- 1 tbsp. Worcestershire sauce
- 1 lb. grass-fed organic beef
- 1 tbsp. fresh parsley, chopped
- 1 seeded & diced green bell pepper
- 4 tsp chili powder
- 4 chopped small big large carrots
- 26 oz. tomatoes, neatly chopped
- A pinch of cumin
- Diced onions, if desired
- Sliced jalapeños, if desired
- Dairy-free sour cream, if desired

Directions:

Using a medium-sized skillet, add in the ground beef and brown over high heat, occasionally stirring until there is no pink.

Put the browned beef inside the slow cooker, including the fat.

Add the onion, green bell pepper, tomatoes, and carrots to the slow cooker.

Mix all the fixing, then put in all the remaining seasonings and spices.

Stir all the ingredients together again, then cover and cook for 8 hours on low settings or 5 on high settings.

Serve then top with sour cream (dairy-free) with extra jalapenos, if desired, and enjoy.

Nutrition:

Calories: 241

Carbs: 24g

Fat: 8g

Protein: 20g

99. DAIRY-FREE CHILI CHICKEN SOUP

Preparation Time: 30 minutes

Cooking Time: 6 hours

Servings: 10

Ingredients:

- 1/4 tsp white pepper
- 1 cup of coconut milk
- 1 tsp chili powder
- 1 big diced yellow onion
- 1 tbsp minced garlic
- 1 tbsp coarse-real salt
- 2 tsp cumin
- 2 cups chicken broth
- 2 (8 ounces) cans green chilies, diced
- 2 & ½-pounds boneless chicken thighs
- 3 cans Great Northern beans
- (Optional)
- 1/4 cup arrowroot starch
- 1/2 cup water
- (For toppings)
- 1/3 cup chopped cilantro
- Sour cream
- Tortilla chips
- Juiced lime

Directions:

Put all the items into the slow cooker, then cover and cook for 5-6 hours on high settings.

Remove the chicken from the slow cooker, then transfer into a medium-sized bowl, then shred.

Take the chicken back inside the slow cooker, then stir until properly distributed, then allow to cook for an extra 30 minutes.

Taste for seasoning as desired.

Serve then garnish with any toppings of your choice and enjoy.

Nutrition:

Calories: 137

Carbs: 9g

Fat: 2g

Protein: 0g

100. LOW CARBOHYDRATE SLOW COOKER SOUP

Preparation Time: 15 minutes

Cooking Time: 4 hours

Servings: 8

Ingredients:
- 1/2 cup shredded cheese, to garnish
- 1-2 tbsp fresh cilantro
- 2 pounds ground pork beef
- 2 tbsp taco seasonings
- 2 (10-ounces) diced tomato cans
- 2 (8-ounces) cream cheese packages
- 4 cups chicken broth

Directions:

Cook the ground pork beef over medium-high heat in a large skillet.

In the meantime, place the diced tomatoes, cream cheese, and taco seasoning into the slow cooker.

Drain the meat of the grease and transfer it into the slow cooker.

Mix the ingredients, then add the chicken broth over the meat.

Cover the chicken then cook for 4 hours on low or 2 hours on high settings.

Stir in the cilantro before serving. Serve the garnish with the shredded cheese.

Nutrition:

Calories: 131

Carbs: 11g

Fat: 9g

Protein: 5g

101. SLOW COOKER CHEESEBURGER SOUP

Preparation Time: 15 minutes

Cooking Time: 3 hours

Servings: 5

Ingredients:
- 1/2 tsp salt
- 1/2 tsp pepper
- 1/2 cup cheese
- 1/2 cup chopped onions
- 1/2 chopped red bell pepper
- 1 tsp garlic powder
- 1 tsp Worcestershire sauce
- 1 1/2 tsp parsley
- 1 1/2 chopped tomatoes
- 1 1/2 pounds ground beef
- 2 chopped & cooked bacon slices
- 3 cups beef broth
- 3 chopped celery sticks
- 8 ounces tomato paste

Directions:

Using a large saucepan, add in the ground beef and brown.

Halfway through the browning process, drain off every fat, add in the red pepper, onions, celery, and continue cooking.

Add the remaining ingredients and beef mixture into the slow cooker then stir to combine.

If desired, add in more beef broth, cover, and cook for 6-8 hours on a low setting or 3-5 hours on a high setting, occasionally stirring.

Serve then top with a full spoon of cheese and bacon slices (if desired), then enjoy.

Nutrition:

Calories: 200

Carbs: 14g

Fat: 13g

Protein: 7g

102. DELICIOUS KERNEL CORN TACO SOUP

Preparation Time: 10 minutes

Cooking Time: 8 hours

Servings: 8

Ingredients:
- 1 package taco seasoning mix
- 1-pound ground beef
- 1 can whole kernel corn, with liquid
- 1 onion, chopped
- 1 can dice green chili peppers
- 1 can tomato sauce
- 2 cans peeled and diced tomatoes
- 1 can chili beans, with liquid
- 2 cups of water
- 1 can kidney beans with liquid

Directions:

Sauté your beef in a skillet until it is brown on all sides and keep aside.

Put your browned beef into your slow cooker and add all other ingredients and toss together to blend evenly.

Cook within 8 hours, low.

Nutrition:

Calories: 83

Carbs: 14g

Fat: 3g

Protein: 1g

103. SUMPTUOUS HAM AND LENTIL CONSOMMÉ

Preparation Time: 15 minutes

Cooking Time: 11 hours

Servings: 6

Ingredients:
- 8 tsp tomato sauce

- 1 cup onion, diced
- 1 cup dried lentils
- 1 cup of water
- 1 cup celery, chopped
- 1/2 tsp dried basil
- 32 ounces chicken broth
- 1 cup carrots, diced
- 1/4 tsp dried thyme
- 1/4 tsp black pepper
- 2 cloves garlic, minced
- 1/2 tsp dried oregano
- 1 1/2 cups diced cooked ham
- 1 bay leaf

Directions:

Put all your fixing into your slow cooker and mix very well to blend well.

Cook within 11 hours, low heat settings. Remove your bay leaf before serving it.

Nutrition:

Calories: 194
Carbs: 21g
Fat: 4g
Protein: 20g

104. BEEF BARLEY VEGETABLE SOUP

Preparation Time: 15 minutes
Cooking Time: 8 hours
Servings: 10

Ingredients:

- 1 package frozen mixed vegetables
- Ground black pepper to taste
- 1 beef chuck roast
- 1 onion, chopped
- Salt to taste
- 1/2 cup barley
- 4 cups of water
- 1 can chop stewed tomatoes
- 1 bay leaf
- 3 stalks celery, chopped
- 1/4 tsp ground black pepper
- 3 carrots, chopped
- 4 cubes beef bouillon cube
- 2 tbsp oil
- 1 tbsp Stevia or other Keto-approved sugar

Directions:

Season your beef with salt, adding bay leaf and barley in the last hour; cook your beef in your slow cooker for 8 hours or until tender.

Set your beef aside; keep your broth also aside.

Stir fry your onion, celery, carrots, and frozen vegetable mix until soft.

Add your bouillon cubes, pepper, water, salt, beef mixture, barley mixture, chopped stewed tomatoes, and broth.

Bring to boiling point and simmer at lowered heat for 20 minutes.

Nutrition:

Calories: 69
Carbs: 10g
Fat: 2g
Protein: 5g

105. DELICIOUS CHICKEN SOUP WITH LEMONGRASS

Preparation Time: 5 minutes
Cooking Time: 8 hours
Servings: 10

Ingredients:

- 1 stalk of lemongrass, cut into big hunks
- 1 whole chicken
- 1 tbsp of salt
- 5 thick slices of fresh ginger
- 20 fresh basil leaves (10 -slow cooker; 10 -spices)
- 1 lime

Directions:

Put your lemongrass, ginger, 10 basil leaves, salt, and chicken into the slow cooker.

Fill the slow cooker up with water. Boil the chicken mixture for 480 - 600 minutes.

Scoop the soup into a bowl and adjust your salt to taste. Juice in the lime to taste and spice up with the chopped basil leaves.

Nutrition:

Calories: 105
Carbs: 1g
Fat: 2g
Protein: 15g

106. SLOW COOKER PORK STEW WITH TAPIOCA

Preparation Time: 15 minutes
Cooking Time: 10 hours
Servings: 6

Ingredients:

- 3 tbsp quick-cooking tapioca
- 1 tbsp vegetable oil
- 1/4 tsp pepper
- 1 large onion, chopped
- 1 1/2 lb. pork stew meat, cut into bite-size pieces

- 2 tsp Worcestershire sauce
- 1 stalk celery, chopped
- 4 carrots, sliced
- 1 tbsp beef bouillon granules
- 1 cup cauliflower
- 3 cups vegetable juice

Directions:

Heat your oil over medium-high heat using a Dutch oven; brown your beef on all sides.

Mix your browned beef with all other ingredients in the slow cooker.

Cover and cook on low heat settings for 9-10 hours.

Nutrition:

Calories: 190

Carbs: 0g

Fat: 10g

Protein: 23g

107. DELICIOUS BACON CHEESE CAULIFLOWER SOUP

Preparation Time: 15 minutes

Cooking Time: 10 hours

Servings: 8

Ingredients:

- 3 lb. cauliflower
- 1/4 cup chopped fresh chives
- 8 slices bacon, diced
- 1 carton fat-free reduced-sodium chicken broth, divided
- 1/2 cup milk
- 1 onion, finely chopped
- 1 pkg. Shredded Triple Cheddar Cheese, divided
- 1/2 cup Sour Cream
- 2 tbsp almond flour

Directions:

Stir fry bacon over medium heat in a large skillet. Remove bacon with your slotted spoon and leave the drippings in the skillet.

Stir fry your onions in the skillet for few minutes until it is soft and crisp. Add in your flour and cook for 1 minute, stirring it frequently.

Add 1 cup of your chicken broth and cook for 2-3 minutes or until sauce is thick and simmers. Pour the sauce into your slow cooker.

Add your remaining chicken broth and cauliflower and cook with a slow cooker cover for 8-10 hours on low heat settings.

Transfer 4 cups of your cauliflower to a bowl and mash it until smooth, adding 1.5 cups of cheese to the remaining mixture in the slow cooker; stir until melted.

Stir your mashed cauliflower into the slow cooker with milk added and cook again within 5 minutes with the lid.

Microwave your bacon on a microwavable plate within 30 seconds or until heated.

Serve your soup with bacon, using sour cream, chives, and remaining cheese as toppings.

Nutrition:

Calories: 100

Carbs: 18g

Fat: 0g

Protein: 2g

108. TASTY TOMATO SOUP WITH PARMESAN AND BASIL

Preparation Time: 15 minutes

Cooking Time: 3 hours

Servings: 6

Ingredients:

- 28 oz of tomatoes, chopped
- 1/2 cup heavy cream
- 1/2 cup grated Parmesan cheese
- 10-12 large basil leaves
- 3 tbsp chopped garlic
- 2-3 servings of Erythritol
- 1/2 tbsp dried thyme
- 1/4 tsp of red pepper flakes
- 1 tbsp onion powder

Directions:

Add all ingredients except your parmesan and heavy cream to your slow cooker and cook on high heat for 3 hours.

Add your cheese and cream and stir. Adjust seasoning to taste. Enjoy

Nutrition:

Calories: 110

Carbs: 16g

Fat: 3g

Protein: 5g

109. LUSCIOUS CARROT BEEF STEW WITH CAULIFLOWER

Preparation Time: 15 minutes

Cooking Time: 10 hours

Servings: 8

Ingredients:

- 32 oz beef broth
- One tsp oregano
- 2 cups baby carrots
- 2 pounds beef stew meat, bite-sized

- 2 celery ribs, chopped
- 1 tbsp dried parsley
- ¼ cup of water
- 1 tsp Salt
- 1 cup of frozen corn
- 2 tbsp Worcestershire sauce
- 2-3 cloves of garlic, grated
- ¼ cup almond flour
- 6oz can tomato paste
- 1 tsp pepper
- 2 cups cauliflower
- 1 cup frozen pea
- 1 medium onion, finely chopped

Directions:

Add your tomato paste, beef, beef broth, celery, Worcestershire sauce, carrots, oregano, red onions, parsley, cauliflower, garlic, salt, and pepper into your slow cooker and mix.

Cook on low heat for 10 hours.

Mix the flour plus water in a small bowl and pour it into your slow cooker 30 minutes before serving and mix until well combined.

Stir in your corn and frozen peas and cook for another 30 minutes in the slow cooker, covered.

Nutrition:

Calories: 262

Carbs: 9g

Fat: 10g

Protein: 20g

110. DELICIOUS LASAGNA CONSOMMÉ

Preparation Time: 15 minutes

Cooking Time: 7 hours

Servings: 8

Ingredients:

- 2 cups uncooked shell pasta
- 1 tbsp dried parsley
- 1 can of diced tomatoes
- 1 cup of water
- 3 cups of beef broth
- ¼ tsp pepper
- 1 tbsp dried basil
- ¼ tsp salt
- ½ cup chopped onion
- 1 cup V8
- 4-5 cloves of garlic, grated
- 1, 6oz can of tomato paste
- 1 lb. ground beef
- Shredded cheese- topping

Directions:

Mix your tomato pastes and can tomatoes in your slow cooker.

Add your garlic, salt, broth, V8, pepper, basil, beef, and parsley.

Mix, then cook on low heat for 7 hours.

Precisely 30 minutes left of cooking time, add 1 cup of water and noodles into your slow cooker. Stir together and cook with the lid back on for 30 minutes.

Nutrition:

Calories: 68

Carbs: 5g

Fat: 0g

Protein: 12g

111. CHEESE BROCCOLI BOUILLABAISSE

Preparation Time: 15 minutes

Cooking Time: 8 hours

Servings: 8

Ingredients:

- 1 tbsp butter
- 1 1/2 lbs. cauliflower, chopped into 3/4 in cubes
- 2 1/2 cups boiling water
- 1 cup onion, sliced
- 1 package frozen broccoli, chopped
- 1 package cheddar cheese, minced
- 2 chicken bouillon cubes

Directions:

Butter the saucepan and fry your onions until crisp.

Add your water, bouillon cubes, sautéed onions, and cauliflower into a pot and cover it up. Cook under medium heat until cauliflower is soft.

Place your cheddar cheese and broccoli in your slow cooker while you cook your cauliflower. Melt and defrost your cheese and broccoli on low heat settings.

Blend your soft cauliflower contents using a food processor to your desired consistency and pour it into your slow cooker.

Heat up on low heat settings until it is warm.

Nutrition:

Calories: 240

Carbs: 5g

Fat: 9g

Protein: 34g

112. CHICKEN THIGH & BREAST LOW CARB SOUP

Preparation Time: 5 minutes

Cooking Time: 6 hours

Servings: 6

Ingredients:
- 1/2 tsp fresh ground pepper
- 1 tsp sea salt
- 1 chopped medium onion
- 1 tsp apple cider vinegar
- 1 tbsp. herbs de Provence
- 2 organic skin on & bone chicken thighs
- 2 organic skin on & bone-in chicken breasts
- 3 diced carrots
- 3 diced celery stalks
- 3-4 cups filtered water

Directions:

Place the ingredients in layers inside the slow cooker.

Make sure the bone side of the chicken is down on top of the veggies.

Add in surplus water until the veggies are submerged, and the chicken is covered halfway.

Cover the slow cooker then cook for 6-8 hours.

Remove the chicken from the slow cooker once done and cool, then remove the bones and skin.

Shred the chicken, then return into the slow cooker, season to taste, reheat, then serve and enjoy.

Nutrition:

Calories: 97
Carbs: 6g
Fat: 2g
Protein: 14g

113. BEEF & PUMPKIN STEW

Preparation Time: 5 minutes
Cooking Time: 4 hours
Servings: 4

Ingredients:
- 1 tsp sage
- 1 tsp mixed herbs
- 2 tbsp rosemary
- 2 tbsp thyme
- 6 tbsp coconut oil
- 200g pumpkin
- 300g stewing steak
- Salt & pepper, to taste

Directions:

Trim off every excess fat from the stewing steak then transfer it into the slow cooker.

Season the steak with half of the coconut oil then and in the salt & pepper.

Cover the slow cooker then cook on a high setting for 1 hour.

Remove the steak from the slow cooker to a serving platter alongside all the remaining seasoning and coconut oil.

Mix everything, then transfer back into the slow cooker with the pumpkin and cook for 3 hours on a low setting.

Serve with fresh mixed herbs and enjoy.

Nutrition:

Calories: 324
Carbs: 37g
Fat: 11g
Protein: 23g

114. PEPPER JALAPENO LOW CARB SOUP

Preparation Time: 10 minutes
Cooking Time: 7 hours
Servings: 8

Ingredients:
- 1/4 tsp paprika
- 1/2 tsp pepper
- 1/2 chopped onion
- 1/2 tsp xanthan gum
- 1/2 chopped green pepper
- 1/2 cup heavy whipping cream
- 1/2 lb. cooked & crumbled bacon
- 3/4 cup cheddar Cheese
- 3/4 cup Monterrey Jack Cheese
- 1 tsp salt
- 1 tsp cumin
- 1 & ½-pounds chicken breasts, boneless
- 2 minced garlic cloves
- 2 seeded & chopped jalapenos
- 3 tbsp. butter
- 3 cups chicken broth
- 6 oz. cream cheese

Directions:

Dissolve the butter, then cook the green peppers, seasoning, jalapenos, and onions until translucent in a medium-sized pan.

Scoop the mixture into the slow cooker, then add in the chicken broth and breast.

Cover the slow cooker then cook for 3-4 hours on high or 6-7 hours on a low setting.

Separate the chicken, and shred it, then return it to the slow cooker.

Put in the heavy whipping cream, cream cheese, remaining cheeses, bacon then stir until the cheese melts.

Sprinkle the soup with xantham gum to thicken, then allow it to simmer uncovered on low for 10 minutes.

Serve, then top with cheddar cheese, bacon, or jalapenos and enjoy.

Nutrition:
Calories: 240
Carbs: 1g
Fat: 20g
Protein: 11g

115. LEAN BEEF & MIXED VEGGIES SOUP

Preparation Time: 8 minutes
Cooking Time: 6 hours
Servings: 6

Ingredients:
- 1/2 tsp garlic salt, if desired
- 1 peeled small onion
- 1 diced small green pepper
- 1 tsp garlic & herb seasoning
- 1 small zucchini, sliced into rounds
- 1 can rinse & drained cannellini beans
- 1 small yellow squash, sliced into rounds
- 1 (14 1/2 ounces) can diced roasted tomatoes
- 1 & ½-pounds beef stew meat
- 1-2 tsp ground pepper
- 1-3 bay leaves
- 2 cups of frozen mixed vegetables
- 4 cups low salt beef broth
- 4 peeled & chopped garlic cloves

Directions:
Add all the ingredients except the zucchini cannellini beans, mixed vegetables, and yellow squash into the slow cooker.
Cover the pot then cook on high for 4 hours.
After 4 hours, add in the zucchini, cannellini beans, yellow squash, and mixed vegetables.
Season to taste, and cook for an extra 2 hours on high.
Once done, stir then serve and enjoy.

Nutrition:
Calories: 50
Carbs: 10g
Fat: 0g
Protein: 2g

116. CHICKEN & TORTILLA SOUP

Preparation Time: 7 minutes
Cooking Time: 2 hours & 10 minutes
Servings: 6

Ingredients:
- 1 diced sweet onion
- 1 tsp cumin
- 1 tsp chili powder
- 1 neatly chopped cilantro bunch
- 1 (28 ounces) can diced tomatoes
- 1-2 cups water
- 2 cups celery, chopped
- 2 cups carrots, shredded
- 2 tbsp tomato paste
- 2 diced & de-seeded jalapenos
- 2 big skinned chicken breasts, sliced into 1/2" strips
- 4 minced garlic cloves
- 32 ounces organic chicken broth
- Olive oil
- Sea salt & fresh cracked pepper, as desired

Directions:
Pour a dash of olive oil, 1/4 cup of chicken broth, garlic, onions, pepper, jalapeno, and sea salt into a Dutch oven, and cook over medium-high heat until soft.
Transfer the mixture into the slow cooker and ass in the remaining ingredients and cook for 2 hours on low settings.
Shred the chicken, then top with the cilantro, avocado slices and enjoy.

Nutrition:
Calories: 130
Carbs: 16g
Fat: 5g
Protein: 8g

117. CHICKEN CHILE VERDE

Preparation Time: 12 minutes
Cooking Time: 6 hours
Servings: 9

Ingredients:
- 1/4 tsp sea salt
- 2 pounds chopped boneless chicken.
- 3 tbsp divided butter
- 3 tbsp neatly chopped & divided cilantro
- 5 minced & divided garlic cloves
- 1 extra tbsp cilantro, to garnish
- 1 1/2 cups salsa Verde

Directions:
Dissolve 2 tbsp of butter in the slow cooker on high.
Add in 4 of the garlic along with 2 tbsp cilantro then stir.
Use a stovetop, melt 1 tbsp butter in a big frypan over medium-high heat, and add 1 tbsp minced garlic and cilantro.

Put in the chopped chicken, then sear until all the sides are browned but not cooked through.

Add the cilantro, garlic, and butter mixture with browned chicken into the slow cooker.

Pour in the salsa Verde and stir together.

Cover the slow cooker and cook on high settings for 2 hours, then reduce to a low setting for 3-4 extra hours.

Serve the chicken Verde in a lettuce cup or over cauliflower rice.

Nutrition:

Calories: 140

Carbs: 6g

Fat: 4g

Protein: 18g

118. CAULIFLOWER & HAM CAULIFLOWER STEW

Preparation Time: 5 minutes

Cooking Time: 4 hours

Servings: 6

Ingredients:

- 1/4 tsp salt
- 1/4 cup heavy cream
- 1/2 tsp onion powder
- 1/2 tsp garlic powder
- 3 cups diced ham
- 4 garlic cloves
- 8 oz. grated cheddar cheese
- 14 1/2 oz. chicken broth
- 16 oz. bag frozen cauliflower florets
- A dash peppers

Directions:

Put all the items except the cauliflower inside the slow cooker and mix.

Cover the slow cooker then cook for 4 hours on a high setting.

Once done, add in the cauliflower and cook for an extra 30 minutes on high. Serve and enjoy.

Nutrition:

Calories: 71

Carbs: 2g

Fat: 4g

Protein: 6g

119. MINESTRONE GROUND BEEF SOUP

Preparation Time: 15 minutes

Cooking Time: 8 hours

Servings: 1

Ingredients:

- 1/2 tsp basil, dried
- 1/2 tsp oregano, dried
- 1/2 cup vegetable broth
- 1 diced carrot
- 1 lb. ground beef
- 1 diced yellow onion
- 1 diced celery stalk
- 1 tbsp. garlic, minced
- 1 (28 ounces) can diced tomatoes
- 2 diced small zucchini

Directions:

Using a medium-sized pan on a stovetop, place in the ground beef and brown.

Boil 3 cups of water. Transfer the boiled water and browned beef into the slow cooker

Put the remaining fixing into the slow cooker.

Cook for 5-8 hours on low settings. Serve and enjoy.

Nutrition:

Calories: 180

Carbs: 24g

Fat: 4g

Protein: 13g

120. VEGETABLE STEW

Preparation Time: 15 minutes

Cooking Time: 6 hours

Servings: 5

Ingredients:

- Olive oil – 1 tbsp.
- Onion – 1, chopped
- Garlic – 2 cloves, chopped
- Cauliflower – ½, cut into florets
- Red bell peppers – 1, chopped
- Carrot – 1, sliced
- Parsnip – 1, cubed
- Zucchini – ½, cubed
- Cherry tomatoes – ½ cup, halved
- Tomato sauce – ¼ cup, no sugar added
- Vegetable stock – 1 cup
- Bay leaf – 1
- Salt and pepper to taste
- Butter – 2 tbsp.

Directions:

Heat-up the oil, then put the onion and garlic in a skillet. Cook for 2 minutes to soften, then place in the Crock-Pot.

Add the remaining ingredients, mix, and season with salt and pepper, then cook on low within 6 hours. Serve.

Nutrition:
Calories: 76
Fat: 5.7g
Carbs: 7.1g
Protein: 1.3g

121. DELICIOUS BEEF, MEATBALL AND SOUR CREAM SOUP

Preparation Time: 15 minutes
Cooking Time: 6 hours
Servings: 4

Ingredients:
- 1 diced red bell pepper
- 8-10 halved pearl onions
- 2 cloves of minced garlic
- 2 tbsp of olive oil
- 3 cups of lean ground beef
- 1 large egg
- 1 tsp of dry savory
- Salt and pepper to taste
- 1 cup of beef broth
- 2 cups of hot water
- 1 cup of sour cream

Directions:
Preheat the slow cooker on low. Add the oil and vegetables.

Mix the egg, salt, pepper, dry savory, and meat in a large bowl. Shape into approximately 30 small meatballs.

Cook the broth in a pot, add the meatballs, and cook for 2 minutes.

Add the broth and the meatballs to the slow cooker—cover and cook for 6 hours.

Take out a spoonful of the broth, add it to the sour cream, mix, and then put it back inside the slow cooker. Stir gently, spoon into bowls and serve.

Nutrition:
Carbs: 11 g
Protein: 27 g
Fat: 28 g
Calories: 409

122. VEGGIE SOUP WITH MINTY BALLS

Preparation Time: 15 minutes
Cooking Time: 6 hours
Servings: 45

Ingredients:
- 3 cups of beef broth
- 1 medium zucchini sliced into sticks
- 2 diced celery sticks
- 1 diced yellow onion
- 5 crushed cloves of garlic
- 1 cubed medium tomato
- 3 cups of ground veal
- ½ cup of Parmesan cheese
- 1 large egg
- ½ cup of chopped fresh mint
- 1 tsp of dry oregano
- 1 tsp of sweet paprika
- Salt and pepper to taste

Directions:
Preheat the slow cooker on low. Add the tomato, onion, celery, zucchini, and broth.

Mix the meat, salt, pepper, seasoning, mint, egg, garlic, and cheese in a large bowl. Shape the meat into small, approximately 45 small meatballs.

Heat-up the olive oil in a pan, then put the meatballs and brown.

Put the meatballs inside the slow cooker, then put one cup of hot water if more liquid is required.

Cook within 6-8 hours, low. Spoon into bowls and serve.

Nutrition:
Carbs: 11 g
Protein: 32 g
Fat: 25 g
Calories: 395 g

123. CHICKEN CORDON BLEU SOUP

Preparation Time: 15 minutes
Cooking Time: 6 hours
Servings: 4

Ingredients:
- 12 ounces of diced ham
- 1 pound of chicken breast
- 4 ounces of diced onion
- 5 ounces of chopped mushrooms
- 3 tbsp of minced garlic
- 6 cups of chicken broth
- 2 tsp of tarragon
- 3 tbsp of salted butter
- 1 tsp of sea salt
- 1 tsp of black pepper
- 1 ½ cups of heavy cream
- ½ cup of sour cream
- ½ cup of grated parmesan cheese
- 4 ounces of Swiss cheese

Directions:

Place the onion, tarragon, salt, pepper, ham, mushroom, and broth into the slow cooker.

Heat-up the butter in a saucepan, then sauté the garlic. Add the chicken and sear it.

Place the chicken, garlic, and cheese in the slow cooker—cover and cook on low within six hours.

Add cream, and cook for another hour. Serve.

Nutrition:

Calories: 178

Fat: 12 g

Carbs: 2.75 g

Protein: 16 g

124. GINGER PUMPKIN SOUP

Preparation Time: 15 minutes

Cooking Time: 4 hours

Servings: 4

Ingredients:

- 1 diced onion
- 1 tsp of crushed ginger
- 1 tsp of crushed garlic
- ½ stick of butter
- 1 pound of pumpkin chunks
- 2 cups of vegetable stock
- 1 2/3 cups of coconut cream
- Salt and pepper to taste

Directions:

Place all the items inside a slow cooker. Cook on high for 4-6 hours.

Puree the soup using an immersion blender. Spoon into bowls and serve.

Nutrition:

Calories: 234

Fat: 21.7 g

Carbs: 11.4 g

Fiber: 1.5 g

Protein: 2.3 g

125. PUMPKIN SOUP

Preparation Time: 10 min

Cooking Time: 20 min

Servings: 2

Ingredients:

- 1 lb pumpkin peeled-1/2-1inch cubes
- 1 cup vegetable broth or water
- 1 tsp dried rosemary
- 1/4 tsp grated cinnamon
- 1/2 tsp salt
- 1 cup coconut milk
- 2 tbsp butter
- 1 tbsp almond flour

Directions:

Mix the pumpkin cubes, broth, rosemary, cinnamon, and salt in a slow cooker.

Open the slow cooker. Add coconut milk.

Bring the soup to a simmer, stirring often. In the meantime, place the butter in a small bowl or measuring container and place it in the microwave in 5-second increments. Use a fork to mix the flour and make a thin paste.

When the soup is boiling, Whisk the butter mixture into the pan. Continue whisking until the soup is a bit thick, about 1 minute. Turn off the Sauté function and allow it to cool for a few minutes before serving.

Nutrition:

Calories 415,

Total Fat 41g,

Saturated Fat 32. 9g,

Cholesterol 31mg,

Sodium 1064mg,

Total Carbohydrate 11. 5g,

Dietary Fiber 3. 3g,

Total Sugars 5. 2g,

Protein 5. 9g.

126. SPINACH SOUP

Preparation Time:15 min

Cooking Time: 6-8 hours

Servings: 4

Ingredients:

- 2 pounds spinach
- 1/4 cup cream cheese
- 1 onion, diced
- 2 cups heavy cream
- 1 garlic clove, minced
- 2 cups water
- salt, pepper, to taste

Directions:

Pour water into the slow cooker. Add spinach, salt, and pepper.

Add cream cheese, onion, garlic, and heavy cream.

Close the lid and cook on Low for 6-8 hours.

Puree soup with blender and serve.

Nutrition:

Calories 322,

Total Fat 28.2g,

Cholesterol 31mg,

Total Carbohydrate 10.1 g,

Protein 12.2 g

127. MEXICAN CHICKEN SOUP

Preparation Time: 15 minutes

Cooking Time: 8 hours

Servings: 6

Ingredients:
- 6 cups chicken broth
- 4 tsp garlic
- 0.25 cups jalapeno
- 1 tbsp cumin
- 1 tbsp chili powder
- 0.5 cups cilantro
- 2 tbsp lime juice
- 1.5 cups carrots
- 0.66 cups onion
- 0.5 cups Roma tomato
- 0.75 cups tomato juice
- 1 tsp coriander
- 2 tsp sea salt
- 4 cups chicken breast

Directions:

Chop herbs and vegetables. Put everything in the cooker. Low cook for 8 hours. Serve.

Nutrition:

Calories 296

Fat 16 g

Protein 27 g

Carbs 10 g

128. BUTTERNUT SQUASH SOUP

Preparation Time: 10 minutes

Cooking Time: 8 hours

Servings: 9

Ingredients:
- 2-pound butternut squash
- 4 tsp minced garlic
- ½ cup onion, chopped
- 1 tsp salt
- ¼ tsp ground nutmeg
- 1 tsp ground black pepper
- 8 cups chicken stock
- 1 tbsp fresh parsley

Directions:

Peel the butternut squash and cut it into chunks.

Toss the butternut squash in the slow cooker.

Add chopped onion, minced garlic, and chicken stock.

Close the slow cooker lid and cook the soup for 8 hours on low.

Meanwhile, combine the ground black pepper, ground nutmeg, and salt.

Chop the fresh parsley.

When the time is done, remove the soup from the slow cooker and blend it with a blender until you get a creamy soup.

Sprinkle the soup with the spice mixture and add chopped parsley. Serve the soup warm. Enjoy!

Nutrition:

Calories 129,

Fat 2.7g,

Fiber 2g,

Carbs 20.85g,

Protein 7g.

129. CABBAGE, KIELBASA, AND ONION SOUP

Preparation Time: 5 minutes

Cooking Time: 8 hours

Servings: 6

Ingredients:
- 2 ½ lb. cabbage head, cut into wedges
- 1 cup vegetable broth
- 1 onion, thinly sliced
- 1 tbsp. brown mustard
- ½ tsp black pepper
- 1 lb. kielbasa, sliced into 3-inch pieces
- ½ tsp kosher salt
- Cooking spray, as required

Directions:

Put all the items in the slow cooker, excluding the kielbasa, and combine them well.

Make sure that the cabbage is well coated with the seasoning broth mixture.

Now, top it with the kielbasa and cover the slow cooker.

Cook for 7 hours on low heat. Stir it again and cook it for an additional 1 hour.

Nutrition:

Calories: 278

Carbs: 11g

Protein: 11.8g

Fat: 21g

130. BROCCOLI CHEDDAR SOUP

Preparation Time: 10 minutes

Cooking Time: 6 to 8 hours

Servings: 20

Ingredients:

- 1 ½ lb. broccoli
- 2 tbsp. butter
- 1 medium onion, chopped
- 2 leeks, rinsed and trimmed
- 2 cups heavy cream
- 1 cauliflower, medium head
- 2 cups parmesan cheese, grated
- 5 garlic cloves, minced
- 4 cups of sharp cheddar cheese, shredded
- 32 oz. chicken broth
- Salt and pepper, to taste

Directions:

Heat-up a medium-sized skillet over medium heat. Stir in the onion, garlic, butter, salt, and pepper, and cook until the onions become translucent and caramelized.

After that, take the slow cooker and heat it on high, and then toss the cauliflower, leeks, and broccoli to it.

Pour in the heavy cream, broth along with salt and pepper, and combine them well.

Stir in the caramelized onions and mix well until well incorporated.

Cook in the slow cooker within 5 to 6 hours on high heat. Once it is cooked, mash the vegetables.

Finally, add the parmesan and cheddar cheese, salt plus pepper, and cook them for another additional hour. Serve.

Nutrition:

Calories: 235

Carbs: 5g

Protein: 13g

Fat: 18g

131. CREAM OF ZUCCHINI SOUP

Preparation Time: 15 minutes

Cooking Time: 2 hours & 10 minutes

Servings: 4

Ingredients:

- 3 cups vegetable stock
- 2 pounds chopped zucchini
- 2 minced garlic cloves
- ¾ cup chopped onion
- ¼ cup basil leaves
- 1 tbsp extra-virgin olive oil
- Salt and pepper to taste

Directions:

Heat-up olive oil in a skillet. When hot, cook garlic and onion for about 5 minutes.

Pour into your slow cooker with the rest of the fixings. Close the lid.

Cook on low for 2 hours. Puree the soup with an immersion blender. Serve.

Nutrition:

Calories: 96

Protein: 7g

Carbs: 11g

Fat: 5g

Fiber: 2.3g

132. TOMATO SOUP

Preparation Time: 15 minutes

Cooking Time: 4 hours

Servings: 4

Ingredients:

- 1 can crushed tomatoes
- 1 cup vegetable broth
- ½ cup heavy cream
- 2 tbsp chopped parsley
- ½ tsp onion powder
- ½ tsp garlic powder
- Salt and pepper to taste

Directions:

Put all the fixings except heavy cream in the slow cooker, then cook on low for 4 hours.

Blend then stir in the cream using an immersion blender. Taste and season with more salt and pepper if necessary.

Nutrition:

Calories: 165

Protein: 3g

Carbs: 15g

Fat: 13g

Fiber: 3.7g

133. MEXICAN CORN AND SHRIMP SOUP

Preparation Time: 15 minutes

Cooking Time: 4 hours & 10 minutes

Servings: 2

Ingredients:

- 1 c. reduced-sodium vegetable broth
- 2½ c. whole kernel corn
- 1/3 c. onion, chopped
- 1 small jalapeno chili, minced
- 1 minced garlic clove
- 1 tbsp. chopped epazote leaves
- 6 oz. peeled and deveined shrimp
- Salt to taste
- Cayenne pepper to taste

- Roasted Red Pepper Sauce:
- 1 halved large red bell pepper
- ½ tsp. Stevia

Directions:

In a slow cooker, mix all the ingredients, except the epazote, shrimp, salt, and cayenne pepper. Cook on high for 4 hours.

Blend the soup into a food processor or blender and add the epazote leaves. Blend until smooth and pour back into a slow cooker. Add the shrimp. Cook within 10 minutes on high. Season with salt and pepper.

To make the Roasted Red Pepper Sauce, put the pepper with the skin side up on a broiler pan. Broil until the skin becomes blackened and blistered.

Transfer the roasted pepper into a plastic bag and set aside for 5 minutes. Then, peel off the skin. Blend with the Stevia in a food processor or blender until smooth.

Soup can be served warm or chilled. Add 3 tbsp of Roasted Red Pepper Sauce into each serving bowl.

Nutrition:

Calories: 194.9

Carbs: 24.2 g

Fat: 6.3 g

Protein: 13.6 g

134. TUSCAN FISH SOUP

Preparation Time: 15 minutes

Cooking Time: 4 hours

Servings: 3

Ingredients:

- ½ qt chicken broth
- ¼ c. dry red wine or chicken broth
- 1½ lb. chopped tomatoes
- 1 chopped medium onion
- 1½ minced garlic cloves garlic
- ½ tsp dried oregano
- ½ tsp dried sage
- ½ tsp. dried rosemary leaves
- 1/8 tsp. red pepper, crushed
- ¾ lb. assorted skinless fish fillets
- 3 oz. peeled and deveined shrimp
- Salt and pepper to taste
- 3 slices Italian bread, toasted
- 1 halved clove garlic

Directions:

In a slow cooker, mix all of the ingredients except the seafood, salt, pepper, bread, and halved garlic cloves. Cook on high for 4 hours.

In the last 15 minutes, add the seafood—season with salt and pepper.

In the meantime, rub the garlic cloves on the bread. Place bread into soup bowls and ladle the soup on top. Serve piping hot.

Nutrition:

Calories: 132.2

Fat: 3.3g

Carbs: 18.9g

Protein: 7.6g

135. SEAFOOD STIR-FRY SOUP

Preparation Time: 30 minutes

Cooking Time: 3 hours & 10 minutes

Servings: 2

Ingredients:

- 7.25 oz low-carb Udon noodle, beef flavor
- 1/2 lb. shrimp
- 1/4 lb. scallops
- 3 cups low-sodium broth
- 1 carrot, shredded

Directions:

Add all ingredients except noodles, shrimp, and scallops to the slow cooker. Include seasonings such as garlic, ginger, salt, and pepper to taste. Add vinegar, soy sauce, and fish sauce, 1/2 tbsp each. Stir to mix well.

Cook on high for 2-3 hours. Add udon noodles, shrimp, and scallops. Cook on high for additional 10-15 minutes.

Nutrition:

Calories: 266

Fat: 19g

Carbs: 8g

Protein: 27.5g

Cholesterol: 173mg

Sodium: 489mg

136. CHICKEN KALE SOUP

Preparation Time: 15 minutes

Cooking Time: 6 hours

Servings: 6

Ingredients:

- 1 tbsp olive oil
- 14 ounces chicken broth
- 0.5 cups olive oil
- 5 ounces kale
- Salt to taste
- 2 pounds of chicken
- 0.33 cups onion

- 32 ounces chicken stock
- 0.25 cups lemon juice

Directions:

Cook the chicken until it achieves approximately 165F. Do this in a pan.

Shred and put it into the cooker.

Process the onion, broth, and oil and put it into the cooker. Add other ingredients and mix.

Low cook for 6 hours. Serve.

Nutrition:

Calories 261

Fat 21 g

Protein 14 g

Carbs 2 g

137. PORK RAMEN

Preparation Time: 10 minutes

Cooking Time: 6 hours

Servings: 5

Ingredients:

- 2-3 lbs pork shoulder
- 1 tbsp ramen seasoning
- 10 oz. ramen noodles
- 4 cups chicken stock
- 1 tsp salt
- 3 tbsp soy sauce
- 1 tsp paprika
- 1 tbsp butter

Directions:

Add pork, chicken stock, butter, ramen, paprika, all other ingredients to the Slow Cooker. Put the cooker's lid on and set the cooking time on High settings. Serve warm. Transfer the pork to a cutting board and shred.

Return the broth and pork to the slow cooker and season to taste. Cook on low-heat setting.

Cook the noodles according to package instructions.

Divide the noodles among the bowls then ladle the pork and broth over noodles. Serve.

Nutrition:

Calories: 405,

Total Fat: 19.2g,

Fiber: 6g,

Total Carbs: 29.93g,

Protein: 15g

138. SHRIMP FAJITA SOUP

Preparation Time: 10 minutes

Cooking Time: 2 hours 10 minutes

Servings: 4

Ingredients:

- 1 lb shrimp
- 1 bell pepper, sliced
- 64 oz chicken stock
- 2 tbsp fajita seasoning
- 1 onion, sliced

Directions:

Add all ingredients except shrimp into the cooking pot and stir well.

Add shrimp and cook for 10 minutes more.

Stir well and serve.

Nutrition:

Calories 189

Fat 3.1 g

Carbohydrates 11.1 g

Sugar 4 g

Protein 27.7 g

Cholesterol 239 mg

139. CHINESE OYSTER SOUP

Preparation Time: 15 minutes

Cooking Time: 6 hours

Servings: 2

Ingredients:

- 1¼ cup chicken broth
- 1 tbsp. soy sauce
- 1 cup sliced Napa cabbage
- 4 o sliced mushrooms
- ½ tbsp. ginger root, minced
- ½ pint fresh oysters
- Salt and pepper to taste

Directions:

In a slow cooker, mix the broth, soy sauce, cabbage, mushrooms, bean sprouts, green onions, and ginger root. Cook for 6 hours on low.

In the last 15 minutes, put the oysters and liquid—season with salt and pepper before serving.

Nutrition:

Calories: 206.89

Fat: 5.93 g

Carbs: 5.1 g

Protein: 30.98 g

140. VEGAN CREAM OF MUSHROOM SOUP

Preparation Time: 15 minutes

Cooking Time: 1 hour & 40 minutes

Servings: 2

Ingredients:

- ¼ tsp sea salt
- ½ diced yellow onion
- ½ tsp. extra-virgin olive oil
- 1 ½ cup chopped white mushrooms
- 1 2/3 cup unsweetened almond milk
- 1 tsp. onion powder
- 2 cups cauliflower florets

Directions:

Add cauliflower, pepper, salt, onion powder, and milk to the slow cooker. Stir and set to cook on high for 1 hour.

With olive oil, sauté onions, and mushrooms together for 8 to 10 minutes till softened.

Allow cauliflower mixture to cool off a bit and add to blender. Blend until smooth. Then blend in mushroom mixture.

Pour back into the slow cooker and heat 30 minutes.

Nutrition:

Calories: 281

Carbs: 3g

Fat: 16g

Protein: 11g

141. VEGGIE-NOODLE SOUP

Preparation Time: 15 minutes

Cooking Time: 8 hours

Servings: 2

Ingredients:

- 1/2 cup chopped carrots, chopped
- 1/2 cup chopped celery, chopped
- 1 tsp Italian seasoning
- 7 oz zucchini, cut spiral
- 2 cups spinach leaves, chopped

Directions:

Except for the zucchini and spinach, add all the ingredients to the slow cooker.

Add 3 cups of water.

Cover and cook within 8 hours on low. Add the zucchini and spinach at the last 10 minutes of cooking.

Nutrition:

Calories: 56

Fat: 0.5 g

Carbs: 0.5 g

Protein: 3 g

VEGETABLES

142. KETO SPINACH-FETA QUICHE

Preparation Time: 20 minutes
Cooking Time: 7 to 8 hours
Servings: 4

Ingredients:
- 2 cups fresh spinach
- 8 eggs
- 2 cups of milk
- ½ cup shredded Parmesan cheese
- ¾ cup crumbled feta cheese
- ¼ cup shredded cheddar cheese
- 2 garlic cloves, minced
- ¼ tsp salt

Directions:

Mix the eggs plus milk in a large bowl.

Add the spinach, feta cheese, garlic, Parmesan cheese, and salt, then stir until well combined.

Put the batter into the greased slow cooker then sprinkle cheddar cheese on top.

Cover then cook for 7 to 8 hours on low.

Nutrition:

Calories: 337
Carbs: 9.4g
Protein: 25g
Fat: 22.4g

143. CHEESY ZUCCHINI-ASPARAGUS FRITTATA

Preparation Time: 30 minutes
Cooking Time: 1 hour 10 minutes
Servings: 6

Ingredients:
- 8 oz. asparagus, trimmed then sliced diagonally into 2" pieces
- 3 tbsp olive oil
- 1 medium-size zucchini, cut into ½" thickness
- 2 medium-size shallots, diced
- 12 large eggs
- 1 cup Parmesan cheese, grated
- ¼ cup minced fresh basil (or flat-leaf parsley leaves)
- Fresh ground black pepper and sea salt to taste

Directions:

Heat-up oil in a medium-size skillet over medium-high heat then add the asparagus, shallots, and zucchini. Cook for some minutes until the asparagus starts to soften and the zucchini a bit browned.

Remove the veggies from heat then let them cool for 10 minutes. Grease the bottom and sides about 2" up of your 5 to 7 qt oval slow cooker using a cooking spray and then pour the cooled veggies into the slow cooker.

Beat the eggs, basil, and parmesan together in a medium-size bowl, then add a small salt and some black pepper. Put the batter inside the slow cooker, then mix until the veggies are well mixed.

Cover the cooker then cook for 60 to 70 minutes on high until ready. Slice into 4 portions, then use a spatula to lift it out into plates. Serve at once.

Nutrition:

Calories: 520

Carbs: 4g

Protein: 41g

Fat: 37g

144. SLOW-COOKED YELLOW SQUASH ZUCCHINI

Preparation Time: 5 minutes

Cooking Time: 6 hours

Servings: 6

Ingredients:

- 2 medium yellow squash, sliced and quartered
- 2 medium zucchinis, sliced and quartered
- ¼ tsp pepper
- 1 tsp Italian seasoning
- 1 tsp powdered garlic
- ¼ cup Asiago or Parmesan cheese, grated
- ¼ cup butter, cubed
- ½ tsp sea salt

Directions:

Combine the sliced yellow squash and zucchini in your slow cooker. Sprinkle Italian seasoning, pepper, sea salt, and garlic powder on top.

Place the butter pieces, and cheese on top. Cover the cooker then cook for 4 to 6 hours on low.

Nutrition:

Calories: 122

Carbs: 5.4g

Protein: 4.2g

Fat: 9.9g

145. PARMESAN MUSHROOMS

Preparation Time: 5 minutes

Cooking Time: 4 hours

Servings: 4

Ingredients:

- 16 oz. cremini mushrooms, fresh
- ½ oz. ranch dressing mix
- 2 tbsp. parmesan cheese, add more if desired
- ½ cup butter, melted and unsalted

Directions:

Place the mushrooms in the slow cooker.

Combine melted butter and ranch dressing in a small-sized bowl. Stir in the butter mixture over the mushrooms and mix well.

Now, toss the parmesan cheese over the top. Cover the slow cooker and cook for 4 hours on low heat.

Nutrition:

Calories: 240

Carbs: 4g

Protein: 4.9g

Fat: 24g

146. MASHED GARLIC CAULIFLOWER

Preparation Time: 5 minutes

Cooking Time: 6 hours

Servings: 6

Ingredients:

- 2 medium cauliflower head, sliced into florets
- 3 tbsp. butter
- 4 garlic cloves
- 2 tsp Celtic sea salt
- 8 to 10 cups of water
- ½ tsp black pepper
- Dill, to taste

Directions:

Place the garlic and cauliflower along with a sufficient amount of water in the slow cooker.

Cook within 6 hours on low heat or until the cauliflower becomes tender.

Discard the water then place the cauliflower in the food processor. Add butter, then pulse until it is mashed.

Now, to this, stir in the seasoning and check for taste. Finally, toss the herbs into it and serve it immediately.

Nutrition:

Calories: 58

Carbs: 0.5g

Protein: 0.2g

Fat: 1.4g

147. ELBOWS CASSEROLE

Preparation Time: 5 minutes

Cooking Time: 5 ½ hours

Servings: 4

Ingredients:

- 1 packet low carb elbows or ravioli, cooked
- ¼ cup Romano cheese, preferably grated
- ¼ cup black olives, sliced
- 2 cup low carb BBQ sauce
- 2 cup mushrooms, preferably sliced
- 1 cup of small curd cottage cheese

Directions:

Coat your slow cooker with oil.

Spoon the BBQ sauce into it and then top with ½ of the cooked elbows, half of the Romano cheese and mushrooms along with 2 tbsp of the olives.

Continue layering with the remaining ingredients.

Cook within 5 ½ hours on low heat or until cooked.

Sprinkle with the cottage cheese and cook again for another half an hour.

Nutrition:

Calories: 400

Carbs: 9.6g

Protein: 10.5g

Fat: 30.5g

148. CHEESY BEER DIP SALSA

Preparation Time: 5 minutes

Cooking Time: 4 hours

Servings: 5 ½ cups

Ingredients:

- 16 oz. salsa
- 2/3 cup beer
- 1 lb. American cheese, shredded
- 8 oz. cream cheese, sliced
- 8 oz. Monterey jack cheese, shredded

Directions:

Begin by combining all the ingredients until they are properly mixed.

Cover the slow cooker and cook for 4 hours on low heat. Serve immediately.

Nutrition:

Calories: 177

Carbs: 5g

Protein: 9g

Fat: 14g

149. BRUSSELS SPROUT DIP

Preparation Time: 10 minutes

Cooking Time: 1 to 2 hours

Servings: 4

Ingredients:

- 1 lb. Brussels sprouts, quartered
- ¼ cup parmesan cheese, grated
- 1 garlic clove, unpeeled
- ¼ cup sour cream
- 1 tbsp. olive oil
- ½ tsp thyme, chopped
- ¾ cup mozzarella, shredded
- 4 oz. cream cheese, room temperature
- Salt and pepper, to taste
- ¼ cup mayonnaise

Directions:

Combine Brussels sprouts with pepper, olive oil, and salt and then spread them on a baking sheet in a single layer along with garlic.

Roast in a preheated oven at 400 degrees F for about 25 to 30 minutes while flipping them repeatedly.

Place all the other remaining ingredients into the slow cooker and stir well. Stir in the Brussels sprouts.

Cook within 1 to 2 hours on high heat or until the cheese has melted.

Nutrition:

Calories: 196

Carbs: 6g

Protein: 13g

Fat: 33g

150. BRAISED CABBAGE

Preparation Time: 5 minutes

Cooking Time: 5 hours

Servings: 2

Ingredients:

- 1 green cabbage head, tough ends discarded and cut into 12 wedges
- ½ cup bone broth
- 1 sweet onion, preferably large and chopped
- ¼ cup bacon fat, melted
- 4 garlic cloves
- Celtic sea salt, preferably coarse
- Caraway seeds

Directions:

Heat the slow cooker on high heat and then add melted bacon fat and onions to it.

After that, place the cabbage wedges in a layer in the slow cooker. Spoon the broth over it along with the salt and caraway seeds.

Cover the slow cooker, then cook within 1 hour. In between, stir the cabbage once to shift the top ones to the bottom. Pour in more stock if required.

Cook it again for another 4 hours on high heat. Once cooked, you can add some apple cider vinegar if you like.

Nutrition:

Calories: 122

Carbs: 2g

Protein: 8.7g

Fat: 3.4g

151. HOMEMADE VEGETABLE STOCK

Preparation Time: 15 minutes
Cooking Time: 12 hours & 30 minutes
Servings: 4

Ingredients:
- 4 quarts cold filtered water
- 12 whole peppercorns
- 3 peeled and chopped carrots
- 3 chopped celery stalks
- 2 bay leaves
- 4 smashed garlic cloves
- 1 large quartered onion
- 2 tbsp apple cider vinegar
- Any other vegetable scraps

Directions:
Put everything in your slow cooker and cover. Do not turn it on; let it sit for 30 minutes.

Cook on low for 12 hours. Strain the broth and discard the solids.

Before using, keep the stock in a container in the fridge for 2-3 hours.

Nutrition:
Calories: 11
Protein: 0g
Carbs: 3g
Fat: 0g
Fiber: 0g

152. VEGETABLE KORMA

Preparation Time: 15 minutes
Cooking Time: 8 hours
Servings: 4

Ingredients:
- 1 head's worth of cauliflower florets
- ¾ can of full-fat coconut milk
- 2 cups chopped green beans
- ½ chopped onion
- 2 minced garlic cloves
- 2 tbsp curry powder
- 2 tbsp coconut flour
- 1 tsp garam masala
- Salt and pepper to taste

Directions:
Add vegetables into your slow cooker. Mix coconut milk with seasonings.

Pour into the slow cooker. Sprinkle over coconut flour and mix until blended.

Close and cook on low for 8 hours. Taste and season more if necessary. Serve!

Nutrition:
Calories: 206
Protein: 5g
Carbs: 18g
Fat: 14g
Fiber: 9.5g

153. STUFFED EGGPLANT

Preparation Time: 15 minutes
Cooking Time: 1 hour & 30 minutes
Servings: 6

Ingredients:
- 1 seeded and chopped green bell pepper
- 1 tbsp. tomato paste
- 1 tsp. cumin
- 1 tsp. raw Stevia
- 2 chopped red onions
- 3 tbsp. chopped parsley
- 4 chopped tomatoes
- 4 minced garlic cloves
- 4 tbsp. olive oil
- 6 eggplants

Directions:
Remove eggplant skins with a vegetable peeler. Slice eggplants lengthwise and sprinkle with salt. Set aside for half an hour to sweat.

Place eggplants into your slow cooker. Cook on high for 20 minutes.

Sauté onions in a heated pan with olive oil. Stir bell pepper and garlic with onions and sauté for an additional 1 to 2 minutes.

Pour mixture into eggplants into the slow cooker—Cook 20 minutes on high.

Put pepper plus salt and add parsley, tomato paste, cumin, Stevia, and tomato. Cook another 10 minutes, stir well and serve!

Nutrition:
Calories: 180
Carbs: 2g
Fat: 13g
Protein: 9g

154. BACON CHEDDAR BROCCOLI SALAD

Preparation Time: 15 minutes
Cooking Time: 2 hours
Servings: 15

Ingredients:

Dressing:
- ¼ cup sweetener of choice
- 1 cup keto mayo
- 2 tbsp. organic vinegar
- Broccoli Salad:
- ½ diced red onion
- 4 ounces cheddar cheese
- ½ pound bacon, cooked and chopped
- 1 large head of broccoli
- 1/8 cup sunflower seeds
- 1/8 cup pumpkin seeds

Directions:

For the dressing, whisk all dressing components together, adjusting taste pepper and salt, and add to your slow cooker. Set to a low setting to cook for 2 hours until everything is combined. Serve warm!

Nutrition:

Calories: 189

Carbs: 8g

Fat: 21g

Protein: 8g

155. CRACKED-OUT KETO SLAW

Preparation Time: 15 minutes

Cooking Time: 1 hour & 35 minutes

Servings: 2

Ingredients:
- ½ cup chopped macadamia nuts
- 1 tbsp. sesame oil
- 1 tsp. chili paste
- 1 tsp. vinegar
- 2 garlic cloves
- 2 tbsp. tamari
- 4 cups shredded cabbage

Directions:

Toss cabbage with chili paste, sesame oil, vinegar, and tamari. Add to slow cooker.

Add minced garlic and mix well. Set to cook on high for 1 ½ hour.

Stir in macadamia nuts. Cook 5 minutes more. Garnish with sesame seeds before serving.

Nutrition:

Calories: 360

Carbs: 5g

Fat: 33g

Protein: 7g

156. ZUCCHINI PASTA

Preparation Time: 15 minutes

Cooking Time: 2 hours

Servings: 4

Ingredients:
- ¼ cup olive oil
- ½ cup basil
- ½ tsp. red pepper flakes
- 1-pint halved cherry tomatoes
- 1 sliced red onion
- 2 pounds spiralized zucchini
- 4 minced garlic cloves

Directions:

Sauté onion and garlic 3 minutes till fragrant in olive oil.

Add zucchini noodles to your slow cooker and season with pepper and salt—Cook 60 minutes on high heat.

Mix in tomatoes, basil, onion, garlic, and red pepper. Cook another 20 minutes.

Add parmesan cheese to the slow cooker. Mix thoroughly and cook for 10 minutes to melt the cheese. Devour!

Nutrition:

Calories: 181

Carbs: 6g

Fat: 13g

Protein: 5g

157. TWICE BAKED SPAGHETTI SQUASH

Preparation Time: 15 minutes

Cooking Time: 6 hours

Servings: 4

Ingredients:
- ¼ tsp. Pepper
- ¼ tsp. salt
- ½ cup grated parmesan cheese
- 1 tsp. oregano
- 2 minced garlic cloves
- 2 small spaghetti squashes
- 2 tbsp. butter
- 4 slices Provolone cheese

Directions:

Cut spaghetti squash in half lengthwise, discarding innards. Set gently into your pot.

Cook on high heat for 4 hours.

Take squash innards and mix with parmesan cheese and butter. Then mix in pepper, salt, garlic, and oregano.

Add squash innards mixture to the middle of cooked squash halves.

Cook on high for another 1-2 hours till middles are deliciously bubbly.

Nutrition:

Calories: 230

Carbs: 4g

Fat: 17g

Protein: 12g

158. MUSHROOM RISOTTO

Preparation Time: 15 minutes

Cooking Time: 4 hours

Servings: 4

Ingredients:

- ¼ cup vegetable broth
- 1-pound sliced Portobello mushrooms
- 1-pound sliced white mushrooms
- 1/3 cup grated parmesan cheese
- 2 diced shallots
- 3 tbsp. chopped chives
- 3 tbsp. coconut oil
- 4 ½ cups riced cauliflower
- 4 tbsp. butter

Directions:

Heat-up oil and sauté mushrooms for 3 minutes till soft. Discard the liquid and set it to the side.

Add oil to skillet and sauté shallots 60 seconds.

Pour all recipe components into your pot and mix well to combine.

Cook 3 hours on high heat. Serve topped with parmesan cheese.

Nutrition:

Calories: 438

Carbs: 5g

Fat: 17g

Protein: 12g

159. VEGAN BIBIMBAP

Preparation Time: 15 minutes

Cooking Time: 45 minutes

Servings: 4

Ingredients:

- ½ cucumber, sliced into strips
- 1 grated carrot
- 1 sliced red bell pepper
- 1 tbsp. soy sauce
- 1 tsp. sesame oil
- 10-ounces riced cauliflower
- 2 tbsp. rice vinegar
- 2 tbsp. sesame seeds
- 2 tbsp. sriracha sauce
- 4-5 broccoli florets
- 7-ounces tempeh, sliced into squares
- Liquid sweetener

Directions:

In a bowl, combine tempeh squares with 1 tbsp soy sauce and 2 tbsp vinegar. Set aside to soak. Slice veggies.

Add carrot, broccoli, and peppers to the slow cooker. Cook on high for 30 minutes.

Add cauliflower rice to the slow cooker; cook for 5 minutes.

Add sweetener, oil, soy sauce, vinegar, and sriracha to the slow cooker. Don't hesitate to add a bit of water if you find the mixture to be too thick.

Nutrition:

Calories: 119

Carbs: 0g

Fat: 18g

Protein: 8g

160. AVOCADO PESTO KELP NOODLES

Preparation Time: 15 minutes

Cooking Time: 1 hour & 30 minutes

Servings: 2

Ingredients:

- Pesto:
- ¼ cup basil
- ½ cup extra-virgin olive oil
- 1 avocado
- 1 cup baby spinach leaves
- 1 tsp. salt
- 1-2 garlic cloves
- 1 package of kelp noodles

Directions:

Add kelp noodles to the slow cooker with just enough water to cover them. Cook on high for 45-60 minutes.

In the meantime, combine pesto ingredients in a blender, blending till smooth and incorporated.

Stir in pesto and heat noodle mixture for 10 minutes.

Nutrition:

Calories: 321

Carbs: 1g

Fat: 32g

Protein: 2g

161. CREAMY CURRY SAUCE NOODLE BOWL

Preparation Time: 15 minutes

Cooking Time: 2 hours
Servings: 4

Ingredients:
- ½ head chopped cauliflower
- 1 diced red bell pepper
- 1 pack of Kanten Noodles
- 2 chopped carrots
- 2 handfuls of mixed greens
- Chopped cilantro
- Curry Sauce:
- ¼ cup avocado oil mayo
- ¼ cup water
- ¼ tsp./ ginger
- ½ tsp. pepper
- 1 ½ tsp. coriander
- 1 tsp. cumin
- 1 tsp turmeric
- 2 tbsp. apple cider vinegar
- 2 tbsp. avocado oil
- 2 tsp. curry powder

Directions:
Add all ingredients, minus curry sauce components, to your slow cooker. Set to cook on high for 1-2 hours.

In the meantime, add all of the curry sauce ingredients to a blender. Puree until smooth.

Pour over veggie and noodle mixture. Stir well to coat.

Nutrition:
Calories: 110
Carbs: 1g
Fat: 9g
Protein: 7g

162. SPINACH ARTICHOKE CASSEROLE

Preparation Time: 15 minutes
Cooking Time: 4 hours
Servings: 10

Ingredients:
- ½ tsp. pepper
- ¾ cup coconut flour
- ¾ cups unsweetened almond milk
- 1 cup grated parmesan cheese
- 1 tbsp. baking powder
- 1 tsp. salt
- 3 minced garlic cloves
- 5-ounces chopped spinach
- 6-ounces chopped artichoke hearts
- 8 eggs

Directions:
Grease the inside of your slow cooker.

Whisk ½ of parmesan cheese, pepper, salt, garlic, artichoke hearts, spinach, eggs, and almond milk.

Add baking powder and coconut flour, combining well.

Spread into the slow cooker. Sprinkle with remaining parmesan cheese.

Cook within 2 to 3 hours on high, or you can cook 4 to 6 hours on a lower heat setting.

Nutrition:
Calories: 141
Carbs: 7g
Fat: 9g
Protein: 10g

163. ASPARAGUS WITH LEMON

Preparation Time: 15 minutes
Cooking Time: 2 hours
Servings: 2

Ingredients:
- 1 lb. asparagus spears
- 1 tbsp lemon juice

Directions:
Prepare the seasonings: 2 crushed cloves of garlic and salt and pepper to taste.

Put the asparagus spears on the bottom of the slow cooker. Add the lemon juice and the seasonings.

Cook on low for 2 hours.

Nutrition:
Calories: 78
Fat: 2 g
Carbs: 3.7 g
Protein: 9 g

164. ZUCCHINI AND YELLOW SQUASH

Preparation Time: 15 minutes
Cooking Time: 6 hours
Servings: 2

Ingredients:
- 2/3 cup zucchini, sliced
- 2/3 cups yellow squash, sliced
- 1/3 tsp Italian seasoning
- 1/8 cup butter

Directions:
Place zucchini and squash on the bottom of the slow cooker.

Sprinkle with the Italian seasoning with salt, pepper, and garlic powder to taste. Top with butter.

Cover and cook within 6 hours on low.

Nutrition:

Calories: 122
Fat: 9.9 g
Carbs: 3.7 g
Protein: 4.2 g

165. GLUTEN-FREE ZUCCHINI BREAD

Preparation Time: 15 minutes
Cooking Time: 3 hours
Servings: 2

Ingredients:
- 1/2 cup coconut flour
- 1/2 tsp baking powder and baking soda
- 1 egg, whisked
- 1/4 cup butter
- 1 cup zucchini, shredded

Directions:
Combine all dry ingredients and add a pinch of salt and sweetener of choice. Combine the dry ingredients with the eggs and mix thoroughly.
Fold in zucchini and spread inside the slow cooker. Cover and cook within 3 hours on high.

Nutrition:
Calories: 174
Fat: 13 g
Carbs: 2.9 g
Protein: 4 g

166. EGGPLANT PARMESAN

Preparation Time: 40 minutes
Cooking Time: 4 hours
Servings: 2

Ingredients:
- 1 large eggplant, 1/2-inch slices
- 1 egg, whisked
- 1 tsp Italian seasoning
- 1 cup marinara
- 1/4 cup Parmesan cheese, grated

Directions:
Put salt on each side of the eggplant, then let stand for 30 minutes.
Spread some of the marinara on the bottom of the slow cooker and season with salt and pepper, garlic powder, and Italian seasoning.
Spread the eggplants on a single slow cooker and pour over some of the marinara sauce. Repeat up to 3 layers. Top with Parmesan. Cover and cook for 4 hours. l

Nutrition:
Calories: 159
Fat: 12 g
Carbs: 8 g
Protein: 14 g

167. ZUCCHINI LASAGNA

Preparation Time: 15 minutes
Cooking Time: 4 hours
Servings: 2

Ingredients:
- 1 large egg, whisked
- 1/8 cup Parmesan cheese, grated
- 1 cup spinach, chopped
- 2 cups tomato sauce
- 2 zucchinis, 1/8-inch thick, pre-grilled

Directions:
Mix egg with spinach and parmesan. Spread some of the tomato sauce inside the slow cooker and season with salt and pepper. lo
Spread the zucchini on a single slow cooker and pour over some of the tomato sauce. Repeat until 3 layers. Top with Parmesan. Cover and cook for 4 hours.

Nutrition:
Calories: 251
Fat: 13.9 g
Carbs: 4.8 g
Protein: 20.8 g

168. CAULIFLOWER BOLOGNESE ON ZUCCHINI NOODLES

Preparation Time: 15 minutes
Cooking Time: 4 hours
Servings: 2

Ingredients:
- 1 cauliflower head, floret cuts
- 1 tsp dried basil flakes
- 28 oz diced tomatoes
- 1/2 cup vegetable broth
- 5 zucchinis, spiral cut

Directions:
Place ingredients in the slow cooker except for the zucchini. Season with 2 garlic cloves, 3.4 diced onions, salt, pepper to taste, and desired spices. Cover and cook for 4 hours.
Smash florets of the cauliflower with a fork to form "Bolognese."
Transfer the dish on top of the zucchini noodles.

Nutrition:
Calories: 164
Fat: 5 g
Carbs: 6 g

Protein: 12 g

169. GARLIC TOMATO, ZUCCHINI, AND YELLOW SQUASH

Preparation Time: 15 minutes

Cooking Time: 6 hours

Servings: 3

Ingredients:

- 1 medium yellow squash, quartered, sliced
- 1 medium zucchini, quartered, sliced
- 1 tomato, cut into wedges
- ½ tsp Italian seasoning
- ¼ tsp of sea salt
- 2 tbsp parmesan cheese or Asiago cheese, grated
- Pepper to taste
- ½ tsp garlic powder
- 2 tbsp cold butter, cubed

Directions:

Add squash, tomato, and zucchini to the slow cooker. Sprinkle salt, garlic powder, garlic slices, pepper, and Italian seasoning.

Place butter cubes all over the vegetables, then sprinkle cheese on top. Close the lid. Cook on 'Low' for 4-6 hours or until tender. Stir and serve.

Nutrition:

Calories 126

Fat 10.2g

Carbohydrate 6g

Protein 4.9g

170. PARMESAN ZUCCHINI AND TOMATO GRATIN

Preparation Time: 15 minutes

Cooking Time: 4 hours

Servings: 3

Ingredients:

- 3 small zucchinis, sliced
- 1 small onion, chopped
- 1 medium tomato, sliced
- ¼ cup parmesan cheese, shredded
- 1 tbsp garlic, minced
- ½ tsp garlic powder
- 1 tsp dried basil
- 1 tbsp olive oil + extra to drizzle
- ¼ tsp salt

Directions:

Place a skillet over medium heat. Put the oil, then onions, and cook until soft. Add garlic and cook until fragrant.

Transfer into the slow cooker. Place alternate layers of zucchini slices and a tomato slice.

Drizzle olive oil all over the top layer. Sprinkle dried herbs, salt, garlic powder, and finally, Parmesan cheese. Close the lid. Cook on 'Low' for 3-4 hours or until tender.

Nutrition:

Calories 89

Fat 5.5g

Carbohydrate 9.1g

Protein 3.1g

171. SLOW-COOKED SUMMER VEGETABLES

Preparation Time: 15 minutes

Cooking Time: 45 minutes

Servings: 5

Ingredients:

- 1 cup okra slices
- 1 medium onion, chopped into chunks
- 1 medium zucchini, sliced
- ½ cup grape tomatoes
- 1 yellow bell pepper, sliced
- ½ cup mushroom, sliced
- ¼ cup olive oil
- ¼ cup balsamic vinegar
- ½ tbsp fresh thyme, chopped
- 1 tbsp fresh basil, chopped

Directions:

Put all the fixings into the slow cooker and stir well. Close the lid. Cook on 'High' for 45 minutes. Serve.

Nutrition:

Calories 125

Fat 10.4g

Carbohydrate 7.9g

Protein 1.8g

172. CHEESY CAULIFLOWER GARLIC BREAD

Preparation Time: 15 minutes

Cooking Time: 4 hours

Servings: 6

Ingredients:

- 1 ½ pounds cauliflower, grated to a rice-like texture
- 4 cups mozzarella cheese, shredded, divided
- 3 tsp garlic
- 2 tsp red pepper flakes
- Pepper to taste
- 6 tsp Italian seasoning
- 6 tbsp coconut flour

- 1 tsp salt
- 4 large eggs, beaten
- Cooking spray

Directions:

Grease the slow cooker with cooking spray. Add all the ingredients (left out 2 cups of cheese and garlic) into a bowl and mix it until well.

Transfer into the slow cooker. Scatter garlic and remaining cheese on top.

Close the lid. Cook on 'High' for 2-4 hours or until brown and crisp. Cut slices and serve.

Nutrition:

Calories 184

Fat 11.2g

Carbohydrate 9.5g

Protein 13.7g

173. CHEESY CAULIFLOWER GRATIN

Preparation Time: 15 minutes

Cooking Time: 4 hours & 10 minutes

Servings: 3

Ingredients:

- 2 cups cauliflower florets
- 3 tbsp heavy whipping cream
- 3 deli slices pepper Jack cheese
- 2 tbsp butter
- Salt to taste
- Pepper to taste

Directions:

Add cauliflower, cream, butter, salt, and pepper to the slow cooker. Close the lid. Cook on 'Low' for 3-4 hours or until tender.

When done, mash with a fork. Taste and adjust the seasoning if necessary.

Place cheese slices on top. Cover and cook within 10 minutes or until cheese melts. Serve right away.

Nutrition:

Calories 216

Fat 19.3g

Carbohydrate 4g

Protein 5.7g

174. CREAMY RICOTTA SPAGHETTI SQUASH

Preparation Time: 15 minutes

Cooking Time: 6 hours

Servings: 8

Ingredients:

- 2 spaghetti squash, halved, deseeded
- 2 tsp garlic powder
- 4 tbsp fresh basil or parsley, chopped
- 2 cups part-skim ricotta cheese
- 2 tsp lemon zest, grated
- Salt to taste
- Pepper to taste
- Cooking spray

Directions:

Spray the cut part of the spaghetti squash with cooking spray. Place it in the slow cooker with the cut side facing down.

Close the lid. Cook on 'Low' for 4-6 hours or until tender. When done, using a fork, scrape the squash, and add into a bowl.

Add ricotta cheese, lemon zest, garlic powder, salt, pepper, and basil, and mix well.

Nutrition:

Calories 112

Fat 5.4g

Carbohydrate 9.1g

Protein 7.7g

175. CREAMY KETO MASH

Preparation Time: 15 minutes

Cooking Time: 2 hours

Servings: 8

Ingredients:

- 2 large heads cauliflower, chopped into small floret's
- 4 cloves garlic, minced
- 1 large onion, chopped
- 8 tbsp butter or ghee+ extra to top
- 1 cup cream cheese or sour cream
- ½ cup of water
- Salt to taste
- Pepper to taste

Directions:

Place the cauliflower florets in the slow cooker. Pour about ½ a cup of water.

Close the lid. Cook on 'Low' for 1-2 hours or until tender.

Place a skillet over medium heat. Add 2 tbsp butter or ghee. When it melts, add onions and garlic and sauté until the onions are translucent.

Add remaining butter and stir, then remove from heat. Transfer into a blender. Add cauliflower and blend until smooth or blend in the food processor. Add cream cheese and pulse until well combined.

Transfer into a bowl, then add salt and pepper to taste. Top with butter plus ghee and serve.

Nutrition:

Calories 219
Fat 21.7g
Carbohydrate 4.3g
Protein 3.1g

176. GARLIC RANCH MUSHROOMS

- Preparation Time: 15 minutes
- Cooking Time: 2 hours
- Servings: 2

Ingredients:

1 package of Ranch Dressing
4 packages of whole mushrooms
1 cube butter, melted

Directions:

Place 5 cloves of garlic at the bottom of the slow cooker and pour in the melted butter.

Add in the mushrooms and pour the dressing—season with salt and pepper to taste.

Cover and cook on high within 2 hours.

Nutrition:

Calories: 97
Fat: 20 g
Carbs: 3 g
Protein: 10 g

177. EASY CREAMED SPINACH

Preparation Time: 15 minutes
Cooking Time: 3 hours
Servings: 2

Ingredients:

- 10 oz spinach, defrosted
- 3 tbsp Parmesan cheese
- 3 oz cream cheese
- 2 tbsp sour cream

Directions:

Combine all the fixings in the slow cooker.

Add some seasonings: salt and pepper to taste and half a tsp of onion and garlic powder. Mix thoroughly—cover and cook within 3 hours on low.

Nutrition:

Calories: 165
Fat: 13.22 g
Carbs: 3.63 g
Protein: 7.33 g

178. ZOODLES WITH CAULIFLOWER-TOMATO SAUCE

Preparation Time: 15 minutes
Cooking Time: 3 hours & 31 minutes
Servings: 4

Ingredients:

- 5 large spiralized zucchinis
- Two 24-ounce cans of diced tomatoes
- 2 small heads' worth of cauliflower florets
- 1 cup chopped sweet onion
- 4 minced garlic cloves
- ½ cup veggie broth
- 5 tsp Italian seasoning
- Salt and pepper to taste
- Enough water to cover zoodles

Directions:

Put everything but the zoodles into your slow cooker. Cook on high for 3 ½ hours.

Smash into a chunky sauce with a cauliflower masher or another utensil.

To cook the zoodles, boil a large pot of water. When boiling, cook zoodles for just 1 minute, then drain—Season with salt and pepper. Serve sauce over zoodles!

Nutrition:

Calories: 113
Protein: 7g
Carbs: 22g
Fat: 2g
Fiber: 10.5g

179. SPAGHETTI SQUASH CARBONARA

Preparation Time: 15 minutes
Cooking Time: 8 hours & 10 minutes
Servings: 4

Ingredients:

- 2 cups of water
- One 3-pound spaghetti squash
- ½ cup coconut bacon
- ½ cup fresh spinach leaves
- 1 egg
- 3 tbsp heavy cream
- 3 tbsp unsweetened almond milk
- ½ cup grated Parmesan cheese
- 1 tsp garlic powder
- Salt and pepper to taste

Directions:

Put squash in your cooker and pour in 2 cups of water. Close the lid.

Cook on low for 8-9 hours. When the spaghetti squash cools, mix egg, cream, milk, and cheese in a bowl.

When the squash is cool enough for you to handle with oven mitts, cut it open lengthwise and scrape out noodles. Mix in the egg mixture right away.

Add spinach and seasonings. Top with coconut bacon and enjoy!

Nutrition:
Calories: 211
Protein: 5g
Carbs: 26g
Fat: 11g
Fiber: 5.1g

180. SUMMERY BELL PEPPER + EGGPLANT SALAD

Preparation Time: 15 minutes
Cooking Time: 7 hours
Servings: 4

Ingredients:
- One 24-ounce can of whole tomatoes
- 2 sliced yellow bell peppers
- 2 small eggplants (smaller ones tend to be less bitter)
- 1 sliced red onion
- 1 tbsp paprika
- 2 tsp cumin
- Salt and pepper to taste
- A squeeze of lime juice

Directions:
Mix all the fixings in your slow cooker. Close the lid. Cook on low for 7-8 hours.
When time is up, serve warm, or chill in the fridge for a few hours before eating.

Nutrition:
Calories: 128
Protein: 5g
Carbs: 27g
Fat: 1g
Fiber: 9.7g

181. ZUCCHINI PASTA

Preparation Time: 15 minutes
Cooking Time: 1 hour
Servings: 4

Ingredients:
- 2 zucchinis
- 1 tsp dried oregano
- 1 tsp dried basil
- 2 tbsp butter
- ¼ tsp salt
- tbsp water

Directions:
Peel the zucchini and spiralize it with a veggie spiralizer.
Melt the butter and mix it with the dried oregano, dried basil, salt, and water.
Place the spiralized zucchini in the slow cooker and add the spice mixture.
Close the lid and cook the meal for 1 hour on Low.
Let the cooked pasta cool slightly.
Serve it!

Nutrition:
Calories 68,
Fat 6g,
Fiber 1.2g,
Carbs 3.5g,
Protein 1.3g.

182. CHINESE BROCCOLI

Preparation Time: 15 minutes
Cooking Time: 1 hour
Servings: 4

Ingredients:
- 1 tbsp sesame seeds
- 1 tbsp olive oil
- Oz broccoli
- 1 tsp chili flakes
- 1 tbsp apple cider vinegar
- 1 tbsp water
- ¼ tsp garlic powder

Directions:
Cut the broccoli into the florets and sprinkle with olive oil, chili flakes, apple cider vinegar, and garlic powder.
Stir the broccoli and place it in the slow cooker.
Add water and sesame seeds.
Cook the broccoli for 1 hour on High.
Transfer the cooked broccoli to serving plates and enjoy!

Nutrition:
Calories 69,
Fat 4.9g,
Fiber 2.1g,
Carbs 5.4g,
Protein 2.4g.

183. SLOW COOKER SPAGHETTI SQUASH

Preparation Time: 15 minutes
Cooking Time: 4 hours
Servings: 5

Ingredients:
- 1-pound spaghetti squash
- 1 tbsp butter

- ¼ cup water
- 1 tsp ground black pepper
- ¼ tsp ground nutmeg

Directions:
Peel the spaghetti squash and sprinkle it with the ground black pepper and ground nutmeg.
Pour water into the slow cooker.
Add butter and spaghetti squash.
Close the lid and cook for 4 hours on Low.
Chop the spaghetti squash into small pieces and serve!

Nutrition:
Calories 50,
Fat 2.9g,
Fiber 6.6g,
Carbs 0.1g,
Protein 0.7g.

184. MUSHROOM STEW

Preparation Time: 15 minutes
Cooking Time: 6 hours
Servings: 8

Ingredients:
- Oz white mushrooms, sliced
- 2 eggplants, chopped
- 1 onion, diced
- 1 garlic clove, diced
- 2 bell peppers, chopped
- 1 cup water
- 1 tbsp butter
- ½ tsp salt
- ½ tsp ground black pepper

Directions:
Place the sliced mushrooms, chopped eggplant, and diced onion into the slow cooker.
Add the garlic clove and bell peppers.
Sprinkle the vegetables with salt and ground black pepper.
Add butter and water and stir it gently with a wooden spatula.
Close the lid and cook the stew for 6 hours on Low.
Stir the cooked stew one more time and serve!

Nutrition:
Calories 71,
Fat 1.9g,
Fiber 5.9g,
Carbs 13g,
Protein 3g.

185. CABBAGE STEAKS

Preparation Time: 15 minutes
Cooking Time: 2 hours
Servings: 4

Ingredients:
- Oz white cabbage
- 1 tbsp butter
- ½ tsp cayenne pepper
- ½ tsp chili flakes
- 1 tbsp water

Directions:
Slice the cabbage into medium steaks and rub them with the cayenne pepper and chili flakes.
Rub the cabbage steaks with butter on each side.
Place them in the slow cooker and sprinkle with water.
Close the lid and cook the cabbage steaks for 2 hours on High.
When the cabbage steaks are cooked, they should be tender to the touch.
Serve the cabbage steak after 10 minutes of chilling.

Nutrition:
Calories 44,
Fat 3g,
Fiber 1.8g,
Carbs 4.3g,
Protein 1g.

186. MASHED CAULIFLOWER

Preparation Time: 20 minutes
Cooking Time: 3 hours
Servings: 5

Ingredients:
- tbsp butter
- 1-pound cauliflower
- 1 tbsp full-fat cream
- 1 tsp salt
- 1 tsp ground black pepper
- 1 oz dill, chopped

Directions:
Wash the cauliflower and chop it.
Place the chopped cauliflower in the slow cooker.
Add butter and full-fat cream.
Add salt and ground black pepper.
Stir the mixture and close the lid.
Cook the cauliflower for 3 hours on High.
When the cauliflower is cooked, transfer it to a blender and blend until smooth.

Place the smooth cauliflower in a bowl and mix with the chopped dill.

Stir it well and serve!

Nutrition:

Calories 101,

Fat 7.4g,

Fiber 3.2g,

Carbs 8.3g,

Protein 3.1g.

187. BACON-WRAPPED CAULIFLOWER

Preparation Time: 15 minutes

Cooking Time: 7 hours

Servings: 4

Ingredients:
- Oz cauliflower head
- Oz bacon, sliced
- 1 tsp salt
- 1 tsp cayenne pepper
- 1 oz butter, softened
- ¾ cup water

Directions:

Sprinkle the cauliflower head with salt and cayenne pepper then rub with butter.

Wrap the cauliflower head in the sliced bacon and secure it with toothpicks.

Pour water into the slow cooker and add the wrapped cauliflower head.

Cook the cauliflower head for 7 hours on Low.

Then let the cooked cauliflower head cool for 10 minutes.

Serve it!

Nutrition:

Calories 187,

Fat 14.8g,

Fiber 2.1g,

Carbs 4.7g,

Protein 9.5g.

188. CAULIFLOWER CASSEROLE

Preparation Time: 15 minutes

Cooking Time: 7 hours

Servings: 5

Ingredients:
- 2 tomatoes, chopped
- Oz cauliflower chopped
- Oz broccoli, chopped
- 1 cup water
- 1 tsp salt
- 1 tbsp butter
- Oz white mushrooms, chopped
- 1 tsp chili flakes

Directions:

Mix the water, salt, and chili flakes.

Place the butter in the slow cooker.

Add a layer of the chopped cauliflower.

Add the layer of broccoli and tomatoes.

Add the mushrooms and pat down the mix to flatten.

Add the water and close the lid.

Cook the casserole for 7 hours on Low.

Cool the casserole to room temperature and serve!

Nutrition:

Calories 61,

Fat 2.6g,

Fiber 3.2g,

Carbs 8.1g,

Protein 3.4g.

189. CAULIFLOWER RICE

Preparation Time: 15 minutes

Cooking Time: 2 hours

Servings: 5

Ingredients:
- 1-pound cauliflower
- 1 tsp salt
- 1 tbsp turmeric
- 1 tbsp butter
- ¾ cup water

Directions:

Chop the cauliflower into tiny pieces to make cauliflower rice. You can also pulse in a food processor to get very fine grains of 'rice'.

Place the cauliflower rice in the slow cooker.

Add salt, turmeric, and water.

Stir gently and close the lid.

Cook the cauliflower rice for 2 hours on High.

Strain the cauliflower rice and transfer it to a bowl.

Add butter and stir gently.

Serve it!

Nutrition:

Calories 48,

Fat 2.5,

Fiber 2.6,

Carbs 5.7,

Protein 1.9.

190. CURRY CAULIFLOWER

Preparation Time: 15 minutes
Cooking Time: 5 hours
Servings: 2

Ingredients:
- Oz cauliflower
- 1 tsp curry paste
- 1 tsp curry powder
- ½ tsp dried cilantro
- 1 oz butter
- ¾ cup water
- ¼ cup chicken stock

Directions:
Chop the cauliflower roughly and sprinkle it with the curry powder and dried cilantro.
Place the chopped cauliflower in the slow cooker.
Mix the curry paste with the water.
Add chicken stock and transfer the liquid to the slow cooker.
Add butter and close the lid.
Cook the cauliflower for 5 hours on Low.
Strain ½ of the liquid off and discard. Transfer the cauliflower to serving bowls.
Serve it!

Nutrition:
Calories 158,
Fat 13.3g,
Fiber 3.9g,
Carbs 8.9g,
Protein 3.3g.

191. GARLIC CAULIFLOWER STEAKS

Preparation Time: 15 minutes
Cooking Time: 3 hours
Servings: 4

Ingredients:
- 1 oz cauliflower head
- 1 tsp minced garlic
- tbsp butter
- tbsp water
- 1 tsp paprika

Directions:
Wash the cauliflower head carefully and slice it into the medium steaks.
Mix up together the butter, minced garlic, and paprika.
Rub the cauliflower steaks with the butter mixture.
Pour the water into the slow cooker.
Add the cauliflower steaks and close the lid.
Cook the vegetables for 3 hours on High.
Transfer the cooked cauliflower steaks to a platter and serve them immediately!

Nutrition:
Calories 129,
Fat 11.7g,
Fiber 2.7g,
Carbs 5.8g,
Protein 2.2g.

192. ZUCCHINI GRATIN

Preparation Time: 10 minutes
Cooking Time: 5 hours
Servings: 3

Ingredients:
- 1 zucchini, sliced
- Parmesan, grated
- 1 tsp ground black pepper
- 1 tbsp butter
- ½ cup almond milk

Directions:
Sprinkle the sliced zucchini with the ground black pepper.
Chop the butter and place it in the slow cooker.
Transfer the sliced zucchini to the slow cooker to make the bottom layer.
Add the almond milk.
Sprinkle the zucchini with the grated cheese and close the lid.
Cook the gratin for 5 hours on Low.
Then let the gratin cool until room temperature.
Serve it!

Nutrition:
Calories 229,
Fat 19.6g,
Fiber 1.8g,
Carbs 5.9g,
Protein 10.9g.

193. EGGPLANT GRATIN

Preparation Time: 15 minutes
Cooking Time: 5 hours
Servings: 7

Ingredients:
- 1 tbsp butter
- 1 tsp minced garlic
- 2 eggplants, chopped
- 1 tsp salt

- 1 tbsp dried parsley
- Oz Parmesan, grated
- tbsp water
- 1 tsp chili flakes

Directions:
Mix the dried parsley, chili flakes, and salt together.
Sprinkle the chopped eggplants with the spice mixture and stir well.
Place the eggplants in the slow cooker.
Add the water and minced garlic.
Add the butter and sprinkle with the grated Parmesan.
Close the lid and cook the gratin for 5 hours on Low.
Open the lid and cool the gratin for 10 minutes.
Serve it.

Nutrition:
Calories 107,
Fat 5.4g,
Fiber 5.6g,
Carbs 10g,
Protein 6.8g.

194. MOROCCAN EGGPLANT MASH

Preparation Time: 15 minutes
Cooking Time: 7 hours
Servings: 4

Ingredients:
- 1 eggplant, peeled
- 1 jalapeno pepper
- 1 tsp curry powder
- ½ tsp salt
- 1 tsp paprika
- ¾ tsp ground nutmeg
- 2 tbsp butter
- ¾ cup almond milk
- 1 tsp dried dill

Directions:
Chop the eggplant into small pieces.
Place the eggplant in the slow cooker.
Chop the jalapeno pepper and combine it with the eggplant.
Then sprinkle the vegetables with curry powder, salt, paprika, ground nutmeg, and dried dill.
Add almond milk and butter.
Close the lid and cook the vegetables for 7 hours on Low.
Cool the vegetables and then blend them until smooth with a hand blender.
Transfer the cooked eggplant mash into the bowls and serve!

Nutrition:
Calories 190,
Fat 17g,
Fiber 5.6g,
Carbs 10g,
Protein 2.5g.

195. SAUTÉED BELL PEPPERS

Preparation Time: 15 minutes
Cooking Time: 5 hours
Servings: 6

Ingredients:
- 10 Oz bell peppers
- 7 Oz cauliflower, chopped
- 2 oz bacon, chopped
- 1 tsp salt
- 1 tsp ground black pepper
- ¾ cup coconut milk, unsweetened
- 1 tsp butter
- 1 tsp thyme
- 1 onion, diced
- 1 tsp turmeric

Directions:
Remove the seeds from the bell peppers and chop them roughly.
Place the bell peppers, cauliflower, and bacon in the slow cooker.
Add the salt, ground black pepper, coconut milk, butter, milk, and thyme.
Stir well then add the diced onion.
Add the turmeric and stir the mixture.
Close the lid and cook for 5 hours on Low.
When the meal is cooked, let it chill for 10 minutes and serve it!

Nutrition:
Calories 195,
Fat 12.2g,
Fiber 4.2g,
Carbs 13.1g,
Protein 6.7g.

196. GARLIC ARTICHOKE

Preparation Time: 15 minutes
Cooking Time: 2 hours
Servings: 4

Ingredients:

- 8 Oz artichoke, trimmed, chopped
- 2 tsp butter
- 1 garlic clove, peeled
- ¼ cup water
- ½ tsp ground black pepper

Directions:

Chop the garlic clove.

Melt the butter and mix it with the chopped garlic.

Add the ground black pepper and stir the mixture.

Place the artichoke in the slow cooker and cover it with the butter mixture.

Add water and close the lid.

Cook the artichoke for 2 hours on High.

Transfer the cooked artichoke to a platter and serve!

Nutrition:

Calories 45,

Fat 2g,

Fiber 3.2g,

Carbs 6.4g,

Protein 2g.

197. SPINACH PORTOBELLO

Preparation Time: 15 minutes

Cooking Time: 3 hours

Servings: 8

Ingredients:

- 4 large Portobello mushrooms, stems removed
- 1 tablespoons olive oil
- 1/2 onion, chopped
- 2 cups fresh spinach, rinsed and chopped
- garlic cloves, minced
- 1 cup chicken broth
- 3 tablespoons parmesan cheese, grated
- 1/3 teaspoon dried thyme
- salt, pepper, to taste

Directions:

Heat oil in a medium pan over high heat. Add onion, cook until translucent, stirring regularly. Add spinach and thyme, cook for 1-2 minutes until spinach is wilted.

Brush each mushroom with olive oil.

Insert 1 tablespoon of onion and spinach stuffing into each mushroom.

Pour chicken broth into the slow cooker. Lay stuffed mushrooms on the bottom.

Close the lid and cook on High for 3 hours.

Once cooked, sprinkle mushrooms with parmesan cheese and serve.

Nutrition:

Calories 310,

Fat 21g,

Fiber 3.2g,

Carbs 3g,

Protein 12g.

198. KALE QUICHE

Preparation Time: 15 minutes

Cooking Time: 3-5 hours

Servings: 3

Ingredients:

- 1 cup almond milk 1 tablespoons olive oil
- 4 eggs
- 1 cup Carbquick Baking Mix
- 2 cups spinach, chopped
- 1/2 bell pepper, chopped
- cups fresh baby kale, chopped
- 1 teaspoon garlic, chopped
- 1/3 cup fresh basil, chopped
- 1 tablespoon olive oil
- salt, pepper, to taste

Directions:

Add oil to a slow cooker or use a cooking spray.

Beat eggs into the slow cooker; add almond milk, Baking Mix, and combine.

Add spinach, bell pepper, garlic, and basil, stir to combine.

Close the lid and cook on Low for 5 hours or on High for 3 hours.

Make sure the quiche is ready, check the center with a toothpick, it should be dry.

Nutrition:

Calories 273,

Fat 24.4g,

Carbs 5.8g,

Protein 10.5g.

FISH & SHELLFISH

199. BUTTERFLY TILAPIA

Preparation Time: 15 minutes

Cooking Time: 2 hours

Servings: 4

Ingredients:
- 4 tilapia fillets
- For the garlic-butter compound:
- 8 tbsp. butter
- 8 chopped garlic cloves
- 8 tsp chopped parsley

Directions:

Mix all of the garlic-butter compound ingredients in a mixing bowl.

Place each tilapia fillet in the middle of a large sheet of aluminum foil. Generously season fillets with salt and pepper. Divide the garlic butter compound into each fillet, then seal all the fish's sides using a foil. Place into the slow cooker. Cover with lid—Cook for 2 hours on high.

Nutrition:

Calories: 309

Fat: 24.1 g

Protein: 21.9 g

200. TUNA AND OLIVE-ORANGE TAPENADE

Preparation Time: 15 minutes

Cooking Time: 1 hour

Servings: 4

Ingredients:
- 12 oz. tuna
- 5 oz. pitted brine-cured black olives
- 5 oz. pitted mild green olives
- 5 tbsp. extra-virgin olive oil, and extra for the spinach
- 6 oz. fresh baby spinach
- 3 fresh bay leaves
- 2 thinly sliced garlic cloves
- ¼ cup fish stock or vegetable broth
- ¼ cup dry white or rose wine
- ½ tsp. kosher salt
- ½ medium finely chopped onion
- 1 tsp. red or white wine vinegar
- 1 orange zest
- Black pepper

Directions:

In the slow cooker, combine the broth, wine, 4 tbsp olive oil, bay leaves, and salt. Season with pepper to taste. Stir to combine. Cover the slow cooker with a lid. Cook for 30 minutes on low.

Add in the tuna. Turn to coat each piece evenly with the cooked broth wine mix. Cover and cook for 25-35 minutes on low or until the fish is opaque. When the fish is opaque, remove with a slotted spoon and transfer to a serving platter. Shred the fish into large flakes. Cover with foil to keep warm. Discard the cooking liquid.

While the fish is cooking, put the orange zest, garlic, olives, vinegar, and the remaining 1 tbsp olive oil in a food processor. Pulse until the mix is a thick puree.

When ready to serve, put the spinach in a mixing bowl. Toss with a little olive oil—season with salt and pepper. Divide into the number of servings indicated, creating a bed for the tuna. Evenly distribute the tuna flakes into the number of servings. Top with the tapenade. Serve at room temperature.

Nutrition:

Calories: 414
Fat: 31 g
Protein: 25.1 g
Carbs: 9 g

201.HEART AND TUNA STUFFED MUSHROOM

Preparation Time: 15 minutes
Cooking Time: 5 hours
Servings: 15

Ingredients:

- 8 oz. shredded Italian cheese blend
- 3 tbsp. mayonnaise
- 3 sliced scallions
- 3 oz. softened cream cheese
- 2 lbs. cleaned mushrooms
- ¼ c. minced fresh parsley
- ½ tsp. pepper
- 7 oz. drained tuna
- 14 oz drained chopped artichoke hearts
- ¼ tsp. hot sauce

Directions:

Place artichoke hearts, scallions, and the tuna in a mixing bowl and heat until well combined.

Then add in the Italian cheese, cream cheese, pepper, hot sauce, mayo, and parsley. Mash all your ingredients until well blended.

Stuff the tuna-artichoke mix into the mushroom caps.

Place a basket-type steamer in the slow cooker. Arrange a layer of the stuffed mushrooms on the basket steamer.

Take a piece of aluminum foil, then make holes in the foil using a fork. Fit the holed aluminum foil down the first layer of the stuffed mushrooms. Make a hole in the middle.

Arrange another layer of stuffed mushrooms on the foil. Do the process again to ensure that the mushrooms are well arranged. Close the lid—Cook for about 4-5 hours on low.

When cooked, serve in the slow cooker to keep warm or transfer them into a serving platter.

Nutrition:

Calories: 142
Fat: 9 g
Protein: 10.7 g
Carbs: 6.2 g

202.ETOUFFEE

Preparation Time: 15 minutes
Cooking Time: 7 hours
Servings: 9

Ingredients:

- 1½ lbs. peeled and deveined raw shrimp
- 1½ lbs. quartered scallops
- 4 tbsp. olive oil
- 2 medium onions diced
- 9 scallions, chopped
- 3 celery stalks, diced
- 2 diced small green bell peppers
- 2 diced small jalapeno peppers
- 3 minced garlic cloves
- 20oz. diced tomatoes
- 5 tbsp tomato paste
- ¾ tsp dried basil
- ¾ tsp dried thyme
- ¾ tsp dried oregano
- 1/3 tsp cayenne pepper
- 3 tsp almond meal
- 1½ tbsp. cold water
- Hot sauce
- Sea salt

Directions:

Combine the olive oil and onion in the slow cooker. Add the scallions, bell pepper, jalapeno, and celery. Mix well. Cook within 30 minutes, high.

Add the tomato paste and garlic—cover and cook for 15 minutes on high.

Add the tomatoes, cayenne, thyme, oregano, basil, and salt—Cook within 6 hours on low.

Add the shrimp and scallops. Set heat to high, cover, and cook for 15 minutes.

Combine the almond meal and water. Add the mixture to your slow cooker for about 6 minutes to thicken. Add a few drops of hot sauce and stir.

Nutrition:

Calories: 247

Protein: 19 g

Fat: 1.3 g

Carbs: 6.2 g

203. POACHED SALMON

Preparation Time: 15 minutes

Cooking Time: 1 hour

Servings: 8

Ingredients:

- 2 tbsp. butter
- 1 sliced large sweet onion
- 3 cup water
- 2 tbsp. lemon juice
- 2 sprigs of fresh dill
- 8 salmon fillets
- Sea salt
- 2 quartered lemons

Directions:

Butter the inside of the slow cooker. Place the onion rings on the bottom in a single layer.

Slowly pour the water into the slow cooker—Cook within half an hour on high.

On top of the onion slices, place salmon fillets—season with the fresh dill, salt, and some lemon juice.

Cover the cooker and cook for 30 mins on high or until the salmon is no longer pink on the outside.

Drain the fillets very well and serve with the lemon wedges.

Nutrition:

Calories: 100

Protein: 40.1 g

Fat: 3.4 g

Carbs: 3.75 g

204. COD AND VEGETABLES

Preparation Time: 15 minutes

Cooking Time: 1-3 hours

Servings: 4

Ingredients:

- (5-6 oz.) cod fillets
- 1 bell pepper, sliced or chopped
- 1/2 fresh lemon, sliced
- 2 1 onion, sliced
- 1 zucchini, sliced
- garlic cloves, minced
- 1/4 cup low-sodium broth
- 1 tsp rosemary
- 1/4 teaspoon red pepper flakes
- Salt, pepper, to taste

Directions:

Season the cod fillets with salt and pepper.

Pour the broth into a slow cooker, add garlic, bell pepper, rosemary, onion, and zucchini into the slow cooker.

Put fish into your slow cooker, add lemon slices on top.

Close the lid and cook on Low for 2-3 hours or on High for 1 hour.

Nutrition:

Calories: 150

Protein: 26.9 g

Fat: 11.6 g

Carbs: 6.2 g

205. MAHI-MAHI TACO WRAPS

Preparation Time: 5 minutes

Cooking Time: 2 hours

Servings: 6

Ingredients:

- 1-pound Mahi-Mahi, wild-caught
- ½ cup cherry tomatoes
- 1 green bell pepper
- 1/4 medium red onion
- ½ tsp garlic powder
- 1 tsp of sea salt
- ½ tsp ground black pepper
- 1 tsp chipotle pepper
- ½ tsp dried oregano
- 1 tsp cumin
- 2 tbsp avocado oil
- 1/4 cup chicken stock
- 1 medium avocado, diced
- 1 cup sour cream
- 6 large lettuce leaves

Directions:

Grease a 6-quart slow cooker with oil, place fish in it and then pour in chicken stock.

Stir together garlic powder, salt, black pepper, chipotle pepper, oregano, and cumin, and then season fish with half of this mixture.

Layer fish with tomatoes, pepper, and onion, season with remaining spice mixture, and shut with lid.

Plugin the slow cooker, then cook fish for 2 hours at a high heat setting or until cooked.

When done, evenly spoon fish among lettuce, top with avocado and sour cream, and serve.

Nutrition:

Calories: 193.6

Fat: 12g

Protein: 17g

Carbs: 5g

Fiber: 3g

Sugars: 2.5g

206. SHRIMP SCAMPI

Preparation Time: 5 minutes

Cooking Time: 2 hours & 30 minutes

Servings: 4

Ingredients:

- 1 pound wild-caught shrimps, peeled & deveined
- 1 tbsp minced garlic
- 1 tsp salt
- ½ tsp ground black pepper
- 1/2 tsp red pepper flakes
- 2 tbsp chopped parsley
- 2 tbsp avocado oil
- 2 tbsp unsalted butter
- 1/2 cup white wine
- 1 tbsp lemon juice
- 1/4 cup chicken broth
- ½ cup grated parmesan cheese

Directions:

Place all the ingredients except for shrimps and cheese in a 6-quart slow cooker and whisk until combined.

Add shrimps and stir until evenly coated and shut with lid.

Cook in the slow cooker for 1 hour and 30 minutes to 2 hours and 30 minutes at a low heat setting or until cooked.

Then top with parmesan cheese and serve.

Nutrition:

Calories: 234

Total Fat: 14.7g

Protein: 23.3g

Carbs: 2.1g

Fiber: 0.1g

Sugars: 2g

207. SHRIMP TACOS

Preparation Time: 5 minutes

Cooking Time: 3 hours

Servings: 6

Ingredients:

- 1 pound medium wild-caught shrimp, peeled and tails off
- 12-ounce fire-roasted tomatoes, diced
- 1 small green bell pepper, chopped
- ½ cup chopped white onion
- 1 tsp minced garlic
- ½ tsp of sea salt
- ½ tsp ground black pepper
- ½ tsp red chili powder
- ½ tsp cumin
- ¼ tsp cayenne pepper
- 2 tbsp avocado oil
- 1/2 cup salsa
- 4 tbsp chopped cilantro
- 1 ½ cup sour cream
- 2 medium avocados, diced

Directions:

Rinse shrimps, layer into a 6-quart slow cooker, and drizzle with oil.

Add tomatoes, stir until mixed, then add peppers and remaining ingredients except for sour cream and avocado and stir until combined.

Plugin the slow cooker, shut with lid, and cook for 2 to 3 hours at low heat setting or 1 hour and 30 minutes to 2 hours at high heat setting or until shrimps turn pink.

When done, serve shrimps with avocado and sour cream.

Nutrition:

Calories: 369

Fat: 27.5g

Protein: 21.2g

Carbs: 9.2g

Fiber: 5g

Sugars: 5g

208. FISH CURRY

Preparation Time: 5 minutes

Cooking Time: 4 hours 7 30 minutes

Servings: 6

Ingredients:

- 2.2 pounds wild-caught white fish fillet, cubed
- 18-ounce spinach leaves
- 4 tbsp red curry paste, organic
- 14-ounce coconut cream, unsweetened and full-fat
- 14-ounce water

Directions:

Plug in a 6-quart slow cooker and let preheat at a high heat setting.

In the meantime, whisk together coconut cream and water until smooth.

Place fish into the slow cooker, spread with curry paste, and then pour in coconut cream mixture.

Cook within 2 hours at a high setting or 4 hours at low heat setting until tender.

Then add spinach and continue cooking for 20 to 30 minutes or until spinach leaves wilt.

Serve straight away.

Nutrition:

Calories: 323

Fat: 51.5g

Protein: 41.3g

Carbs: 7g

Fiber: 2.2g

Sugars: 2.3g

209.SALMON WITH CREAMY LEMON SAUCE

Preparation Time: 5 minutes

Cooking Time: 2 hours & 15 minutes

Servings: 6

Ingredients:

- For the Salmon:
- 2 pounds wild-caught salmon fillet, skin-on
- 1 tsp garlic powder
- 1 ½ tsp salt
- 1 tsp ground black pepper
- 1/2 tsp red chili powder
- 1 tsp Italian Seasoning
- 1 lemon, sliced
- 1 lemon, juiced
- 2 tbsp avocado oil
- 1 cup chicken broth
- For the Creamy Lemon Sauce:
- Chopped parsley, for garnish
- 1/8 tsp lemon zest
- 1/4 cup heavy cream
- 1/4 cup grated parmesan cheese

Directions:

Line a 6-quart slow cooker with parchment sheet spread its bottom with lemon slices, top with salmon, and drizzle with oil.

Stir together garlic powder, salt, black pepper, red chili powder, Italian seasoning, and oil until combined, and rub this mixture all over salmon.

Pour lemon juice and broth around the fish and shut with lid.

Cook in the slow cooker within 2 hours at a low heat setting.

In the meantime, set the oven at 400 degrees F and let preheat.

When fish is done, lift out an inner pot of slow cooker, place into the oven, then cook within 5 to 8 minutes or until the top is nicely browned.

Lift out the fish using a parchment sheet and keep it warm.

Remove, transfer juices to a medium skillet pan, place it over medium-high heat, and then bring to boil and cook for 1 minute.

Turn heat to a low level, whisk the cream into the sauce, and lemon zest, and parmesan cheese, and cook for 2 to 3 minutes or until thickened.

Cut salmon in pieces, then top each portion with lemon sauce and serve.

Nutrition:

Calories: 340

Fat: 20g

Protein: 32g

Carbs: 8g

Fiber: 2g

Sugars: 2g

210.SALMON WITH LEMON-CAPER SAUCE

Preparation Time: 5 minutes

Cooking Time: 1 hour & 30 minutes

Servings: 6

Ingredients:

- 1 pound wild-caught salmon fillet
- 2 tsp capers, rinsed and mashed
- 1 tsp minced garlic
- 1 tsp salt
- ½ tsp ground black pepper
- 1/2 tsp dried oregano
- 1 tsp lemon zest
- 2 tbsp lemon juice
- 4 tbsp unsalted butter

Directions:

Cut salmon into 4 pieces, then season with salt and black pepper and sprinkle lemon zest on top.

Arrange a 6-quart slow cooker with parchment paper, place seasoned salmon pieces on it, and shut with a lid.

Set to cook in the slow cooker within 1 hour and 30 minutes or until salmon is cooked through.

Prepare lemon-caper sauce and for this, place a small saucepan over low heat, add butter and let it melt.

Then add capers, garlic, lemon juice, stir until mixed, and simmer for 1 minute.

Remove saucepan from heat and stir in oregano.

When salmon is cooked, spoon lemon-caper sauce on it and serve.

Nutrition:

Calories: 368.5

Fat: 26.6g

Protein: 19.5g

Carbs: 2.7g

Fiber: 0.3g

Sugars: 2g

211. SPICY BARBECUE SHRIMP

Preparation Time: 5 minutes

Cooking Time: 1 hour & 30 minutes

Servings: 6

Ingredients:
- 1 1/2 pounds large wild-caught shrimp, unpeeled
- 1 green onion, chopped
- 1 tsp minced garlic
- 1 ½ tsp salt
- ¾ tsp ground black pepper
- 1 tsp Cajun seasoning
- 1 tbsp hot pepper sauce
- ¼ cup Worcestershire Sauce
- 1 lemon, juiced
- 2 tbsp avocado oil
- 1/2 cup unsalted butter, chopped

Directions:

Place all the ingredients except for shrimps in a 6-quart slow cooker and whisk until mixed.

Plugin the slow cooker, then shut with lid and cook for 1 hour and 30 minutes at a high heat setting.

Then take out ½ cup of this sauce and reserve.

Add shrimps to the slow cooker.

Nutrition:

Calories: 321

Fat: 21.4g

Protein: 27.3g

Carbs: 4.8g

Fiber: 2.4g

Sugars: 1.2g

212. LEMON DILL HALIBUT

Preparation Time: 15 minutes

Cooking Time: 2 hours

Servings: 2

Ingredients:
- 12-ounce wild-caught halibut fillet
- 1 tsp salt
- ½ tsp ground black pepper
- 1 1/2 tsp dried dill
- 1 tbsp fresh lemon juice
- 3 tbsp avocado oil

Directions:

Cut an 18-inch piece of aluminum foil, halibut fillet in the middle, and then season with salt and black pepper.

Whisk the remaining ingredients, drizzle this mixture over halibut, then crimp foil's edges and place it into a 6-quart slow cooker.

Cook within 1 hour and 30 minutes or 2 hours at a high heat setting or until cooked.

When done, carefully open the crimped edges and check the fish; it should be tender and flaky.

Serve straight away.

Nutrition:

Calories: 321.5

Fat: 21.4g

Protein: 32.1g

Carbs: 0g

Fiber: 0g

Sugars: 0.6g

213. COCONUT CILANTRO CURRY SHRIMP

Preparation Time: 15 minutes

Cooking Time: 2 hours & 30 minutes

Servings: 4

Ingredients:
- 1 pound wild-caught shrimp, peeled and deveined
- 2 ½ tsp lemon garlic seasoning
- 2 tbsp red curry paste
- 4 tbsp chopped cilantro
- 30 ounces coconut milk, unsweetened
- 16 ounces of water

Directions:

Whisk together all the ingredients except for shrimps and 2 tbsp of cilantro and add to a 4-quart slow cooker.

Plugin the slow cooker, shut with lid, and cook for 2 hours at a high heat setting or 4 hours at a low heat setting.

Then add shrimps, toss until evenly coated and cook for 20 to 30 minutes at high heat settings or until shrimps are pink.

Garnish shrimps with remaining cilantro and serve.

Nutrition:

Calories: 160.7

Total Fat: 8.2g

Protein: 19.3g

Carbs: 2.4g
Fiber: 0.5g
Sugars: 1.4g

214. SHRIMP IN MARINARA SAUCE

Preparation Time: 15 minutes
Cooking Time: 5 hours & 10 minutes
Servings: 5

Ingredients:
- 1 pound cooked wild-caught shrimps, peeled and deveined
- 14.5-ounce crushed tomatoes
- ½ tsp minced garlic
- 1 tsp salt
- 1/2 tsp seasoned salt
- ¼ tsp ground black pepper
- ½ tsp crushed red pepper flakes
- 1/2 tsp dried basil
- 1/2 tsp dried oregano
- ½ tbsp avocado oil
- 6-ounce chicken broth
- 2 tbsp minced parsley
- 1/2 cup grated Parmesan cheese

Directions:
Place all the ingredients except for shrimps, parsley, and cheese in a 4-quart slow cooker and stir well.
Then plug in the slow cooker, shut with lid, and cook for 4 to 5 hours at a low heat setting.
Then add shrimps and parsley, stir until mixed and cook for 10 minutes at a high heat setting.
Garnish shrimps with cheese and serve.

Nutrition:
Calories: 358.8
Fat: 25.1g
Protein: 26g
Carbs: 7.2g
Fiber: 1.5g
Sugars: 3.6g

215. GARLIC SHRIMP

Preparation Time: 5 minutes
Cooking Time: 1 hour
Servings: 5

Ingredients:
For the Garlic Shrimp:
- 1 1/2 pounds large wild-caught shrimp, peeled and deveined
- 1/4 tsp ground black pepper
- 1/8 tsp ground cayenne pepper
- 2 ½ tsp minced garlic
- 1/4 cup avocado oil
- 4 tbsp unsalted butter

For the Seasoning:
- 1 tsp onion powder
- 1 tbsp garlic powder
- 1 tbsp salt
- 2 tsp ground black pepper
- 1 tbsp paprika
- 1 tsp cayenne pepper
- 1 tsp dried oregano
- 1 tsp dried thyme

Directions:
Stir together all the ingredients for seasoning, garlic, oil, and butter and add to a 4-quart slow cooker.
Plugin the slow cooker, shut with lid, and cook for 25 to 30 minutes at a high heat setting or until cooked.
Then add shrimps, toss until evenly coated, and continue cooking for 20 to 30 minutes at a high heat setting or until shrimps are pink.
When done, transfer shrimps to a serving plate, top with sauce, and serve.

Nutrition:
Calories: 233.6
Fat: 11.7g
Protein: 30.9g
Carbs: 1.2g
Fiber: 0g
Sugars: 0g

216. SALMON POACHED IN WHITE WINE AND LEMON

Preparation Time: 15 minutes
Cooking Time: 2 hours
Servings: 4

Ingredients:
- 2 cups of water
- 1 cup cooking wine, white
- 1 lemon, sliced thin
- 1 small mild onion, sliced thin
- 1 bay leaf
- 1 mixed bunch of fresh tarragon, dill, and parsley
- 2.2 pounds salmon fillet, skin on
- 1 tsp salt
- 1 tsp ground black pepper

Directions:

Add all fixings, except salmon and seasoning, to the slow cooker. Cover, cook on low for 1 hour.

Season the salmon, place in the slow cooker skin-side down.

Cover, cook on low for another hour. Serve.

Nutrition:

Calories: 216

Carbs: 1g

Fat: 12g

Protein: 23

217. LEMON PEPPER TILAPIA

Preparation Time: 5 minutes

Cooking Time: 3 hours

Servings: 6

Ingredients:

- 6 wild-caught Tilapia fillets
- 4 tsp lemon-pepper seasoning, divided
- 6 tbsp unsalted butter, divided
- 1/2 cup lemon juice, fresh

Directions:

Put each fillet in the center of the foil, then season with lemon-pepper seasoning, drizzle with lemon juice, and top with 1 tbsp butter.

Gently crimp the edges of foil to form a packet and place it into a 6-quart slow cooker.

Plugin the slow cooker, shut with lid, and cook for 3 hours at high heat or until cooked.

Serve straight away.

Nutrition:

Calories: 201.2

Fat: 12.9g

Protein: 19.6g

Carbs: 1.5g

Fiber: 0.3g

Sugars: 0.7g

218. POACHED SALMON IN COURT-BOUILLON RECIPE

Preparation Time: 5 minutes

Cooking Time: 2 hours 30 minutes

Servings: 2

Ingredients:

- 2 whole black peppercorns
- 1/2 medium carrot, thinly sliced
- 1/2 celery rib, thinly sliced
- 2 salmon steaks in 1-inch-thick slices
- 1 1/2 tbsp white wine vinegar

Directions:

Put all the items in the slow cooker except for the salmon. You can also add parsley and bay leaf for extra flavor.

Rub salmon slices with salt and pepper to taste.

Cook within 2 hours on high.

Put some of the liquid over the top. Cook again within 30 minutes, high.

Nutrition:

Calories: 197

Fat: 7.7g

Carbs: 4.8g

Protein: 18.3g

Cholesterol: 95mg

Sodium: 366mg

219. BRAISED SQUID WITH TOMATOES AND FENNEL

Preparation Time: 20 minutes

Cooking Time: 4 hours

Servings: 2

Ingredients:

- 1 1/2 cups clam juice
- 1 can plum tomatoes
- 1/2 fennel bulb, minced
- 3 tbsp almond flour
- 1 lb. squid in 1-inch pieces

Directions:

Add chopped onions, fennel, and garlic to the flameproof insert of a slow cooker and cook on a stove in medium heat for about 5 minutes.

Whisk in flour and tomato paste until thoroughly mixed, then add the clam juice, tomatoes, 1 tsp salt, and pepper. Boil for about 2 minutes.

Transfer to the slow cooker, cover, and cook for 3 hours on low.

Uncover, add the squid and mix well—Cook for another 1 hour.

Nutrition:

Calories: 210

Fat: 25g

Carbs: 6g

Protein: 29g

220. FISH AND TOMATOES

Preparation Time: 7 minutes

Cooking Time: 3 hours

Servings: 2

Ingredients:

- 1/2 bell pepper, sliced

- 1/8 cup low-sodium broth
- 8 oz diced tomatoes
- 1/2 tbsp rosemary
- 1/2 lb. cod

Directions:

Put all the listed fixing except the fish in the slow cooker. Add garlic, salt, and pepper to taste.

Season fish with your favorite seasoning and place other ingredients in the pot. Cook for 3 hours on low.

Nutrition:

Calories: 204

Fat: 16.8g

Carbs: 5g

Protein: 25.3g

Cholesterol: 75mg

Sodium: 296mg

221. HOT CRAB DIP

Preparation Time: 10 minutes

Cooking Time: 3 hours

Servings: 2

Ingredients:

- 1/8 cup grated Parmesan cheese
- 1/4 package cream cheese, softened
- 1/8 cup mayonnaise
- 6 oz crabmeat, drained and flaked

Directions:

In a slow cooker, combine the ingredients. Add sweetener to taste and a sliced clove of garlic.

Stir, cover, and cook on low for 2-3 hours.

Nutrition:

Calories: 190

Fat: 16g

Carbs: 3g

Protein: 8g

Cholesterol: 55mg

Sodium: 231mg

222. COD AND ZOODLES STEW

Preparation Time: 5 minutes

Cooking Time: 2 hours

Servings: 2

Ingredients:

- 1/8 cup low-sodium broth
- 1/2 bell pepper, diced
- 1/2 lb. sablefish or any whitefish
- 14 oz diced tomatoes
- 1 zucchini, made into zoodles

Directions:

Prepare seasonings: onion, garlic, pepper, and salt to taste.

Place all the ingredients in the slow cooker and add the prepared seasonings—cook on high for 2 hours.

Nutrition:

Calories: 209

Fat: 20g

Net Carbs: 3g

Protein: 15g

Cholesterol: 74mg

Sodium: 291mg

223. SLOW-COOKED TILAPIA

Preparation Time: 10 minutes

Cooking Time: 4 hours

Servings: 2

Ingredients:

- 1 lb. tilapia, sliced
- 1/2 fresh lemon, juiced
- 1/2 cup mayonnaise

Directions:

Whisk mayo and lemon juice in a bowl. Add some chops of garlic.

Spread the mixture on all sides of the tilapia. Cook on low for 3-4 hours.

Nutrition:

Calories: 189

Fat: 18g

Carbs: 4g

Protein: 22g

224. SALMON LEMON AND DILL

Preparation Time: 10 minutes

Cooking Time: 2 hours

Servings: 2

Ingredients:

- 1 tsp extra-virgin olive oil
- 2 lb. salmon
- 1 lemon, sliced
- A handful of fresh dill

Directions:

Rub salmon with oil, salt, pepper, garlic, and fresh dill.

Put the salmon in the slow cooker and place lemon slices on top. Cook on high for 1 hour or low for 2.

Nutrition:

Calories: 159

Fat: 16g

Carbs: 2g
Protein: 37g
Cholesterol: 114mg
Sodium: 209mg

225. CREAMY CRAB ZUCCHINI CASSEROLE

Preparation Time: 20 minutes
Cooking Time: 5 hours
Servings: 2

Ingredients:
- 1/4 cup heavy cream
- 1 medium zucchini squash
- 2 oz. cream cheese
- 4 oz. crab meat
- 1/3 tbsp butter

Directions:
Spiralize zucchini squash on wide ribbons and season with salt. Place the ribbons in a steamer basket and heat for 5 to 7 minutes.

Put all ingredients in a slow cooker, including seasonings such as garlic, onions, pepper, and salt to taste. Put the zucchini spirals on top—Cook within 5 hours on low.

Nutrition:
Calories: 162.6
Fat: 11.9g
Carbs: 2.8g
Protein: 7.2g
Cholesterol: 114mg
Sodium: 209mg

226. LOBSTER BISQUE

Preparation Time: 20 minutes
Cooking Time: 6 hours
Servings: 2

Ingredients:
- 1 1/3 lobster tails, fan parts cut out
- 2/3 tsp Worcestershire sauce
- 2 tbsp tomato paste
- 2/3 cup lobster stock
- 2/3 cup heavy cream

Directions:
Enhance the broth: slowly add broth to an onion-garlic sauté.

Put the broth plus all the other listed fixing except the heavy cream in the slow cooker, including desired spices to taste (paprika, thyme, black pepper)—Cook within 6 hours on low.

Nutrition:
Calories: 400
Fat: 30g
Carbs: 7g
Protein: 23g
Cholesterol: 163mg
Sodium: 1758mg

227. CLAM CHOWDER

Preparation Time: 15 minutes
Cooking Time: 6 hours
Servings: 6

Ingredients:
- 20-ounce wild-caught baby clams, with juice
- ½ cup chopped scallion
- ½ cup chopped celery
- 1 tsp salt
- 1 tsp ground black pepper
- 1 tsp dried thyme
- 1 tbsp avocado oil
- 2 cups coconut cream, full-fat
- 2 cups chicken broth

Directions:
Grease a 6-quart slow cooker with oil, then add ingredients and stir until mixed.

Plugin the slow cooker, shut with lid, and cook for 4 to 6 hours at a low heat setting or until cooked.

Serve straight away.

Nutrition:
Calories: 357
Fat: 28.9g
Protein: 15.2g
Carbs: 8.9g
Fiber: 2.1g
Sugars: 3.9g

228. SOY-GINGER STEAMED POMPANO

Preparation Time: 5 minutes
Cooking Time: 1 hour
Servings: 4

Ingredients:
- 1 wild-caught whole pompano, gutted and scaled
- 1 bunch scallion, diced
- 1 bunch cilantro, chopped
- 3 tsp minced garlic
- 1 tbsp grated ginger
- 1 tbsp swerve sweetener
- ¼ cup of soy sauce
- ¼ cup white wine
- ¼ cup sesame oil

Directions:

Place scallions in a 6-quart slow cooker and top with fish.

Whisk together the remaining ingredients, except for cilantro, and pour the mixture all over the fish.

Plugin the slow cooker, shut with lid, and cook for 1 hour at high heat or until cooked.

Garnish with cilantro and serve.

Nutrition:

Calories: 202.5

Fat: 24.2g

Protein: 22.7g

Carbs: 4g

Fiber: 0.5g

Sugars: 1.1g

229. VIETNAMESE BRAISED CATFISH

Preparation Time: 5 minutes

Cooking Time: 6 hours

Servings: 3

Ingredients:

- 1 fillet of wild-caught catfish, cut into bite-size pieces
- 1 scallion, chopped
- 3 red chilies, chopped
- 1 tbsp grated ginger
- 1/2 cup swerve sweetener
- 2 tbsp avocado oil
- 1/4 cup fish sauce, unsweetened

Directions:

Put a small saucepan over medium heat, put the sweetener, and cook until it melts.

Then add scallion, chilies, ginger, and fish sauce and stir until mixed.

Transfer this mixture to a 4-quart slow cooker, add fish and toss until coated.

Plugin the slow cooker, shut with lid, and cook for 6 hours at a low heat setting until cooked.

Drizzle with avocado oil and serve straight away.

Nutrition:

Calories: 110.7

Fat: 8g

Protein: 9.4g

Carbs: 0.3g

Fiber: 0.2g

230. CHILI SHRIMPS

Preparation Time: 15 minutes

Cooking Time: 2 hours

Servings: 6

Ingredients:

- 1½ pounds peeled and deveined raw shrimps
- 1-pound tomatoes, fire-roasted
- 2 tbsp spicy salsa
- ½ cup chopped bell pepper
- Sea salt
- Black pepper
- ½ tsp cumin
- ½ tsp cayenne pepper
- ½ tsp minced garlic
- 4 tbsp chopped cilantro
- 2 tbsp olive oil

Directions:

Drizzle the slow cooker with a generous amount of olive oil. Place the shrimps at the bottom of it.

Put the rest of the fixing into the slow cooker. Cook on high for 2 hours.

Nutrition:

Calories: 185

Fat: 6.7 g

Carbs: 5.2 g

Protein: 28.4 g

231. FENNEL SCENTED FISH STEW

Preparation Time: 15 minutes

Cooking Time: 6 hours

Servings: 4

Ingredients:

- ½ qt clam juice
- ¼ cup dry white wine
- 2½ peeled and chopped medium tomatoes
- ½ cup carrots, chopped
- ½ cup onion, chopped
- 1½ minced garlic cloves
- ½ tbsp minced orange zest
- ½ tsp. lightly crushed fennel seeds
- 1 lb. firm fish fillets, chopped
- 1/8 cup parsley chopped
- Salt & pepper to taste

Directions:

In a slow cooker, mix all the ingredients, except the fish fillets, parsley, salt, and pepper. Cook on low for 6 hours.

Add the fish within the last 15 minutes. Add the parsley and stir to distribute—season with salt and pepper before serving.

Nutrition:

Calories: 342

Fat: 8.2 g
Carbs: 21 g
Protein: 36 g

232. SPICY SHRIMP FRA DIAVOLO

Preparation Time: 10 minutes
Cooking Time: 3 hours
Servings: 2

Ingredients:
- 1 tsp olive oil
- 1 onion, diced
- 5 cloves of garlic, minced
- 1 tsp red pepper flakes
- 1 can fire-roasted tomatoes
- ½ tsp black pepper
- Salt to taste
- ¼ pound shrimp, shelled and deveined
- 1 tbsp Italian parsley

Directions:
Set the slow cooker to high heat and heat the oil. Sauté the onion and garlic for 2 minutes.
Add the pepper flakes and tomatoes—season with black pepper and salt.
Add the shrimps. Adjust the heat setting to low and cook for 2 or 3 hours.
Garnish with parsley.

Nutrition:
Calories: 134
Carbohydrates: 3.41 g
Protein: 13.99g
Fat: 3.44 g
Sugars: 1.5g
Sodium: 609mg
Fiber: 0.4g

233. SHRIMP SCAMPI WITH SPAGHETTI SQUASH

Preparation Time: 10 minutes
Cooking Time: 2 hours and 20 minutes
Servings: 4

Ingredients:
- 1 cup broth
- 2 tsp lemon-garlic seasoning
- 1 onion, chopped
- 1 tbsp butter
- 3 pounds spaghetti squash, cut lengthwise and seeds removed
- ¾-pounds shrimp, shelled and deveined

Directions:
Pour broth in the slow cooker and add the lemon-garlic seasoning, onion, and butter. Place the spaghetti squash inside the slow cooker and cook on high for 2 hours until soft.
Add the shrimps and cook for 20 more minutes on high.

Nutrition:
Calories: 239
Carbohydrates: 16.79g
Protein: 21.19g
Fat: 6.28g
Sugars: 6.63g
Sodium: 1016mg
Fiber: 5.6g

234. TUNA AND WHITE BEANS

Preparation Time: 10 minutes
Cooking Time: 5 hours and 15 minutes
Servings: 4

Ingredients:
- 4 tbsp olive oil
- 1 clove of garlic, minced
- 6 cups of water
- 1-pound white beans, soaked overnight and drained
- 2 cups chopped tomatoes
- 3 cans white tuna, drained and flaked
- 2 sprigs of basil
- Salt and pepper to taste

Directions:
Set the slow cooker to high heat and add oil. Sauté the garlic for 2 minutes and add water.
Stir in the beans—Cook within 5 hours on low.
Add in the tomatoes, tuna, and basil—season with salt and pepper to taste.
Continue cooking on high for 15 minutes.

Nutrition:
Calories: 764
Carbohydrates: 12.05g
Protein: 62.84g
Fat: 25.43g
Sugars: 4 g
Sodium: 559mg
Fiber: 6.03g

235. SLOW COOKER SWORDFISH STEAKS

Preparation Time: 10 minutes
Cooking Time: 2 hours
Servings: 6

Ingredients:

- 6 swordfish steaks
- ½ cup olive oil
- ¼ cup lemon juice
- ½ tsp Worcestershire sauce
- ¼ tsp black pepper
- 1 tsp cayenne pepper powder
- ¼ tsp paprika

Directions:

Place the swordfish steaks in the slow cooker. Pour the other ingredients over the swordfish steaks.

Close the lid and cook on high for 2 hours. Serve.

Nutrition:

Calories: 659
Carbohydrates: 1.63g
Protein: 46.59g
Fat: 50.78g
Sugars: 0.7g
Sodium: 113mg
Fiber: 0.2g

236. SWEET AND SOUR SHRIMP

Preparation Time: 10 minutes
Cooking Time: 5 hours
Servings: 3

Ingredients:

- 1 package Chinese pea pods, cleaned and trimmed
- 1 can pineapple tidbits
- ½ tsp ginger, ground
- ½ pounds shrimps, shelled and deveined
- 1 cup chicken broth
- ½ cup pineapple juice
- 2 tbsp apple cider vinegar
- Salt to taste

Directions:

Put the peas in the bottom of the slow cooker. Add the pineapple tidbits and ginger.

Place the shrimps on top. Add the chicken broth, pineapple juice, and apple cider vinegar.

Season with salt. Cook on low for 5 hours.

Nutrition:

Calories: 236
Carbohydrates: 3.5 g
Protein: 17.12 g
Fat: 1.33 g
Sugars: 1.5g
Sodium: 970 mg
Fiber:0.6g

237. LAZY MAN'S SEAFOOD STEW

Preparation Time: 10 minutes
Cooking Time: 3 hours
Servings: 6

Ingredients:

- 1-pound large shrimp
- 1-pound scallops
- 1 can crushed tomatoes
- 4 cloves of garlic, minced
- 1 tbsp tomato paste
- 4 cups vegetable broth
- 1 tsp dried oregano
- ½ cup onion, chopped
- ½ tsp celery salt
- 1 tsp dried thyme
- 1/8 tsp cayenne pepper
- ¼ tsp red pepper flakes
- 2 tsp salt
- 2 tsp pepper

Directions:

Put all the listed items in the slow cooker, then stir to combine.

Close the lid and cook on high for 3 hours or 30 minutes on a high setting.

Nutrition:

Calories: 135
Carbohydrates: 9.26g
Protein: 20.37g
Fat: 1.29g
Sugars: 3.76g
Sodium: 1906mg
Fiber:1.3g

238. HALIBUT VINAIGRETTE

Preparation Time: 15 minutes
Cooking Time: 3 hours
Servings: 6

Ingredients:

- 2 tbsp fresh lime juice
- 1 tbsp fresh thyme
- ½ tsp crushed red pepper
- Salt and pepper to taste
- 4 fillets of halibut fish
- 1 bunch kale, torn
- 1 cup of water
- 1 shallot, sliced

Directions:

Mix lime juice, thyme, red pepper, salt, and pepper. Sprinkle the spices on the halibut fillet.

Place the kale in the slow cooker and place the halibut fillet at the bottom. Pour in water and sprinkle shallots on top—Cook within 2 to 3 hours, low.

Nutrition:

Calories: 81

Carbohydrates: 1.25g

Protein: 13.68 g

Fat: 2.12g

Sugars: 0.48g

Sodium: 323mg

Fiber:0.2 g

239. SLOW COOKER CRAB LEGS

Preparation Time: 10 minutes

Cooking Time: 3 hours

Servings: 10

Ingredients:

- 5 pounds crab legs
- 1 tbsp butter
- 1 tsp garlic powder
- 2 lemons, juiced
- Salt and pepper to taste

Directions:

Put all ingredients in the pot. Fill the slow cooker with ¼ water.

Cook within 3 hours, low. Serve.

Nutrition:

Calories: 294

Carbohydrates: 1.31g

Protein: 49.27g

Fat: 8.87g

Sugars: 0.48g

Sodium: 175 mg

Fiber: 0.1 g

240. ASIAN-INSPIRED GINGER TUNA STEAKS

Preparation Time: 10 minutes

Cooking Time: 4 hours

Servings: 2

Ingredients:

- 2 pounds tuna steak
- 2 tbsp coconut aminos
- 2 tbsp sherry wine
- ½ cup of water
- 6 sprigs of onion, chopped
- 3 cloves of garlic, minced
- 1 tsp ginger, grated
- Salt and pepper to taste

Directions:

Place the tuna steak at the bottom of the slow cooker.

Add the rest of the ingredients, then marinate.

Cook within 3 to 4 hours, low.

Nutrition:

Calories: 387

Carbohydrates: 12.87g

Protein: 30.65g

Fat: 20.29g

Sugars: 12.9g

Sodium: 91mg

Fiber: 2.4g

241. RUSTIC BUTTERED MUSSELS

Preparation Time: 5 minutes

Cooking Time: 3 hours

Servings: 6

Ingredients:

- 2 pounds mussels, cleaned
- ½ cup white wine
- 2 cloves of garlic, minced
- 1 ¼ tbsp salt
- 2 tbsp butter

Directions:

Place all ingredients in the slow cooker.

Cook within 3 hours, low or until the mussels have opened.

Nutrition:

Calories: 167

Carbohydrates: 6.13g

Protein: 18.19g

Fat: 7.23g

Sugars: 0.23g

Sodium: 1918 mg

Fiber:0g

242. BOILED LOBSTER TAILS

Preparation Time: 15 minutes

Cooking Time: 3 hours

Servings: 4

Ingredients:

- 4 lobster tails
- 1 cup of water
- 4 ounces of white cooking wine
- ½ stick of butter

- ½ tbsp salt
- 2 tbsp lemon juice
- 1 tsp rosemary

Directions:

Place all ingredients in the slow cooker.

Cook within 3 hours, low or until the lobsters are red.

Nutrition:

Calories: 151

Carbohydrates: 0.56 g

Protein: 30.9g

Fat: 2g

Sugars: 0g

Sodium: 1522mg

Fiber: 0g

243. CREAMY SHRIMP CHOWDER

Preparation Time: 15 minutes

Cooking Time: 4 hours

Servings: 8

Ingredients:

- ½ cup butter
- 1 cup heavy whipping cream
- 32-ounce chicken broth
- 2 cups sliced mushroom
- 8-ounce cheddar cheese shredded
- 24-ounce small shrimp

Directions:

Place slow cooker on high settings. Pour in chicken broth and mushrooms.

Cover and cook for two hours. Stir in butter and whipping cream mix well.

Cover and cook for 30 minutes. Stir in cheese.

Cover and cook for 30 minutes, and halfway through, stir to mix.

If needed, cook for another 30 minutes more until cheese is thoroughly melted and incorporated. Stir every 15 minutes. Add shrimp, stir and cook for 30 minutes.

Nutrition:

Calories: 451

Carbohydrates: 4g

Protein: 29g

Fat: 33g

Sugars: 0g

Sodium: 571mg

Fiber: 0g

244. HEARTY WHITE FISH STEW

Preparation Time: 15 minutes

Cooking Time: 6 hours

Servings: 3

Ingredients:

- 1½ pounds sliced white fish
- 2 tbsp. butter
- 1-pound diced tomatoes
- 2 small sliced zucchinis
- 1 minced clove garlic
- 1 chopped large onion
- 1 chopped green bell pepper
- ½ tsp basil, dried
- ½ tsp oregano, dried
- Salt to taste
- Black pepper
- ¼ cup fish stock

Directions:

Stir everything together in the slow cooker pot. Put and secure the lid. Cook the dish on high for 5-6 hours. Serve.

Nutrition:

Calories: 168

Fat: 6.8 g

Carbs: 4.5 g

Protein: 16.4 g

245. CATFISH CREOLE

Preparation Time: 15 minutes

Cooking Time: 4 hours

Servings: 3

Ingredients:

- 8 oz. diced tomatoes
- ¼ cup clam juice or chicken broth
- 1½ tbsp tomato paste
- ¼ cup medium onion, chopped
- ¼ cup green bell pepper, chopped
- 2 sliced green onions
- ½ thinly sliced rib celery
- 2 minced garlic cloves
- ¼ tsp dried marjoram and thyme leaves
- ½ tsp celery seeds
- ½ tsp. ground cumin
- ¾ lb. catfish fillets
- Salt to taste
- Hot pepper sauce
- Red Pepper Rice:
- ¾ cup uncooked long-grain rice

- 1/8 tsp. ground turmeric
- ¼ tsp. paprika
- ½ coarsely chopped roasted red pepper

Directions:

Mix all of the catfish creole ingredients, except the catfish fillets, salt, and red pepper sauce, in the slow cooker. Cook on high for 4 hours.

Add the fish within the last 15 minutes—season with salt and hot pepper sauce. Serve with Red Pepper Rice.

To make Red Pepper Rice, cook the long grain rice-based on package instructions. Add the turmeric into the cooking water.

After the rice is cooked, add the paprika and roasted red pepper and stir gently to distribute.

Nutrition:
Calories: 580
Fat: 5 g
Carbs: 26 g
Protein: 20 g

246. COD WITH FENNEL AND TOMATOES

Preparation Time: 15 minutes
Cooking Time: 7 hours & 45 minutes
Servings: 8

Ingredients:
- 4 medium fennel bulbs, stalks discarded
- ½ cup olive oil
- 2 large sliced onions
- 4 minced cloves garlic
- 48 ounces diced tomatoes
- 1 cup white wine, dry
- 2 tbsp lemon zest, grated
- 1 cup lemon juice
- 2 tbsp fennel seeds, crushed
- 4 pounds cod fillets
- Sea salt and black pepper to taste

Directions:

Rinse the fennel, then remove the core and outermost flesh. Slice thinly and set aside.

Place a skillet over a medium-high flame and heat the oil. Sauté the onion and garlic until the onion becomes translucent. Stir in the fennel and cook for 2 minutes. Transfer into the slow cooker.

Stir the tomatoes, lemon zest and juice, wine, and fennel seeds into the slow cooker—Cook within 7 hours on low. Season the fish with salt and pepper.

Increase heat to high and add the fish into the slow cooker. Cook within 45 minutes or until the fish is cooked through.

Nutrition:
Calories: 217
Carbs: 12.9g
Protein: 41.4g
Fat: 29.1g.

247. THAI SHRIMP RICE

Preparation Time: 10 minutes
Cooking Time: 3 hours 30 minutes
Servings: 6

Ingredients:
- 1 lb shrimp, peeled, deveined, & cooked
- 1/2 cup snow peas, cut into thin strips
- 2 cups white rice
- 1/4 cup raisins
- 1/4 cup flaked coconut
- 1 carrot, shredded
- 1 bell pepper, diced
- 1 onion, chopped
- 2 tbsp garlic, minced
- 2 lime juice
- 3/4 tsp cayenne
- 1 tsp cumin
- 1 tsp ground coriander
- 1 cup of water
- 28 oz chicken broth
- 1 tsp salt

Directions:

Add all ingredients except coconut, snow peas, and shrimp into the cooking pot and stir well.

Cover slow cooker with lid.

Select slow cook mode and cook on LOW for 3 hours.

Stir in snow peas and shrimp, cover, and cook on LOW for 30 minutes more.

Top with flaked coconut and serve.

Nutrition:
Calories: 399
Fat: 3.8g
Carbohydrates: 39.8g
Sugars: 7.4g
Protein: 25.8g
Cholesterol: 159mg.

248. CARIBBEAN SHRIMP

Preparation Time: 10 minutes
Cooking Time: 2 hours
Servings: 4

Ingredients:
- 12 oz frozen shrimp, thawed

- 2 cups cooked rice
- 1/2 cup tomatoes, diced
- 1 cup frozen peas, thawed
- 1/2 tsp dried oregano
- 1 tsp chili powder
- 1/2 tsp garlic powder
- 1/2 cup chicken broth

Directions:

Add shrimp, oregano, chili powder, garlic powder, and broth into the cooking pot and stir well.

Cover slow cooker with lid.

Select slow cook mode and cook on LOW for 2 hours.

Stir in rice, tomatoes, and peas. Cover and let it sit for 10 minutes.

Stir well and serve.

Nutrition:

Calories 472

Fat 2.6 g

Carbohydrates 42.1 g

Sugar 2.8 g

Protein 27 g

Cholesterol 128 mg

249. HERB LEMON COD

Preparation Time: 10 minutes

Cooking Time: 2 hours

Servings: 4

Ingredients:

- 4 cod fillets, frozen
- 1/4 cup water
- 1/2 lemon juice
- 2 tbsp herb de Provence

Directions:

Place fish fillets into the cooking pot.

Mix the remaining ingredients and pour over fish fillets.

Cover slow cooker with lid.

Select slow cook mode and cook on LOW for 2 hours.

Serve and enjoy.

Nutrition:

Calories 98

Fat 1.4 g

Carbohydrates 0.1 g

Sugar 0.1 g

Protein 20.9 g

Cholesterol 40 mg

250. WHITE FISH FILLET WITH TOMATOES

Preparation Time: 10 minutes

Cooking Time: 2 hours

Servings: 4

Ingredients:

- 1 lb white fish fillets
- 1/3 cup chicken broth
- 1 tsp dried mix herbs
- 15 oz can tomato, diced
- 1 garlic cloves, minced
- 1 small onion, diced
- 1 bell pepper, diced
- 1/4 tsp black pepper
- 1/2 tsp salt

Directions:

Add tomatoes, broth, bell pepper, onion, and garlic into the cooking pot and stir well.

Add a fish fillet to the cooking pot and season with herbs, pepper, and salt.

Cover slow cooker with lid.

Select slow cook mode and cook on LOW for 2 hours.

Serve and enjoy.

Nutrition:

Calories 241

Fat 8.7 g

Carbohydrates 10.2 g

Sugar 6 g

Protein 29.7 g

Cholesterol 87 mg

251. COCONUT FISH CURRY

Preparation Time: 10 minutes

Cooking Time: 2 hours

Servings: 3

Ingredients:

- 10 oz codfish fillets, cut into 2-inch cubes
- 1 1/2 cups broccoli florets
- 1 cup snow peas, sliced
- 14 oz coconut milk
- 1 stick lemongrass
- 1 1/2 tsp turmeric
- 1 red chili, chopped
- 1 tbsp ginger, chopped
- 2 garlic cloves, chopped

Directions:

Add all ingredients into the cooking pot and stir well.

Cover slow cooker with lid.

Select slow cook mode and cook on LOW for 2 hours.

Serve and enjoy.

Nutrition:

Calories 457

Fat 32.9 g

Carbohydrates 17.3 g

Sugar 7.5 g

Protein 28 g

Cholesterol 52 mg

252. LOUISIANA SHRIMP

Preparation Time: 10 minutes

Cooking Time: 1 hour 30 minutes

Servings: 4

Ingredients:
- 1 lb shrimp, deveined
- 1 tsp garlic, minced
- 1 tsp old bay seasoning
- 1 tbsp Worcestershire sauce
- 1 lemon juice
- 1/2 cup butter, sliced
- 1/2 tsp pepper
- 1/2 tsp salt

Directions:

Add all ingredients into the cooking pot and stir well.

Cover slow cooker with lid.

Select slow cook mode and cook on HIGH for 1 1/2 hours.

Serve and enjoy.

Nutrition:

Calories 343

Fat 25 g

Carbohydrates 2.4 g

Sugar 0.3 g

Protein 26.2 g

Cholesterol 300 mg

253. CAJUN CORN SHRIMP CHOWDER

Preparation Time: 10 minutes

Cooking Time: 5 hours

Servings: 4

Ingredients:
- 16 oz bag frozen sweet corn
- 1/2-pound cauliflower
- 1/4 cup almond flour
- 1 1/2 tsp Cajun seasoning
- 4 cups chicken broth
- 1/2 cup heavy cream
- 12 oz shrimp (small peeled deveined and tail-off)
- Salt and pepper to taste

Directions:

Add all ingredients except shrimp and cream into the cooking pot and stir well.

Cover slow cooker with lid.

Select slow cook mode and cook on LOW for 4 hours.

Add shrimp and cream and stir well, cover, and cook on low for 1 hour.

Serve and enjoy.

Nutrition:

Calories 406

Fat 14 g

Carbohydrates 45 g

Sugar 20.7 g

Protein 28g

Cholesterol 250 mg

254. BBQ SHRIMP

Preparation Time: 10 minutes

Cooking Time: 1 hour

Servings: 4

Ingredients:
- 2 lbs shrimp, peeled & deveined
- 1 cup BBQ sauce
- 2 tsp garlic, minced
- 3 tbsp Worcestershire sauce
- 3 tbsp butter
- Pepper and salt to taste

Directions:

Add all ingredients into the cooking pot and stir well.

Cover slow cooker with lid.

Select slow cook mode and cook on LOW for 1 hour.

Serve and enjoy.

Nutrition:

Calories 453

Fat 12.7 g

Carbohydrates 28.8 g

Sugar 18.6 g

Protein 51.8 g

Cholesterol 501 mg

255. DELICIOUS SHRIMP FAJITAS

Preparation Time: 10 minutes

Cooking Time: 5 hours 30 minutes

Servings: 4

Ingredients:
- 1 lb shrimp, deveined & peeled
- 1/2 tsp paprika
- 1 tsp taco seasoning

- 1/2 cup chicken broth
- 1 onion, sliced
- 1 tomato, quartered
- 2 red bell peppers, sliced
- 2 green bell peppers, sliced
- 1 tsp salt

Directions:

Add all ingredients except shrimp into the cooking pot and stir well.

Cover slow cooker with lid.

Select slow cook mode and cook on LOW for 5 hours.

Add shrimp and stir well, cover, and cook on HIGH for 30 minutes more.

Stir well and serve.

Nutrition:

Calories 195

Fat 2.6 g

Carbohydrates 14.3 g

Sugar 7.7 g

Protein 28.3 g

256. SPICY SHRIMP

Preparation Time: 10 minutes

Cooking Time: 50 minutes

Servings: 8

Ingredients:

- 2 lbs large shrimp, peeled and deveined
- 1 tbsp parsley, minced
- 1/4 tsp red pepper flakes, crushed
- 1 tsp paprika
- 5 garlic cloves, sliced
- 3/4 cup olive oil
- 1/4 tsp pepper
- 1 tsp kosher salt

Directions:

Add all ingredients except shrimp and parsley into the cooking pot and stir well.

Cover slow cooker with lid.

Select slow cook mode and cook on HIGH for 30 minutes.

Add shrimp and stir well, Cover and cook on HIGH for 20 minutes.

Garnish with parsley and serve.

Nutrition:

Calories 257

Fat 19 g

Carbohydrates 2.9 g

Sugar 0.1 g

Protein 21.5 g

Cholesterol 162 mg

257. HEALTHY LIME SALMON

Preparation Time: 10 minutes

Cooking Time: 2 hours

Servings: 6

Ingredients:

- 1 1/2 lbs salmon fillets
- 2 tbsp fresh lime juice
- 2 tbsp fresh ginger, minced
- 1/2 onion, sliced
- 1/2 lime, sliced

Directions:

Place salmon fillets skin side down into the cooking pot.

Pour lime juice over salmon then sprinkle ginger on top.

Arrange onion and lime slices on top of salmon.

Cover slow cooker with lid.

Select slow cook mode and cook on LOW for 2 hours.

Serve and enjoy.

Nutrition:

Calories 165

Fat 7.1 g

Carbohydrates 4 g

Sugar 0.8 g

Protein 22.4 g

Cholesterol 50 mg

258. SHRIMP PASTA

Preparation Time: 10 minutes

Cooking Time: 1 hour 30 minutes

Servings: 4

Ingredients:

- 1 lb shrimp, peeled and deveined
- 1/4 cup fresh parsley, minced
- 1 cup wheat orzo pasta
- 1 tbsp butter
- 1/2 cup dry white wine
- 4 cups vegetable broth
- 2 tsp garlic, minced
- Pepper and salt to taste

Directions:

Add all ingredients into the cooking pot and stir well.

Cover slow cooker with lid.

Select slow cook mode and cook on LOW for 1 1/2 hours.

Stir well and serve.

Nutrition:

Calories 292
Fat 7.1 g
Carbohydrates 16.2 g
Sugar 2.5 g
Protein 33.4 g
Cholesterol 249 mg

259. TASTY SHRIMP CURRY

Preparation Time: 10 minutes
Cooking Time: 2 hours 15 minutes
Servings: 4

Ingredients:
- 1 lb shrimp
- 30 oz coconut milk
- 2 1/2 tsp lemon garlic seasoning
- 1 tbsp curry paste
- 15 oz water

Directions:
Add all ingredients except shrimp into the cooking pot and stir well.
Cover slow cooker with lid.
Select slow cook mode and cook on HIGH for 2 hours.
Add shrimp into the cooking pot and stir well, cover, and cook on HIGH for 15 minutes more.
Stir well and serve.

Nutrition:
Calories 667
Fat 55.2 g
Carbohydrates 17.4 g
Sugar 7.8 g
Protein 30.9 g
Cholesterol 239 mg

260. SWORDFISH AND BLACK BEANS

Preparation Time: 10 minutes
Cooking Time: 5 hours and 15 minutes
Servings: 4

Ingredients:
- 3 cans swordfish, drained and flaked
- 1-pound black beans, soaked overnight and drained
- 4 tbsp olive oil
- 6 cups of water
- 2 cups chopped red bell peppers
- Salt and pepper to taste

Directions:
Set the slow cooker to high heat and add oil. Sauté the garlic for 2 minutes and add water.
Stir in the beans—Cook within 5 hours on low.
Add in the bell peppers, swordfish —s eason with salt and pepper to taste.
Continue cooking on high for 15 minutes.

Nutrition:
Calories: 764
Carbohydrates: 12.05g
Protein: 62.84g
Fat: 25.43g
Sugars: 4 g
Sodium: 559mg
Fiber: 6.03g

261. SALTED COD DIP

Preparation Time: 10 minutes
Cooking Time: 3 hours
Servings: 2

Ingredients:
- 1/8 cup grated Pecorino cheese
- 1/4 package cream cheese, softened
- 1/8 cup butter
- 6 oz salted cod, drained

Directions:

In a slow cooker, combine the ingredients. Add sweetener to taste and a sliced clove of garlic.
Stir, cover, and cook on low for 2-3 hours.

Nutrition:
Calories: 190
Fat: 16g
Carbs: 3g
Protein: 8g
Cholesterol: 55mg
Sodium: 231mg

262. SALMON AND TUNA TACOS

Preparation Time: 5 minutes
Cooking Time: 3 hours
Servings: 6

Ingredients:
- 1/2 pound tuna
- 1/2 pound salmon
- 12-ounce fire-roasted tomatoes, diced
- ½ cup chopped red onion
- ½ tsp of sea salt
- ½ tsp ground black pepper
- 2 tbsp avocado oil
- 1/2 cup salsa
- 1 ½ cup sour cream
- 2 medium avocados, diced

- 6 tacos

Directions:

Rinse shrimps, layer into a 6-quart slow cooker, and drizzle with oil.

Add tomatoes, stir until mixed, then add peppers and remaining ingredients except for sour cream and avocado and stir until combined.

Plugin the slow cooker, shut with lid, and cook for 2 to 3 hours at low heat setting or 1 hour and 30 minutes to 2 hours at high heat setting or until shrimps turn pink.

When done, serve shrimps with avocado and sour cream. If desired, fill the tacos in.

Nutrition:

Calories: 369

Fat: 27.5g

Protein: 21.2g

Carbs: 9.2g

Fiber: 5g

Sugars: 5g

263. CAPERS SALMON

Preparation Time: 10 minutes

Cooking Time: 2 hours

Servings: 2

Ingredients:

- 8 oz salmon
- 1 tbsp capers
- 1/3 cup water
- 2 tbsp lemon juice
- 1/4 tsp fresh rosemary, minced

Directions:

Place salmon into the cooking pot.

Pour lemon juice and water over salmon.

Sprinkle with rosemary and capers.

Cover slow cooker with lid.

Select slow cook mode and cook on LOW for 2 hours.

Serve and enjoy.

Nutrition:

Calories 155

Fat 7.2 g

Carbohydrates 0.6 g

Sugar 0.3 g

Protein 22.2 g

Cholesterol 50 mg

264. EASY CILANTRO LIME SALMON

Preparation Time: 10 minutes

Cooking Time: 2 hours

Servings: 4

Ingredients:

- 1 lb salmon fillets
- 3/4 cup fresh cilantro, chopped
- 1 tbsp olive oil
- 3 tbsp fresh lime juice
- 2 garlic cloves, chopped
- Pepper and salt to taste

Directions:

Place salmon fillet into the cooking pot. Mix remaining ingredients and pour over salmon.

Cover slow cooker with lid.

Select slow cook mode and cook on HIGH for 2 hours.

Serve and enjoy.

Nutrition:

Calories 191

Fat 10.6 g

Carbohydrates 3.4 g

Sugar 0.6 g

Protein 22.3 g

Cholesterol 50 mg

265. CREAMY CURRIED SHRIMP

Preparation Time: 10 minutes

Cooking Time: 4 hours 10 minutes

Servings: 4

Ingredients:

- 2 cups shrimp, cooked
- 1 small onion, chopped
- 10 oz can cream of mushroom soup
- 1 cup sour cream
- 1 tsp curry powder

Directions:

Add all ingredients except cream into the cooking pot and stir well.

Cover slow cooker with lid.

Select slow cook mode and cook on LOW for 4 hours.

Stir in cream and serve.

Nutrition:

Calories 219

Fat 14.1 g

Carbohydrates 10.4 g

Sugar 2.4 g

Protein 12.6 g

Cholesterol 117 mg

266. HERB FLOUNDER FILLET

Preparation Time: 10 minutes

Cooking Time: 4 hours
Servings: 6

Ingredients:
- 2 lbs fresh flounder fillets
- 2 tbsp dried chives
- 2 tbsp lemon juice
- 3/4 cup chicken broth
- 4 tbsp fresh parsley, chopped
- 1 Tsp marjoram
- 2 tbsp dried onion, minced
- 1/2 tsp salt

Directions:
Season fish fillets with salt. Mix lemon juice and broth. Stir in remaining ingredients.
Place rack into the cooking pot.
Place season fish fillet on the rack and pour lemon juice mixture over fish fillets.
Cover slow cooker with lid.
Select slow cook mode and cook on HIGH for 4 hours.
Serve and enjoy.

Nutrition:
Calories 186
Fat 2.6 g
Carbohydrates 0.8 g
Sugar 0.4 g
Protein 37.3 g
Cholesterol 103 mg

267. ONION WHITE FISH FILLET

Preparation Time: 10 minutes
Cooking Time: 4 hours
Servings: 6

Ingredients:
- 1 1/2 lbs white fish fillets
- 1 cup of water
- 2 tbsp butter, melted
- 2 lemons, divided
- 2 onions, sliced
- 4 whole peppercorns
- 1 bay leaf
- 2 Tsp salt

Directions:
Add all ingredients except fish fillets into the cooking pot and mix well.
Place fish fillets into the cooking pot.
Cover slow cooker with lid.
Select slow cook mode and cook on HIGH for 4 hours.
Serve and enjoy.

Nutrition:
Calories 253
Fat 12.5 g
Carbohydrates 6 g
Sugar 2 g
Protein 28.4 g
Cholesterol 97 mg

268. LEMON HALIBUT

Preparation Time: 10 minutes
Cooking Time: 1 hour 30 minutes
Servings: 2

Ingredients:
- 12 oz halibut
- 1 tbsp fresh lemon juice
- 1 tbsp fresh dill
- 1 tbsp olive oil
- Pepper and salt to taste

Directions:
Place halibut middle of the foil and season with pepper and salt.
In a small bowl, whisk together dill, oil, and lemon juice.
Pour dill mixture over halibut. Wrap foil around the halibut.
Place foil packet into the cooking pot.
Cover slow cooker with lid.
Select slow cook mode and cook on HIGH for 1 1/2 hour.
Serve and enjoy.

Nutrition:
Calories 472
Fat 37.3 g
Carbohydrates 1.1 g
Sugar 0.2 g
Protein 31.7 g
Cholesterol 100 mg

269. GARLICKY SHRIMP

Preparation Time: 10 minutes
Cooking Time: 1 hour
Servings: 8

Ingredients:
- 2 lbs large shrimp, peeled and deveined
- 1 tbsp parsley, minced
- 5 garlic cloves, sliced
- 1/4 tsp red pepper flakes, crushed
- 1/4 tsp black pepper
- 1 tsp smoked paprika

- 3/4 cup olive oil
- 1 Tsp kosher salt

Directions:

Add all ingredients except shrimp and parsley into the cooking pot and stir well.

Cover slow cooker with lid.

Select slow cook mode and cook on HIGH for 30 minutes.

Stir in shrimp, cover, and cook on HIGH for 20 minutes.

Garnish with parsley and serve.

Nutrition:

Calories 257

Fat 19 g

Carbohydrates 2.9 g

Sugar 0.1 g

Protein 21.5 g

Cholesterol 162 mg

270. HOT SHRIMP

Preparation Time: 10 minutes

Cooking Time: 1 hour

Servings: 6

Ingredients:

- 1 1/2 lbs large shrimp, unpeeled
- 1/2 cup butter
- 1 tsp Cajun seasoning
- 2 garlic cloves, minced
- 1 green onion, chopped
- 1 lemon juice
- 1 tbsp hot pepper sauce
- 1/4 cup Worcestershire sauce
- Pepper and salt to taste

Directions:

Add all ingredients except shrimp and parsley into the cooking pot and stir well.

Cover slow cooker with lid.

Select slow cook mode and cook on HIGH for 30 minutes.

Stir in shrimp, cover, and cook on HIGH for 30 minutes.

Garnish with green onion and serve.

Nutrition:

Calories 241

Fat 15.4 g

Carbohydrates 4.7 g

Sugar 2.2 g

Protein 21.6 g

Cholesterol 203 mg

271. EASY LEMON DILL SALMON

Preparation Time: 10 minutes

Cooking Time: 2 hours

Servings: 2

Ingredients:

- 2 lbs salmon
- 2 garlic cloves, minced
- 1 lemon, sliced
- 1/4 cup fresh dill
- Pepper and salt to taste

Directions:

Place salmon into the cooking pot. Season with fresh dill, garlic, pepper, and salt.

Arrange lemon slices over salmon.

Cover slow cooker with lid.

Select slow cook mode and cook on HIGH for 2 hours.

Serve and enjoy.

Nutrition:

Calories 628

Fat 28.4 g

Carbohydrates 7.1 g

Sugar 0.8 g

Protein 89.7 g

272. SALMON AND ASPARAGUS

Preparation Time: 10 minutes

Cooking Time: 2 hours

Servings: 4

Ingredients:

- 4 salmon fillets
- 1 bundle asparagus
- 12 tbsp lemon juice
- A pinch of lemon pepper seasoning
- 2 tbsp olive oil

Directions:

Divide salmon fillets into tin foil pieces.

Top each salmon with asparagus spears, lemon juice, lemon pepper, and oil, and wrap them.

Arrange salmon fillets in your slow cooker, cover, and cook on High for 2 hours.

Unwrap salmon and divide fish and asparagus between plates.

Enjoy!

Nutrition:

Calories 172,

Fat 3g,

Carbs 7g,

Protein 3g.

POULTRY

273. AMAZING SOUR CREAM CHICKEN

Preparation Time: 15 minutes
Cooking Time: 6 hours
Servings: 4

Ingredients:
- 1 cup of sour cream
- ½ cup of chicken stock
- 1 can of diced green chilies and tomatoes
- 1 batch of taco seasoning
- 2 pounds of chicken breast

Directions:
Put all the items in the slow cooker. Cook on low for 6 hours. Divide onto plates and serve.

Nutrition:
Calories: 262
Fat: 13 g
Fiber: 2.5 g
Protein: 32 g
Carbs: 23 g

274. FANTASTIC LEMON THYME CHICKEN

Preparation Time: 15 minutes
Cooking Time: 4 hours
Servings: 4

Ingredients:
- 10-15 cloves of garlic
- 2 sliced lemons
- ½ tsp of ground pepper
- 1 tsp of thyme
- 3 ½-pound whole chicken

Directions:
Arrange the lemon and garlic on the base of a slow cooker. Mix the spices and use them to season the chicken.

Put the chicken in the slow cooker. Cook on low within 4 hours. Remove, let it cool within 15 minutes, and then serve.

Nutrition:
Calories: 120
Fat: 8 g
Carbs: 1 g

Fiber: 0 g
Protein: 12 g

275. DELIGHTFUL BALSAMIC OREGANO CHICKEN

Preparation Time: 15 minutes
Cooking Time: 4 hours
Servings: 6

Ingredients:
- 6 pieces of boneless, skinless chicken
- 2 cans of diced tomatoes
- 1 large onion, thinly sliced
- 4 cloves of garlic
- ½ cup of balsamic vinegar
- 1 tbsp of olive oil
- 1 tbsp of dried oregano
- 1 tsp of dried rosemary
- 1 tsp of dried basil
- ½ tsp of thyme
- Salt and pepper to taste

Directions:
Combine all the fixing except the chicken in a small bowl. Mix them thoroughly. Put the chicken inside the slow cooker, then pour the remaining ingredients over the top.
Cook on high for 4 hours.

Nutrition:
Calories: 190
Fat: 6 g
Carbs: 5 g
Fiber: 1 g
Protein: 26 g

276. TANTALIZING CHICKEN BREAST WITH ARTICHOKE STUFFING

Preparation Time: 15 minutes
Cooking Time: 4 hours
Servings: 4

Ingredients:
- 4 boneless, skinless chicken breasts
- 3 cups of finely chopped spinach
- ½ cup of chopped roasted red peppers
- ¼ cup of sliced black olives
- 1 cup of chopped canned artichoke hearts
- 4 ounces of reduced-fat feta cheese
- 1 tsp of dried oregano
- 1 tsp of garlic powder
- 1 ½ cups of low-sodium chicken broth
- Salt and pepper to taste

Directions:
Cut deep in the center of the chicken and season it with salt and pepper.
In a small bowl, combine the garlic, feta, oregano, peppers, spinach, and artichoke hearts.
Stuff the artichoke mixture into the cut in the chicken and put it into the slow cooker.
Cook within low for 4 hours.

Nutrition:
Calories: 222
Fat: 7 g
Carbs: 4 g
Fiber: 0 g
Protein: 52 g

277. CHIPOTLE BARBECUE CHICKEN

Preparation Time: 20 minutes
Cooking Time: 8 hours
Servings: 5

Ingredients:
- ¼ c. water
- 1 14-ounce boneless chicken breasts, skin removed
- 1 14-ounce boneless chicken thighs, skin removed
- Pepper and salt to taste
- 2 tbsp chipotle Tabasco sauce
- 1 c. tomato sauce
- 1/3 cup apple cider vinegar
- 1 onion, chopped
- 4 tbsp unsalted butter
- 2 tbsp yellow mustard
- ¼ tsp garlic powder
- ½ cup water

Directions:
Take all ingredients in a slow cooker. Stir everything so that the chicken is coated with the sauce.
Cook within 8 hours, low. Serve.

Nutrition:
Calories: 482
Carbohydrates: 3g
Protein: 29.4 g
Fat: 18.7g
Sugars: 0g
Sodium: 462mg
Fiber: 0.3g

278. COLOMBIAN CHICKEN

Preparation Time: 10 minutes
Cooking Time: 6 hours

Servings: 4

Ingredients:
- 1 chicken, cut into 8 pieces
- 1 yellow onion, sliced
- 2 bay leaves
- 4 big tomatoes, cut into medium chunks
- Pepper and salt to taste

Directions:

Begin by tossing all the ingredients into the Slow cooker and mix them thoroughly, so that the chicken are well coated with the rest.

Cover it and cook for 6 hours on Low Settings.

Garnish as desired and serve warm. Enjoy.

Nutrition:

Calories: 481

Carbohydrates: 9.1g

Protein: 7g

Fat: 11.1g

Sugars: 3g

Sodium: 203mg

Fiber: 1.7g

279. SPICY SHREDDED CHICKEN LETTUCE WRAPS

Preparation Time: 15 minutes

Cooking Time: 10 hours

Servings: 8

Ingredients:
- 4 chicken breast, skin, and bones removed
- 1 cup tomato salsa
- 1 tsp. onion powder
- 1 can dice green chilies
- 1 tbsp. Tabasco sauce
- 2 tbsp. freshly squeezed lime juice
- Pepper and salt to taste
- 2 large heads of iceberg lettuce, rinsed

Directions:

Take the chicken breast in the slow cooker.

Pour over the tomato salsa, onion powder, green chilies, Tabasco sauce, and lime juice. Season with pepper and salt to taste.

Close the lid and cook for 10 hours. Shred the chicken meat using a fork.

Take on top of lettuce leaves. Garnish with sour cream, tomatoes, or avocado slices if needed.

Nutrition:

Calories: 231

Carbohydrates: 3g

Protein: 23 g

Fat: 12g

Sugars: 0.5g

Sodium: 375mg

Fiber: 2g

280. SLOW COOKER RANCH CHICKEN

Preparation Time: 55 minutes

Cooking Time: 7 hours

Servings: 6

Ingredients:
- 2 pounds boneless chicken breasts
- 3 tbsp dry ranch dressing mix
- 3 tbsp butter
- 4 ounces cream cheese

Directions:

Take the chicken in the slow cooker. Pour the ranch dressing and rub it on the chicken.

Add the butter and cream cheese—Cook within 7 hours, low.

Shred the chicken before serving.

Nutrition:

Calories: 266

Carbohydrates: 0g

Protein: 33g

Fat:12.9g

Sugars: 0g

Sodium: 167mg

Fiber: 0g

281. COCONUT CILANTRO SHRIMP CURRY

Preparation Time: 40 minutes

Cooking Time: 23 hours & 10 minutes

Servings: 4

Ingredients:
- 1 can light coconut milk
- 15-ounces water
- ½ cup Thai red curry sauce
- 2 ½ tsp lemon juice
- 1 tsp. garlic powder
- ¼ cup cilantro
- Pepper and salt to taste
- 1-pound shrimps head removed only

Directions:

Take the coconut milk, water, and curry sauce to the slow cooker.

Stir in the lemon juice, garlic powder, and cilantro—season with pepper and salt to taste.

Cook on high for 23 hours. Add the shrimps and cook on high for 10 minutes.

Nutrition:

Calories: 211

Carbohydrates: 2g

Protein: 18.2g

Fat: 22g

Sugars: 0g

Sodium: 135mg

Fiber: 0.8g

282. SLOW TERIYAKI CHICKEN

Preparation Time: 10 minutes

Cooking Time: 6 hours

Servings: 4

Ingredients:

- 2 lbs. chicken breasts, skinless and boneless
- 1/2 cup of chicken stock
- 1 tablespoon of honey
- 2/3 cup of teriyaki sauce
- a handful green onions, diced
- Pepper and salt to taste

Directions:

Start by tossing all the ingredients into the Slow cooker and mix them thoroughly.

Cap it and cook for 6 hours on Low Settings.

Embellish as desired with the source on the side and serve warm.

Nutrition:

Calories: 609

Carbohydrates: 9.9g

Protein: 29.3g

Fat: 50.5g

Sugars: 0.3g

Sodium: 463mg

Fiber: 1.5g

283. SLOW COOKER BUTTER MASALA CHICKEN

Preparation Time: 45 minutes

Cooking Time: 7 hours

Servings: 8

Ingredients:

- 1 tbsp. olive oil
- 9 cloves of garlic, crushed
- 2 tsp. garam masala
- 2-pounds boneless chicken breasts, cut into strips
- 1 can light coconut milk
- 1 can tomato paste
- ½ tsp. cayenne pepper
- 1 tsp. dried coriander
- 1 tbsp. paprika
- 1 tsp. turmeric powder
- 1 tsp. cumin powder
- 1 ½ tsp salt

Directions:

Heat-up the olive oil in a skillet over medium flame and sauté the garlic for 1 minute. Put the garam masala, then cook for another minute or until fragrant. Set aside. Take the chicken in the slow cooker and add the garlic and garam masala mixture. Stir to coat the chicken meat. Put the rest of the fixing, and cook on low for 7 hours.

Nutrition:

Calories: 520

Carbohydrates: 2.3g

Protein: 32.7g

Fat: 28g

Sugars: 0g

Sodium: 342mg

Fiber: 0.8g

284. CHICKEN WITH BACON GRAVY

Preparation Time: 35 minutes

Cooking Time: 7 hours

Servings: 4

Ingredients:

- 1 ½ pounds chicken breasts, bones, and skin removed
- ¼ tsp. pepper
- 1 tsp. salt
- 1 tsp. minced garlic
- 1 tsp. dried thyme
- 6 slices of bacon, cooked and crumbled
- 1 ½ cup water
- 2/3 cup heavy cream

Directions:

Take all ingredients except the heavy cream in the slow cooker, then cook within 6 hours, low. Put the heavy cream and continue cooking for another hour.

Nutrition:

Calories: 359

Carbohydrates: 0.9g

Protein: 21g

Fat: 25g

Sugars: 0g

Sodium: mg

Fiber: 0 g

285. GARLIC BUTTER CHICKEN WITH CREAM CHEESE

Preparation Time: 20 minutes

Cooking Time: 6 hours

Servings: 8

Ingredients:

- 2 ½ pounds chicken breast
- 1 stick of butter, softened
- 8 cloves of garlic, sliced in half
- 1 onion, sliced
- 1 ½ tsp. salt
- 8 ounces cream cheese
- 1 cup chicken stock

Directions:

Take the chicken in the slow cooker and add the butter. Stir in the garlic and onions. Season with salt.

Cook on low for 6 hours. Meanwhile, prepare the cream cheese sauce by mixing cream cheese and chicken stock in a saucepan, medium flame, and stir until the sauce has reduced. Pour over the chicken.

Nutrition:

Calories: 463

Carbohydrates: 2 g

Protein: 22.4g

Fat: 35g

Sugars: 0g

Sodium: 674mg

Fiber: 0.6g

286. CHEESY ADOBO CHICKEN

Preparation Time: 30 minutes

Cooking Time: 8 hours

Servings: 6

Ingredients:

- 1 pound of chicken breasts, bones removed but the skin on
- 1 tbsp butter
- ½ cup tomatoes, sliced
- 2 tbsp adobo sauce
- ½ cup milk
- ¾ cup cheddar cheese, shredded

Directions:

Take all ingredients in the slow cooker. Mix, then cook on low within 8 hours. Use a fork to shred the chicken. Serve.

Nutrition:

Calories: 493

Carbohydrates: 0g

Protein: 25.8g

Fat: 33.9g

Sugars: 0g

Sodium: 375mg

Fiber: 0g

287. LEMONGRASS COCO-CHICKEN

Preparation Time: 10 minutes

Cooking Time: 5 hours

Servings: 5

Ingredients:

- 10 drumsticks, skin removed
- 1 thick stalk fresh lemongrass
- 4 cloves garlic, minced
- 1 thumb-size piece of ginger
- 1 cup of coconut milk
- 2 tablespoons of Red Boat fish sauce
- 3 tablespoons of coconut aminos
- 1 teaspoon of five-spice powder
- 1 large onion, sliced
- 1/4 cup of fresh scallions, diced
- Kosher salt
- Black pepper

Directions:

Begin by tossing all the ingredients into the Slow cooker. Cover it and cook for 5 hours on Low Settings.

Garnish as desired and serve warm.

Nutrition:

Calories: 372

Carbohydrates: 0.9 g

Protein: 63.5g

Fat: 11.1g

Sugars: 0g

Sodium: 749mg

Fiber: 0.2g

288. KETOGENIC CHICKEN TIKKA MASALA

Preparation Time: 25 minutes

Cooking Time: 8 hours

Servings: 6

Ingredients:

- 1 ½ pounds chicken thighs, bone-in, and skin-on
- 2 tsp onion powder
- 2 tbsp olive oil
- 5 tsp garam masala
- 3 tbsp. tomato paste
- 1-inch ginger root, grated
- 3 cloves of garlic
- 2 tsp smoked paprika

- 1 cup heavy cream
- 1 cup tomatoes, diced
- 1 cup coconut milk
- Salt to taste
- Fresh cilantro for garnish

Directions:

Take all ingredients except the cilantro in the slow cooker. Mix everything until the spices are incorporated well.

Cook within 8 hours, low. Garnish with cilantro once cooked.

Nutrition:

Calories: 493
Carbohydrates: 4.3g
Protein: 26.6g
Fat: 41.2g
Sugars: 1g
Sodium: 457mg
Fiber: 2g

289. BALSAMIC CHICKEN THIGHS

Preparation Time: 30 minutes
Cooking Time: 8 hours
Servings: 8

Ingredients:

- 1 tsp. dried basil
- 2 tsp minced onion
- 1 tsp garlic powder
- ½ tsp salt
- ½ tsp black pepper
- 8 boneless chicken breasts
- 1 tbsp EVOO
- 4 cloves of garlic, minced
- ½ cup balsamic vinegar
- Parsley for garnish

Directions:

In a small bowl, mix the dried basil, onion, garlic, salt, and pepper. Rub the spice mixture onto the chicken. Set aside

Put the olive oil in the slow cooker and sprinkle minced garlic. Arrange the chicken piece on top of the oil and garlic

Pour balsamic vinegar. Cook on low for 8 hours. Garnish with parsley once cooked.

Nutrition:

Calories: 133
Carbohydrates: 5.6g
Protein: 20.1g
Fat: 4g
Sugars: 3g
Sodium: 832mg
Fiber: 0.1g

290. GARLIC DILL CHICKEN THIGHS

Preparation Time: 15 minutes
Cooking Time: 4 hours
Servings: 4

Ingredients:

- 2 tbsp dried parsley
- 2 tsp seasoned salt
- 1 ½ tsp black pepper
- 1 tbsp garlic powder
- ½ tsp dried dill
- ½ tsp onion powder
- 8 boneless, skinless chicken thighs
- 6 oz pesto
- ½ cup chicken broth

Directions:

In a small bowl, combine the spices. Arrange the chicken in a slow cooker. Top with pesto, chicken broth, and spice mixture.

Stir to combine and thoroughly coat each piece of chicken. Cook on high within 3-4 hours.

Nutrition:

Calories: 456
Fats: 30 g
Carbs: 2 g
Fiber: 1 g
Protein: 47 g

291. CHICKEN LO MEIN

Preparation Time: 40 minutes
Cooking Time: 2 hours & 30 minutes
Servings: 6

Ingredients:

- 1 ½ pounds chicken, sliced into strip
- 1 tbsp coconut aminos
- ½ tsp sesame oil
- ½ tsp garlic paste
- 2 cloves of garlic, minced
- 1 tsp ginger, minced
- bunch bok choy washed and sliced
- 12 ounces kelp noodles
- Pepper and salt to taste
- ¾ cup chicken broth
- 1 tbsp. rice vinegar
- 1 tsp. red pepper chili flakes

Directions:

In a small bowl, mix the chicken, coconut aminos, sesame oil, and garlic paste. Let it marinate for 30 minutes inside the fridge.

Cook the marinated chicken in the slow cooker on high for 2 hours. Set aside.

Take the garlic, ginger, and bok choy at the bottom of the slow cooker. Add the chicken and kelp noodles on top—season with pepper and salt to taste.

Mix the chicken broth, rice vinegar, and red pepper flakes in a bowl.

Pour over the chicken mixture and cook for 30 minutes on high.

Nutrition:

Calories: 174
Carbohydrates: 3.1g
Protein: 24.5g
Fat: 8.1g
Sugars: 0.5g
Sodium: 436mg
Fiber: 1.6g

292. ETHIOPIAN DORO WATT CHICKEN

Preparation Time: 35 minutes
Cooking Time: 8 hours
Servings: 6

Ingredients:

- 1 tsp chili powder
- 1 tsp sweet paprika
- ½ tsp ground ginger
- 1 tbsp salt
- 1 tsp ground coriander
- 1/8 tsp ground cardamom
- 1/8 tsp allspice
- 1/8 tsp fenugreek powder
- 1/8 tsp nutmeg
- 1 whole chicken, sliced into different parts
- ½ cup butter
- 1 clove of garlic, minced
- 1/2 cup water
- 2 large onions, chopped
- 8 hard-boiled eggs

Directions:

Combine the first 9 items in a bowl. Use this spice mix and rub it on the chicken parts. Marinate within 30 minutes in the fridge.

Take the butter in the slow cooker and add the onion and garlic. Take the chicken pieces. Arrange the hard-boiled eggs randomly on top of the chicken.

Pour water, then cook on low within 8 hours.

Nutrition:

Calories: 315
Carbohydrates: 4g
Protein: 19g
Fat: 25g
Sugars: 0g
Sodium: 698mg
Fiber: 0.8g

293. DELICIOUS SOUTHWEST CHICKEN

Preparation Time: 10 minutes
Cooking Time: 6 hours
Servings: 8

Ingredients:

- 4 chicken breasts, skinless & boneless
- 1 tsp cumin powder
- 1 tbsp chili powder
- 2 garlic cloves, minced
- 1 small onion, chopped
- 4 oz can green chilies, diced
- 15 oz can corn, drained
- 15 oz can black beans, drained & rinsed
- 1 cup of salsa
- 1 cup chicken broth
- 1/2 tsp salt

Directions:

Add all ingredients into the cooking pot and stir well.

Cover slow cooker with lid.

Select slow cook mode and cook on LOW for 6 hours.

Remove chicken from pot and shred using a fork.

Return shredded chicken to the cooking pot and stir well.

Serve over cooked rice.

Nutrition:

Calories 256
Fat 6.6 g
Carbohydrates 23.9 g
Sugar 3.6 g
Protein 26.9 g
Cholesterol 65 mg

294. FLAVORS PEANUT BUTTER CHICKEN

Preparation Time: 10 minutes
Cooking Time: 8 hours
Servings: 4

Ingredients:

- 3 lbs chicken breasts, bone-in & skinless

- 3 tbsp Stevia
- 1/2 tbsp rice wine vinegar
- 1 tbsp coarse whole grain mustard
- 1 tbsp garlic, minced
- 2 tbsp chili garlic sauce
- 1/2 cup soy sauce
- 1/2 lime juice
- 1/4 cup peanut butter
- Pepper and salt to taste

Directions:

Season chicken with pepper and salt and place into the cooking pot.

Mix the remaining ingredients and pour over the chicken in the cooking pot.

Cover slow cooker with lid.

Select slow cook mode and cook on LOW for 8 hours.

Remove chicken from pot and shred using a fork.

Serve and enjoy.

Nutrition:

Calories 806

Fat 33.5 g

Carbohydrates 17.1 g

Sugar 11.1 g

295. EASY SALSA CHICKEN

Preparation Time: 10 minutes

Cooking Time: 3 hours

Servings: 4

Ingredients:

- 2 1/2 lbs chicken breasts, bone-in & skinless
- 1 1/2 cups salsa
- 3 tsp ranch seasoning
- Pepper and salt to taste

Directions:

Add 1/2 cup salsa into the cooking pot then place chicken on top of salsa. Season with ranch seasoning, pepper, and salt.

Pour remaining salsa over chicken in the cooking pot.

Cover slow cooker with lid.

Select slow cook mode and cook on HIGH for 3 hours.

Remove chicken from pot and shred using a fork.

Serve and enjoy.

Nutrition:

Calories 573

Fat 21.2 g

Carbohydrates 6.1 g

Sugar 3 g

Protein 83.5 g

Cholesterol 252 mg

296. GREEK LEMON CHICKEN

Preparation Time: 10 minutes

Cooking Time: 6 hours

Servings: 4

Ingredients:

- 4 chicken breasts, skinless & boneless
- 3 tbsp parsley, chopped
- 1 cup chicken broth
- 1 tbsp lemon zest
- 1/4 cup lemon juice
- 2 tsp dried oregano
- 1 tbsp garlic, minced
- 1 tsp kosher salt

Directions:

Add all ingredients into the cooking pot and mix well.

Cover slow cooker with lid.

Select slow cook mode and cook on LOW for 6 hours.

Serve and enjoy.

Nutrition:

Calories 296

Fat 11.3 g

Carbohydrates 1.7 g

Sugar 0.6 g

Protein 43.8 g

Cholesterol 130 mg

297. EASY CHICKEN NOODLES

Preparation Time: 10 minutes

Cooking Time: 6 hours 30 minutes

Servings: 8

Ingredients:

- 4 chicken breasts, skinless & boneless
- 12 oz egg noodles
- 14.5 oz chicken broth
- 21 oz cream of chicken soup
- Pepper and salt to taste

Directions:

Add chicken, broth, soup, pepper, and salt into the cooking pot and stir well.

Cover slow cooker with lid.

Select slow cook mode and cook on HIGH for 6 hours.

Remove chicken from pot and shred using a fork, return shredded chicken to the pot and stir well.

Add noodles into the cooking pot and cook for 30 minutes more.

Stir well and serve.

Nutrition:
Calories 273
Fat 10.9 g
Carbohydrates 16.2 g
Sugar 0.7 g
Protein 25.9 g
Cholesterol 83 mg

298. ORANGE CHICKEN

Preparation Time: 10 minutes
Cooking Time: 7 hours
Servings: 6

Ingredients:
- 1 lb chicken breasts, skinless & boneless
- 2 tbsp soy sauce
- 1 cup sweet orange marmalade
- 1/2 cup BBQ sauce

Directions:
Add all ingredients into the cooking pot and stir well.
Cover slow cooker with lid.
Select slow cook mode and cook on LOW for 7 hours.
Remove chicken from pot and shred using a fork, return shredded chicken to the pot and stir well.
Serve and enjoy.

Nutrition:
Calories 342
Fat 5.7 g
Carbohydrates 30.2 g
Sugar 33 g
Protein 22.2 g
Cholesterol 67 mg

299. DELICIOUS BBQ CHICKEN

Preparation Time: 10 minutes
Cooking Time: 4 hours
Servings: 8

Ingredients:
- 3 lbs chicken breasts, skinless & boneless
- 2 tbsp Stevia
- 1 tbsp Worcestershire sauce
- 1 tbsp olive oil
- 1/2 onion, grated
- 1 1/2 cups BBQ sauce

Directions:
Add all ingredients into the cooking pot and stir well.
Cover slow cooker with lid.
Select slow cook mode and cook on HIGH for 4 hours.
Remove chicken from pot and shred using a fork, return shredded chicken to the pot and stir well.
Serve and enjoy.

Nutrition:
Calories 422
Fat 14.5 g
Carbohydrates 20.2 g
Sugar 15.1 g
Protein 49.3 g
Cholesterol 151 mg

300. PARMESAN CHICKEN RICE

Preparation Time: 10 minutes
Cooking Time: 4 hours
Servings: 6

Ingredients:
- 4 chicken breasts, skinless & boneless
- 1/4 cup parmesan cheese, grated
- 1 cup of rice
- 1 3/4 cups milk
- 21 oz can cream of chicken soup
- Pepper and salt to taste

Directions:
Season chicken with pepper and salt and place into the cooking pot.
Mix rice, milk, and soup and pour over chicken and top with parmesan cheese.
Cover slow cooker with lid.
Select slow cook mode and cook on HIGH for 4 hours.
Remove chicken from pot and chop, return chicken to the pot and stir well.
Serve and enjoy.

Nutrition:
Calories 453
Fat 16.7 g
Carbohydrates 35.6 g
Sugar 3.8 g
Protein 38.2 g
Cholesterol 107 mg

301. QUESO CHICKEN TACOS

Preparation Time: 10 minutes
Cooking Time: 4 hours
Servings: 8

Ingredients:
- 2 lbs chicken breasts, boneless & skinless
- 1 1/2 cups Mexican cheese dip
- 10 oz can Rotel

- 1 oz taco seasoning

Directions:

Add all ingredients into the cooking pot and stir well.

Cover slow cooker with lid.

Select slow cook mode and cook on LOW for 4-6 hours.

Remove chicken from pot and shred using a fork, return shredded chicken to the pot and stir well.

Serve and enjoy.

Nutrition:

Calories 349

Fat 17.8 g

Carbohydrates 4.7 g

Sugar 0.9 g

Protein 39.5 g

Cholesterol 120 mg

302. EASY MEXICAN CHICKEN

Preparation Time: 10 minutes

Cooking Time: 6 hours

Servings: 6

Ingredients:

- 2 lbs chicken breasts, boneless & skinless
- 1/3 cup chicken stock
- 1 oz taco seasoning
- 2 cups salsa

Directions:

Add all ingredients into the cooking pot and stir well.

Cover slow cooker with lid.

Select slow cook mode and cook on LOW for 6 hours.

Remove chicken from pot and shred using a fork, return shredded chicken to the pot and stir well.

Serve and enjoy.

Nutrition:

Calories 321

Fat 11.9 g

Carbohydrates 6.2 g

Sugar 2.7 g

Protein 45.7 g

Cholesterol 136 mg

303. MUSTARD MUSHROOM CHICKEN

Preparation Time: 10 minutes

Cooking Time: 6 hours

Servings: 4

Ingredients:

- 4 chicken thighs, bone-in & skin-on
- 1 tsp garlic, minced
- 1 tsp grainy mustard
- 8 oz mushrooms, sliced
- 10.5 oz cream of mushroom soup
- Pepper and salt to taste

Directions:

Season chicken with pepper and salt and place into the cooking pot.

Mix the remaining ingredients and pour over the chicken.

Cover slow cooker with lid.

Select slow cook mode and cook on LOW for 6 hours.

Serve and enjoy.

Nutrition:

Calories 324

Fat 13.3 g

Carbohydrates 4.7 g

Sugar 1.5 g

Protein 44.8 g

Cholesterol 130 mg

304. HERB CHICKEN BREASTS

Preparation Time: 10 minutes

Cooking Time: 5 hours

Servings: 6

Ingredients:

- 6 chicken breasts, boneless & skinless
- 1/3 cup dry white wine
- 1 garlic clove, crushed
- 1 tsp thyme, chopped
- 2 tsp fresh oregano, chopped
- Pepper and salt to taste

Directions:

Season chicken with pepper and salt and place into the cooking pot.

Mix the remaining ingredients and pour over the chicken.

Cover slow cooker with lid.

Select slow cook mode and cook on LOW for 5 hours.

Serve and enjoy.

Nutrition:

Calories 291

Fat 10.9 g

Carbohydrates 1 g

Sugar 0.1 g

Protein 42.4 g

Cholesterol 130 mg

305. BALSAMIC CHICKEN

Preparation Time: 10 minutes

Cooking Time: 4 hours
Servings: 10
Ingredients:
- 4 chicken breasts, boneless & skinless
- 1/2 tsp thyme
- 1 tsp dried rosemary
- 1 tsp dried basil
- 1 tsp dried oregano
- 1 tbsp olive oil
- 1/2 cup balsamic vinegar
- 4 garlic cloves
- 1 onion, sliced
- 30 oz can tomatoes, diced
- Pepper and salt to taste

Directions:
Season chicken with pepper and salt and place into the cooking pot.
Mix remaining ingredients and pour over chicken.
Cover slow cooker with lid.
Select slow cook mode and cook on HIGH for 4 hours.
Serve and enjoy.

Nutrition:
Calories 151
Fat 5.8 g
Carbohydrates 6.1 g
Sugar 3.4 g
Protein 17.9 g
Cholesterol 52 mg

306. CREAMY CHICKEN PENNE
Preparation Time: 10 minutes
Cooking Time: 6 hours
Servings: 6
Ingredients:
- 3 chicken breasts, boneless & skinless
- 1 lb penne pasta, cooked
- 2 cups cheddar cheese, shredded
- 1 cup sour cream
- 1/2 onion, diced
- 1 1/2 cups mushrooms, sliced
- 1/2 tsp dried thyme
- 1/2 cup chicken broth
- 21 oz can cream of chicken soup
- Pepper and salt to taste

Directions:
Add chicken, soup, onions, mushrooms, thyme, pepper, and broth into the cooking pot and stir well.
Cover slow cooker with lid.
Select slow cook mode and cook on LOW for 6 hours.
Remove chicken from pot and shred using a fork, return shredded chicken to the pot and stir well.
Stir in cheddar cheese, penne, and sour cream.
Serve and enjoy.

Nutrition:
Calories 690
Fat 33.6 g
Carbohydrates 52.2 g
Sugar 1.6 g
Protein 43.7 g
Cholesterol 185 mg

307. TASTY CHICKEN FAJITA PASTA
Preparation Time: 10 minutes
Cooking Time: 6 hours
Servings: 6
Ingredients:
- 2 chicken breasts, skinless & boneless
- 2 cups cheddar cheese, shredded
- 16 oz penne pasta, cooked
- 2 cups chicken broth
- 10 oz can tomato, diced
- 2 tsp garlic, minced
- 1 bell peppers, diced
- 1/2 onion, diced
- 2 tbsp taco seasoning

Directions:
Add all ingredients except cheese and pasta into the cooking pot and stir well.
Cover slow cooker with lid.
Select slow cook mode and cook on LOW for 6 hours.
Stir in cheese and pasta.
Serve and enjoy.

Nutrition:
Calories 620
Fat 25.2 g
Carbohydrates 56.2 g
Sugar 3.4 g
Protein 41.3 g
Cholesterol 157 mg

308. MOIST & JUICY CHICKEN BREAST
Preparation Time: 10 minutes
Cooking Time: 3 hours
Servings: 4
Ingredients:
- 4 chicken breasts, skinless and boneless

- 1/8 tsp paprika
- 1 tbsp butter
- 1/4 cup chicken broth
- 1/8 tsp onion powder
- 1/4 tsp garlic powder
- 1/2 tsp dried parsley
- 1/8 tsp pepper
- 1/2 tsp salt

Directions:

In a small bowl, mix paprika, onion powder, garlic powder, parsley, pepper, and salt.

Rub chicken breasts with a spice mixture from both sides.

Add broth and butter to the cooking pot and stir to combine.

Add chicken to the cooking pot.

Cover slow cooker with lid.

Select slow cook mode and cook on LOW for 3 hours.

Serve and enjoy.

Nutrition:

Calories 307

Fat 13.8 g

Carbohydrates 0.4 g

Sugar 0.1 g

Protein 42.6 g

Cholesterol 138 mg

309. ASIAN CHICKEN

Preparation Time: 10 minutes

Cooking Time: 6 hours

Servings: 4

Ingredients:

- 4 chicken breasts, skinless and boneless
- 1/2 cup of soy sauce
- 1 tbsp ginger, minced
- 3 garlic cloves, chopped
- 1 onion, chopped
- 3 tbsp sesame seeds
- 1/3 cup rice vinegar
- 1/3 cup Stevia

Directions:

Add chicken into the cooking pot.

Add ginger, garlic, and onion on top of the chicken.

Add vinegar, Stevia, and soy sauce to the cooking pot.

Season with pepper and salt.

Cover slow cooker with lid.

Select slow cook mode and cook on LOW for 6 hours.

Shred chicken using a fork and stir well.

Serve and enjoy.

Nutrition:

Calories 451

Fat 14.3 g

Carbohydrates 31.6 g

Sugar 25 g

Protein 46.1 g

Cholesterol 130 mg

310. FLAVORFUL CHICKEN CASSEROLE

Preparation Time: 10 minutes

Cooking Time: 8 hours

Servings: 6

Ingredients:

- 4 chicken breasts, boneless & skinless
- 1 1/2 cups chicken stock
- 10.5 oz can cream of chicken soup
- 15 oz can corn kernels, drained
- 2 cups cheddar cheese, shredded
- 1 cup cooked rice
- 1 onion, chopped

Directions:

Add chicken into the cooking pot.

Add chopped onion over chicken.

In a bowl, stir together stock and soup and pour over the chicken.

Cover slow cooker with lid.

Select slow cook mode and cook on LOW for 8 hours.

Remove chicken from cooking pot and shred using a fork.

Return shredded chicken to the cooking pot along with corn, cheese, and rice. Stir well.

Serve and enjoy.

Nutrition:

Calories 561

Fat 23.6 g

Carbohydrates 43.9 g

Sugar 3.6 g

Protein 43.2 g

Cholesterol 130 mg

311. CHICKEN ORZO

Preparation Time: 10 minutes

Cooking Time: 4 hours 30 minutes

Servings: 4

Ingredients:

- 1 lb chicken breasts, skinless and boneless, cut in half
- 3/4 cup whole wheat orzo

- 1 tsp Italian herbs
- 1 lemon juice
- 2 tbsp green onion, chopped
- 1/3 cup olives
- 1 lemon zest, grated
- 1 onion, sliced
- 1 cup chicken stock
- 1/2 cup bell pepper, diced
- 2 tomatoes, chopped

Directions:

Add all ingredients except olives and orzo into the cooking pot and stir well.

Cover slow cooker with lid.

Select slow cook mode and cook on LOW for 4 hours.

Stir in olives and orzo and cook for 30 minutes more.

Serve and enjoy.

Nutrition:

Calories 333

Fat 10.6 g

Carbohydrates 22.3 g

Sugar 4.8 g

Protein 36.4 g

Cholesterol 101 mg

312. GARLIC HERB ROASTED PEPPER CHICKEN

Preparation Time: 10 minutes

Cooking Time: 4 hours

Servings: 6

Ingredients:

- 2 lbs chicken thighs, skinless and boneless
- 1 cup roasted red peppers, chopped
- 1/2 cup chicken stock
- 1 cup olives
- 1 tsp rosemary
- 1 tsp dried thyme
- 1 tsp oregano
- 1 tbsp capers
- 3 garlic cloves, minced
- 1 onion, sliced
- 1 tbsp olive oil
- Pepper and salt to taste

Directions:

Add all ingredients into the cooking pot and stir well.

Cover slow cooker with lid.

Select slow cook mode and cook on LOW for 4 hours.

Stir well and serve.

Nutrition:

Calories 354

Fat 16.1 g

Carbohydrates 6 g

Sugar 2.2 g

Protein 44.7 g

Cholesterol 135 mg

313. SLOW COOK TURKEY BREAST

Preparation Time: 10 minutes

Cooking Time: 4 hours 30 minutes

Servings: 6

Ingredients:

- 4 lbs turkey breast
- 1/2 fresh lemon juice
- 1/2 cup sun-dried tomatoes, chopped
- 1/2 cup olives, chopped
- 3 tbsp almond flour
- 3/4 cup chicken stock
- 4 garlic cloves, chopped
- 1 tsp dried oregano
- 1 onion, chopped
- 1/4 tsp pepper
- 1/2 tsp salt

Directions:

Add turkey breast, garlic, oregano, lemon juice, sun-dried tomatoes, olives, onion, pepper, and salt to the cooking pot.

Pour half stock over turkey.

Cover slow cooker with lid.

Select slow cook mode and cook on LOW for 4 hours.

Whisk together remaining stock and flour and add into the cooking pot and stir well, cover, and cook on LOW for 30 minutes more.

Serve and enjoy.

Nutrition:

Calories 358

Fat 6.5 g

Carbohydrates 19.8 g

Sugar 12 g

Protein 52.7 g

Cholesterol 130 mg

314. SIMPLE CHICKEN & MUSHROOMS

Preparation Time: 10 minutes

Cooking Time: 6 hours

Servings: 2

Ingredients:

- 2 chicken breasts, skinless and boneless
- 1 cup mushrooms, sliced

- 1/2 tsp thyme, dried
- 1 onion, sliced
- 1 cup chicken stock
- Pepper and salt to taste

Directions:

Add all ingredients into the cooking pot and stir well.
Cover slow cooker with lid.
Select slow cook mode and cook on LOW for 6 hours.
Stir well and serve.

Nutrition:

Calories 313
Fat 11.3 g
Carbohydrates 6.9 g
Sugar 3.3 g
Protein 44.3 g
Cholesterol 130 mg

315. LEMON HERB CHICKEN

Preparation Time: 10 minutes
Cooking Time: 4 hours
Servings: 4

Ingredients:

- 20 oz chicken breasts, skinless, boneless, and cut into pieces
- 3/4 cup chicken broth
- 1/2 tsp dried oregano
- 1 tsp dried parsley
- 2 tbsp olive oil
- 2 tbsp butter
- 1/2 cup fresh lemon juice
- 1/8 tsp dried thyme
- 1/4 tsp dried basil
- 3 tbsp rice flour
- 1 tsp salt

Directions:

In a bowl, toss chicken with rice flour.
Add butter and olive oil to a cooking pot and set slow cooker on sauté mode.
Add chicken to the cooking pot and cook until brown.
Add remaining ingredients on top of the chicken.
Cover slow cooker with lid.
Select slow cook mode and cook on LOW for 4 hours.
Serve and enjoy.

Nutrition:

Calories 423
Fat 23.9 g
Carbohydrates 6.9 g
Sugar 0.8 g
Protein 42.7 g
Cholesterol 141 mg

316. CREAMY CHICKEN CURRY

Preparation Time: 10 minutes
Cooking Time: 6 hours
Servings: 6

Ingredients:

- 1 1/2 lbs chicken thighs, boneless
- 1/2 cup chicken broth
- 3 cauliflower, peeled and cut into 1-inch pieces
- 15 oz can coconut milk
- 2 tbsp Stevia
- 1/2 tsp red pepper, crushed
- 1/2 tsp coriander, crushed
- 2 tbsp curry powder
- 3 tbsp fresh ginger, chopped
- 1/2 tsp black pepper
- 1 tsp kosher salt

Directions:

Add all ingredients into the cooking pot and stir well.
Cover slow cooker with lid.
Select slow cook mode and cook on LOW for 6 hours.
Stir well and serve.

Nutrition:

Calories 463
Fat 24.2 g
Carbohydrates 25.7 g
Sugar 4.8 g
Protein 37.1 g
Cholesterol 101 mg

317. TACO CHICKEN

Preparation Time: 10 minutes
Cooking Time: 6 hours
Servings: 8

Ingredients:

- 1 lb chicken breasts, skinless and boneless
- 2 tbsp taco seasoning
- 1 cup chicken broth

Directions:

Add all ingredients into the cooking pot and stir well.
Cover slow cooker with lid.
Select slow cook mode and cook on LOW for 6 hours.
Remove chicken from pot and shred using a fork, return shredded chicken to the pot.
Stir well and serve.

Nutrition:

Calories 118
Fat 4.7 g
Carbohydrates 0.5 g
Sugar 0.1 g
Protein 17.3 g
Cholesterol 51 mg

318. CIDER-BRAISED CHICKEN

Preparation Time: 10 minutes
Cooking Time: 5 hours
Servings: 2

Ingredients:
- 4 chicken drumsticks
- 2 tablespoon of olive oil
- 1/2 cup of apple cider vinegar
- 1 tablespoon of balsamic vinegar
- 1 chili pepper, diced
- 1 yellow onion, minced
- Salt and black pepper- to taste

Directions:
Place all the ingredients into a bowl and mix them thoroughly.
Marinate the chicken for 2 hours in the refrigerator.
Spread the chicken with its marinade in the Slow cooker.
Cover it and cook for 5 hours on Low Settings. Garnish as desired. Serve warm.

Nutrition:
Calories 311
Fat 4.7 g
Carbohydrates 1.4 g
Sugar 0.3 g
Protein 18.4 g
Cholesterol 69 mg

319. BUTTER CHICKEN

Preparation Time: 10 minutes
Cooking Time: 5 hours
Servings: 5

Ingredients:
- 1 lb chicken thighs, boneless and skinless
- 1 lb chicken breasts, boneless and skinless
- 1 1/2 tbsp ginger paste
- 1 tbsp garam masala
- 1 tbsp curry powder
- 1/3 cup heavy whipping cream
- 1 1/2 tbsp butter
- 1/4 cup tomato paste
- 1/2 cup chicken broth
- 3/4 tsp kosher salt

Directions:
Cut chicken into the cooking pot.
pour remaining ingredients except whipping cream over chicken and stir well.
Cover slow cooker with lid.
Select slow cook mode and cook on LOW for 5 hours.
Stir in cream and serve.

Nutrition:
Calories 427
Fat 20.3 g
Carbohydrates 4.7 g
Sugar 1.8 g
Protein 54.1 g
Cholesterol 182 mg

320. SPICY CHILI CHICKEN

Preparation Time: 10 minutes
Cooking Time: 6 hours
Servings: 5

Ingredients:
- 1 lb chicken breasts, skinless and boneless
- 1 jalapeno pepper, chopped
- 1 poblano pepper, chopped
- 12 oz can green chilies
- 1/2 cup dried chives
- 1/2 tsp paprika
- 1/2 tsp dried sage
- 1/2 tsp cumin
- 1 tsp dried oregano
- 14 oz can tomato, diced
- 2 cups of water
- 1 tsp sea salt

Directions:
Add all ingredients into the cooking pot and stir well.
Cover slow cooker with lid.
Select slow cook mode and cook on LOW for 6 hours.
Remove chicken from pot and shred using a fork, return shredded chicken to the pot.
Stir well and serve.

Nutrition:
Calories 212
Fat 7.1 g
Carbohydrates 8.9 g
Sugar 3.4 g
Protein 27.9 g
Cholesterol 81 mg

321. PESTO CHICKEN

Preparation Time: 10 minutes
Cooking Time: 7 hours
Servings: 2

Ingredients:
- 2 chicken breasts, skinless and boneless
- 2 cups cherry tomatoes, halved
- 2 tbsp basil pesto
- 2 cups zucchini, chopped
- 2 cups green beans, chopped

Directions:
Add all ingredients into the cooking pot and stir well.
Cover slow cooker with lid.
Select slow cook mode and cook on LOW for 7 hours.
Stir well and serve.

Nutrition:
Calories 26
Fat 0.8 g
Carbohydrates 1.3 g
Sugar 0.6 g
Protein 3.4 g
Cholesterol 9 mg

322. ROSEMARY TURKEY BREAST

Preparation Time: 10 minutes
Cooking Time: 4 hours
Servings: 12

Ingredients:
6 lbs turkey breast, bone-in
4 fresh rosemary sprigs
1/2 cup water
Pepper and salt to taste

Directions:
Add all ingredients into the cooking pot and stir well.
Cover slow cooker with lid.
Select slow cook mode and cook on LOW for 4 hours.
Serve and enjoy.

Nutrition:
Calories 237
Fat 3.8 g
Carbohydrates 9.8 g
Sugar 8 g
Protein 38.7 g
Cholesterol 98 mg

323. GARLIC OLIVE CHICKEN

Preparation Time: 10 minutes
Cooking Time: 6 hours
Servings: 4

Ingredients:
- 2 1/2 lbs chicken legs
- 1 tbsp capers
- 5 garlic cloves, smashed
- 3 tbsp red wine vinegar
- 1 1/2 tsp dried oregano
- 1/3 cup white wine
- 1/4 cup fresh parsley, chopped
- 1/3 cup olives, pitted
- 1/2 cup prunes
- Pepper and salt to taste

Directions:
Add all ingredients into the cooking pot and stir well.
Cover slow cooker with lid.
Select slow cook mode and cook on LOW for 4 hours.
Serve and enjoy.

Nutrition:
Calories 630
Fat 22.4 g
Carbohydrates 16.9 g
Sugar 8.4 g
Protein 83 g
Cholesterol 252 mg

324. DELICIOUS CHICKPEA CHICKEN

Preparation Time: 10 minutes
Cooking Time: 4 hours
Servings: 4

Ingredients:
- 2 lbs chicken thighs
- 1 tsp paprika
- 1 tbsp lemon juice
- 2 tbsp olive oil
- 1 tsp garlic, minced
- 3 cups grape tomatoes, sliced
- 14 oz can chickpeas, drained and rinsed
- 1 tsp chili powder
- 1 tsp curry powder
- 1 tsp cumin
- 1 tsp oregano
- 1 tsp coriander
- 1 lemon, sliced
- 1 tsp salt

Directions:
Add all ingredients into the cooking pot and stir well.
Cover slow cooker with lid.
Select slow cook mode and cook on LOW for 4 hours.

Serve and enjoy.

Nutrition:

Calories 648

Fat 25.7 g

Carbohydrates 27.8 g

Sugar 4.1 g

Protein 72.3 g

Cholesterol 202 mg

325.CREAMY ITALIAN CHICKEN

Preparation Time: 15 minutes

Cooking Time: 6 hours

Servings: 8

Ingredients:

- 2 pounds of chicken
- 10.5 ounces chicken soup, cream, and canned
- 1 tsp garlic powder
- 0.25 cups onion
- 2 tbsp dressing mix, Italian
- 8 ounces cream cheese

Directions:

Cube the chicken. Place it in the cooker.

Dice and add onions. Stir in cream cheese: mix garlic, soup, and dressing mix.

Pour into the cooker. Low cook for 6 hours.

Nutrition:

Calories 255

Fat 14 g

Protein 23 g

Carbs 7 g

326.CHICKEN AND VEGETABLES

Preparation Time: 15 minutes

Cooking Time: 8 hours

Servings: 8

Ingredients:

- 2 pounds chicken that does not contain any skin or bones
- 2 cups green beans
- 1 cup chicken broth
- 2 tsp herb blend
- 2 cups carrots
- 2 onions
- 4 tsp Worcestershire sauce
- Pepper and salt to taste

Directions:

Prepare and chop the vegetables. Put the chicken in the cooker.

Add the vegetables. Pour the broth and Worcestershire sauce. Low cook for 8 hours.

Nutrition:

Calories 160

Fat 3 g

Protein 23 g

Carbs 13 g

327.CHICKEN GYROS

Preparation Time: 15 minutes

Cooking Time: 8 hours

Servings: 8

Ingredients:

- 0.5 an onion
- 2 pounds ground chicken
- 0.5 cups breadcrumbs, low-carb
- 1 tsp thyme
- 0.25 tsp nutmeg
- 1 tbsp olive oil
- 3 garlic cloves
- 2 eggs
- 1 lemon
- 0.25 tsp cinnamon
- 12 pita bread

Toppings:

- Tomato
- Greek yogurt, plain
- Cucumber
- Lemon

Directions:

Process the garlic and onion. Mix the above with the eggs, lemon, cinnamon, salt, chicken, breadcrumbs, thyme, and nutmeg.

Roll into a ball. Put in a cooker—drizzle olive oil.

Low cook for 8 hours. Once finished, put on pita and apply toppings.

Nutrition:

Calories 248

Fat 13 g

Protein 23 g

Carbs 10 g

328.SLOW COOKER CREAMY SALSA CHICKEN

Preparation Time: 15 minutes

Cooking Time: 4 hours

Servings: 4

Ingredients:

- 1/2 jar salsa

- 1/2 can of cream mushroom soup
- 3 large boneless chicken breasts

Directions:

Lay and settle the chicken breasts inside the slow cooker.

Combine in the salsa plus the mushroom soup. Set it on top of the chicken breasts.

Cook on low within 4 hours, stirring occasionally, and shred once cooked, then serve.

Nutrition:

Calories 254.6

Protein 40.8g

Carbs 5.3g

Fat 6.6g

329. PIZZA CASSEROLE

Preparation Time: 15 minutes

Cooking Time: 4 hours

Servings: 3

Ingredients:

- 2 chicken breasts without bones
- 2 garlic cloves
- 1 tsp seasoning, Italian
- Dash pepper
- 8 ounces tomato sauce
- 1 bay leaf
- 0.25 tsp salt
- 0.5 cups mozzarella

Directions:

Put the chicken in the cooker. Add other ingredients, except cheese.

Low cook for 4 hours. After cooking, top with cheese.

Nutrition:

Calories 228

Fat 9 g

Protein 31 g

Carbs 5 g

330. MOIST AND SPICY PULLED CHICKEN BREAST

Preparation Time: 15 minutes

Cooking Time: 6 hours

Servings: 8

Ingredients:

- 1 tsp dry oregano
- 1 tsp dry thyme
- 1 tsp dried rosemary
- 1 tsp garlic powder
- 1 tsp sweet paprika
- ½ tsp chili powder
- Salt and pepper to taste
- 4 tbsp butter
- 5.5 pounds of chicken breasts
- 1 ½ cups ready-made tomato salsa
- 2 Tbsp of olive oil

Directions:

Mix dry seasoning, sprinkle half on the bottom of the slow cooker.

Place the chicken breasts over it, sprinkle the rest of the spices.

Pour the salsa over the chicken. Cover, cook on low for 6 hours.

Nutrition:

Calories: 42

Carbs: 1g

Fat: 1g

Protein: 9g

331. WHOLE ROASTED CHICKEN

Preparation Time: 15 minutes

Cooking Time: 8 hours

Servings: 6

Ingredients:

- 1 whole chicken (approximately 5.5 pounds)
- 4 garlic cloves
- 6 small onions
- 1 Tbsp olive oil, for rubbing
- 2 tsp salt
- 2 tsp sweet paprika
- 1 tsp Cayenne pepper
- 1 tsp onion powder
- 1 tsp ground thyme
- 2 tsp fresh ground black pepper
- 4 Tbsp butter, cut into cubes

Directions:

Mix all dry ingredients well.

Stuff the chicken belly with garlic and onions.

On the bottom of the slow cooker, place four balls of aluminum foil.

Set the chicken on top of the balls. Rub it generously with olive oil.

Cover the chicken with seasoning, drop in butter pieces. Cover, cook on low for 8 hours.

Nutrition:

Calories: 120

Carbs: 1g

Fat: 6g

Protein: 17g

332. SIMPLE CHICKEN CHILI

Preparation Time: 15 minutes
Cooking Time: 6 hours
Servings: 8

Ingredients:
- 1 Tbsp butter
- 1 red onion, sliced
- 1 bell pepper, sliced
- 2 garlic cloves, minced
- 3 pounds boneless chicken thighs
- 8 slices bacon, chopped
- 1 tsp chili powder
- Salt and pepper to taste
- 1 cup chicken broth
- ¼ cup of coconut milk
- 3 tbsp tomato paste

Directions:
Add all ingredients to the slow cooker, starting with the butter.
Cover, cook on low for 6 hours.
Strip the chicken using a fork in the slow cooker. Serve.

Nutrition:
Calories: 210
Carbs: 32g
Fat: 4g
Protein: 14g

333. CHICKEN IN SALSA VERDE

Preparation Time: 15 minutes
Cooking Time: 6 hours
Servings: 4

Ingredients:
- 2.2 pounds of chicken breasts
- 3 bunches parsley, chopped
- ¾ cup olive oil
- ¼ cup capers, drained and chopped
- 3 anchovy fillets
- 1 lemon, juice, and zest
- 2 garlic cloves, minced
- 1 tsp salt
- 1 tsp fresh ground black pepper

Directions:
Place the chicken breasts in the slow cooker.
Blend the rest of the fixing in a blender, then pour over the chicken.
Cover, cook on low for 6 hours. Shred with a fork and serve.

Nutrition:
Calories: 145
Carbs: 5g
Fat: 2g
Protein: 26g

334. DUCK IN SAUCE

Preparation Time: 10 minutes
Cooking Time: 6 hours
Servings: 4

Ingredients:
- 1 duck, cut into small chunks
- 4 garlic cloves, minced
- 4 tablespoons of swerves
- 2 green onions, roughly diced
- 4 tablespoon of soy sauce
- 4 tablespoon of sherry wine
- 1/4 cup of water
- 1-inch ginger root, sliced
- A pinch salt
- black pepper to taste

Directions:
Mix all the ingredients into the Slow cooker
Cover it and cook for 6 hours on Low Settings.
Garnish as desired.

Nutrition:
Calories: 338
Carbs: 8.3g
Fat: 3.8g
Protein: 15.4mg

335. CHILI GROUND DUCK

Preparation Time: 10 minutes
Cooking Time: 6 hours
Servings: 8

Ingredients:
- 1 yellow onion, cut into half
- 1 top trimmed garlic heat
- 1 bay leaf
- 2 cloves
- 6 cups of water
- Salt- to taste
- 1 cup mixed Italian cheese, grated

For the duck:
- 1 lb. ground duck
- 15 oz. Canned tomatoes diced and their juices

- 1 tablespoon of Vegetable oil
- 4 oz. Canned green chilies and their juice 1 teaspoon of Swerve
- 1 yellow onion, minced
- 2 carrots, diced
- Handful cilantro, diced
- Salt and black pepper to taste

Directions:

Mix all items in a bowl. Put it inside your slow cooker, and set to cook on low for 3 hours. Garnish and serve.

Nutrition:

Calories: 140

Carbohydrates: 3.87g

Protein: 10.93g

Fat: 8.89g

Sugars: 1.27g

Sodium: 309mg

Fiber: 0.3g

336. SPICY HEALTHY CHICKEN

Preparation Time: 10 minutes

Cooking Time: 8 hours

Servings: 4

Ingredients:

- 1 chicken
- 1 tablespoon of olive oil
- 1 tablespoon of dried paprika
- 1 teaspoon of dried turmeric
- 1 tablespoon of curry powder
- 1 teaspoon of salt

Directions:

Begin by combining all the spices and oil in a pan but the chicken.

Now season the chicken with the resulting sauce as desired.

Place the chicken and spices mix in your Slow cooker.

Close the lid and cook for 8 hours on Low Setting. Dish warm and enjoy.

Nutrition:

Calories: 313

Carbohydrates: 6.3g

Protein: 35.2g

Fat: 134g

Sugars: 19g

Sodium: 62mg

Fiber: 0.7g

337. GINGERY CHICKEN

Preparation Time: 10 minutes

Cooking Time: 6 hours

Servings: 4

Ingredients:

- 1 1/2 lbs. chicken drumsticks (approx. 5 drumsticks)
- 1 onion, diced
- 1 (13.5 oz.) can coconut milk
- a 4 cloves garlic, minced
- 1-inch knob fresh ginger, minced
- 1 Serrano pepper, minced
- 1 tablespoon of Garam Masala
- 1/2 teaspoon of turmeric
- 1/2 teaspoon of paprika
- 1/2 teaspoon of cayenne
- Salt and black pepper at will

Directions:

Remove the drumsticks' skin.

Place all the ingredients into the Slow cooker. Close the lid and cook for 6 hours on Low Settings.

Garnish as wished and dish warm.

Nutrition:

Calories: 248

Carbs: 8.4g

Fat: 15.7g

Protein: 14.1g

PORK & LAMB

338. MOUTH-WATERING MINCED PORK ZUCCHINI LASAGNA

Preparation Time: 15 minutes

Cooking Time: 8 hours

Servings: 4

Ingredients:

- 4 medium zucchini
- 1 diced small onion
- 1 minced clove of garlic
- 2 cups of minced lean ground pork
- 2 cans of Italian diced tomatoes
- 2 tbsp of olive oil
- 2 cups of shredded Mozzarella cheese
- 1 large egg
- 1 tbsp of dried basil
- Salt and pepper to taste
- 2 tbsp of butter

Directions:

Slice the zucchini lengthwise into 6 slices. Heat-up the olive oil in a saucepan, then sauté the garlic and onions for 5 minutes.

Put the minced meat, cook for a further 5 minutes, put the tomatoes, and cook for an additional 5 minutes. Add the seasoning and mix thoroughly.

Mix the egg plus cheese in a small bowl, and whisk. Grease the slow cooker using the butter, and then begin to layer the lasagna. First, layer with the zucchini slices, add the meat mixture, then top with the cheese. Repeat and finish with the cheese—Cook for 8 hours on low.

Nutrition:

Carbs: 10 g

Protein: 23 g

Fat: 30 g

Calories: 398

339. BEAUTIFUL BBQ RIBS

Preparation Time: 15 minutes
Cooking Time: 8 hours
Servings: 4

Ingredients:
- 3 pounds of pork ribs
- 1 tbsp of olive oil
- 1 can of tomato paste, 28 ounces
- ½ cup of hot water
- ½ cup of vinegar
- 6 tbsp of Worcestershire sauce
- 4 tbsp of dry mustard
- 1 tbsp of chili powder
- 1 tsp of ground cumin
- 1 tsp of powdered sweetener of your choice
- Salt and pepper to taste

Directions:

Heat the olive oil in a large frying pan and brown the ribs, then put in the slow cooker.

Combine the remainder of the fixing in a small bowl, whisk thoroughly and pour over the ribs—Cook for 8 hours on low.

Nutrition:
Carbs: 14 g
Protein: 38 g
Fat: 28 g
Calories: 410

340. GORGEOUS COCONUT TURMERIC PORK CURRY

Preparation Time: 15 minutes
Cooking Time: 8 hours
Servings: 4

Ingredients:
- 2.2 pounds of cubed pork shoulder
- 1 tbsp of coconut oil
- 1 tbsp of olive oil
- 1 diced yellow onion
- 2 cloves of minced garlic
- 2 tbsp of tomato paste
- 1 can of coconut milk, 12 ounces
- 1 cup of water
- ½ cup of white wine
- 1 tsp of turmeric
- 1 tsp of ginger powder
- 1 tsp of curry powder
- ½ tsp of paprika
- Salt and pepper to taste

Directions:

Heat-up 1 tbsp of olive oil in a saucepan and sauté the garlic and onions for 3 minutes.

Add the pork and brown it, and then add the tomato paste.

Mix the remaining ingredients in the slow cooker and then add the pork.

Cook for 8 hours on low. Divide onto plates and serve

Nutrition:
Carbs: 7 g
Protein: 30 g
Fat: 31 g
Calories: 425

341. KALUA PORK

Preparation Time: 15 minutes
Cooking Time: 8 hours
Servings: 8

Ingredients:
- 4 lbs. pork shoulder roast
- 1 tbsp liquid smoke
- 2 tsp sea salt

Directions:

Place pork roast into the slow cooker. Pour liquid smoke and sea salt all over the pork roast.

Cook within 8 hours, low. Shred the meat, then serve.

Nutrition:
Calories 582
Fat 46.2 g
Carbohydrates 0 g
Sugar 0 g
Protein 38.1 g
Cholesterol 161 mg
Fiber 0 g

342. TASTY CUBAN MOJO PORK

Preparation Time: 15 minutes
Cooking Time: 8 hours
Servings: 6

Ingredients:
- 2 lbs. pork shoulder, boneless and cut into 2 pieces
- 2 bay leaves
- 1/2 tsp paprika
- 1/2 tsp cumin
- 1 1/2 tsp dried oregano
- 1/2 tsp pepper
- 3 garlic cloves, minced
- 1 jalapeno pepper, halved
- 1 small onion, chopped

- 1 lime zest
- 1/4 cup lime juice
- 1/2 cup orange juice
- 1/4 cup vinegar
- 3/4 cup chicken broth
- 1 tsp salt

Directions:

Place pork roast into the slow cooker. Add remaining ingredients into the slow cooker.

Cook within 8 hours, low setting. Discard bay leaves and shred the meat using a fork. Serve and enjoy.

Nutrition:

Calories 468
Fat 32.7 g
Carbohydrates 4.6 g
Sugar 2.5 g
Protein 36.3 g
Cholesterol 136 mg
Fiber 0.7 g
Net carbs 4.6 g

343. SLOW COOKER PORK LOIN

Preparation Time: 15 minutes
Cooking Time: 6 hours
Servings: 4

Ingredients:

- 1/4 cup orange juice
- 1/2 tbsp curry powder
- 1/2 tsp chicken bouillon granules
- 1/4 tsp ground ginger
- 1/8 tsp ground cinnamon
- 1/4 tsp salt
- 1/2 onion, diced
- 1/2 garlic, diced
- 1/8 cup raisins
- 1/8 cup flaked coconut
- 1 tbsp cold water
- 2 pounds boneless pork loin, diced
- 1 tbsp arrowroot powder

Directions:

Mix the salt, cinnamon, chicken bouillon, curry powder, and orange in the slow cooker's bottom.

Mix in the coconut, raisins, garlic, onion, and apple, then place the pork cubes into the mixture.

Put the cauliflower starch into water, mix until it dissolved. Then put it all inside the slow cooker.

Cook on low within 5 to 6 hours.

Nutrition:

Calories 174
Fat 6g
Carbs 8g
Protein 22g

344. GREEN CHILI PORK

Preparation Time: 15 minutes
Cooking Time: 8 hours
Servings: 8

Ingredients:

- 3 lbs. boneless pork, cubed
- 2 garlic cloves, minced
- 16 oz stewed tomatoes
- 4 oz green chilies, chopped
- 1 cup chicken broth
- 1 tsp oregano
- 1 tsp cumin
- 1 small onion, chopped
- 1 tbsp olive oil
- Pepper and salt to taste

Directions:

Heat-up the olive oil in a pan medium-high heat. Brown the pork in hot oil. Transfer pork into the slow cooker.

Add remaining ingredients and stir well—Cook within 8 hours, low. Serve and enjoy.

Nutrition:

Calories 284
Fat 8.1 g
Carbohydrates 4.6 g
Sugar 2.5 g
Protein 45.9 g
Cholesterol 124 mg
Fiber 1 g
Net carbs 3.6 g

345. THAI CURRIED PORK

Preparation Time: 15 minutes
Cooking Time: 8 hours
Servings: 6

Ingredients:

- 4 pork chops, boneless
- 1/2 cup chicken broth
- 1 tsp red pepper flakes
- 2 tsp cardamom
- 2 tsp cumin
- 1 tbsp curry powder
- 1 tbsp turmeric
- 8 oz baby carrots, peeled and chopped

- 1 tbsp fresh ginger, grated
- 4 garlic cloves, minced
- 1 small onion, chopped
- Pepper and sea salt to taste

Directions:

Spray slow cooker from inside with cooking spray. Put all the items into the slow cooker, and stir well.

Cook within 8 hours, low. Shred the pork chops using a fork. Serve and enjoy.

Nutrition:

Calories 211

Fat 14 g

Carbohydrates 7.9 g

Sugar 2.5 g

Protein 13.4 g

Cholesterol 46 mg

Fiber 2.4 g

Net carbs 5.5 g

346. CHINESE 5-SPICE PORK RIBS

Preparation Time: 15 minutes

Cooking Time: 8 hours

Servings: 6

Ingredients:

- 3 lbs. (1.36kg) baby back pork ribs
- Salt and pepper to taste
- 2 tsp Chinese five-spice powder
- 3/4 tsp coarse garlic powder
- 1 fresh jalapeño, cut into rings
- 2 tbsp rice vinegar
- 2 tbsp coconut aminos (or soy sauce)
- 1 tbsp tomato paste

Directions:

Start by cutting the ribs in the pieces so they'll fit into the slow cooker. Massage with salt and pepper.

Mix the Chinese 5-spice mixture and garlic and massage into the meat in a small bowl.

Place the jalapeño rings into the bottom of your slow cooker, followed by the rice vinegar, the coconut aminos, and the tomato paste, and stir it all together until combined.

Add the ribs but stand them up, pop the lid back on and cook for 6-8 hours on high.

Cook until the ribs almost fall apart.

Nutrition:

Calories: 164

Carbs: 6g

Fat: 7g

Protein: 19g

347. PORK STEW WITH OYSTER MUSHROOMS

Preparation Time: 15 minutes

Cooking Time: 8 hours

Servings: 4

Ingredients:

- 2 tbsp butter or lard
- 1 medium onion, chopped
- 1 clove garlic, chopped
- 2lbs (900g) pork loin, cut into 1" cubes and patted dry
- ½ tsp salt
- ½ tsp freshly cracked black pepper
- 2 tbsp dried oregano
- 2 tbsp dried mustard
- ½ tsp ground nutmeg
- 1½ cups (355ml) bone broth or stock
- 2 tbsp white wine vinegar
- 2 lbs. (900g) oyster mushrooms
- ¼ cup (60ml) full-fat coconut milk
- ¼ cup (60ml) ghee
- 3 tbsp capers

Directions:

Turn your slow cooker onto high heat and melt the butter or lard. Add the meat and cook well until brown on both sides. Remove the meat but keep the juices at the bottom.

Add some more fat and add the onions and garlic and cook for around 5 minutes until soft.

Add the oregano, mustard, nutmeg, broth, and vinegar and stir well to combine. Return the meat into the slow cooker, then cover with the lid and cook for 6 hours on low.

Remove the lid, throw in the mushrooms and an extra cup of water and cook for a further 1-2 hours.

Whisk in the coconut milk, ghee, and capers, then serve and enjoy!

Nutrition:

Calories: 190

Carbs: 0g

Fat: 10g

Protein: 23g

348. PAPRIKA PORK TENDERLOIN

Preparation Time: 15 minutes

Cooking Time: 4 hours & 20 minutes

Servings: 4

Ingredients:

- 1 ½ lb. lean pork tenderloin
- ½ tsp salt

- 2 tbsp paprika, smoked
- 1 cup chicken broth
- 1 tbsp oregano
- ½ cup of salsa
- Black pepper to taste

Directions:

Pour chicken stock into a small mixing bowl.

Add salsa, pepper, paprika, salt, and oregano. Mix well.

Remove the fat from the pork before placing it in the slow cooker. Add the liquid mixture.

Cook within 4 hours on high.

Shred the pork, then cook for another 20 minutes without cover.

Nutrition:

Calories: 160

Carbs: 2g

Fat: 8g

Protein: 22g

349. PORK CARNITAS

Preparation Time: 15 minutes

Cooking Time: 8 hours

Servings: 16

Ingredients:

- 8 lb. Boston pork butt
- 1 cup of water
- 2 tbsp butter
- 2 tbsp chili powder
- 4 tbsp garlic, minced
- 1 large onion, sliced thin
- 1 tbsp pepper
- 2 tbsp cumin
- 1 tbsp salt
- 2 tbsp thyme

Directions:

Grease the slow cooker using butter. Distribute onion and garlic evenly to the bottom of the slow cooker.

Remove the fat from the meat and lightly slice the top with a crisscross pattern. Mix the spices in a bowl, then coat the meat with it.

Put meat in the slow cooker with water—Cook for about 8 hours, high.

Nutrition:

Calories: 200

Carbs: 0g

Fat: 14g

Protein: 20g

350. LEMONGRASS COCONUT PULLED PORK

Preparation Time: 15 minutes

Cooking Time: 8 hours

Servings: 8

Ingredients:

- 3 lb. butt roast or pork loin
- ½ cup of coconut milk
- 2-inch ginger, sliced
- 3 tbsp lemongrass, minced
- 1 onion, sliced
- 3 cloves garlic, minced
- 1 tsp ground pepper
- 2 tsp kosher salt
- 1 tbsp apple cider vinegar
- 3 tbsp olive oil

Directions:

Remove fat from the roast and cut a crisscross pattern into it. Distribute onion and ginger slices evenly at the bottom of a slow cooker.

Mix olive oil, pepper, salt, apple cider vinegar, lemongrass, and garlic in a bowl until a loose paste is formed. Coat the pork with the mixture and put it in the slow cooker.

Cover and leave it overnight. Once done, pour coconut milk into the slow cooker and set it on low—Cook for 8 hours. Shred the meat using forks.

Nutrition:

Calories: 120

Carbs: 0g

Fat: 3g

Protein: 23g

351. PORK LOIN ROAST WITH ONION GRAVY

Preparation Time: 15 minutes

Cooking Time: 6 hours

Servings: 6

Ingredients:

- 4 lb. pork loin roast
- 2 tbsp coconut aminos
- 1 tbsp of sea salt
- ¼ cup of water
- 2 tsp black pepper
- 2 medium onions, sliced
- 2 cloves garlic, minced

Directions:

Put pepper, salt, and garlic in a bowl and mix well. Use it to coat all sides of the roast.

Distribute onion slices in the slow cooker. Pour in coconut aminos and water.

Put the roast in the slow cooker.

Cook within 4-6 hours, low.

Transfer the cooking juices and onions into a blender. Process until smooth.

Pour mixture over pork roast.

Nutrition:

Calories: 190

Carbs: 5g

Fat: 10g

Protein: 18g

352. LIME PORK CHOPS

Preparation Time: 15 minutes

Cooking Time: 4 hours

Servings: 8

Ingredients:

- 3.32 lb. pork sirloin
- ¾ tsp black pepper
- 3 tbsp butter
- ½ ground cumin
- ¾ tsp salt
- ½ cup of salsa
- ¾ tsp garlic powder
- 5 tbsp lime juice

Directions:

Mix all of the flavorings in a small bowl. Cover the meat all over with the flavoring mixture.

Using a pan, sear the meat in butter over medium-high heat until brown on both sides.

Combine lime juice and salsa in a separate bowl. Mix well.

Put the pork chops inside the slow cooker and pour the salsa mixture on top.

Cook within 3-4 hours, low.

Nutrition:

Calories: 170

Carbs: 8g

Fat: 6g

Protein: 18g

353. CHILI PULLED PORK

Preparation Time: 15 minutes

Cooking Time: 10 hours

Servings: 10

Ingredients:

- 4 1/2 lb. (2kg) pork butt / shoulder
- 2 tbsp chili powder
- 1 tbsp salt
- 1 ½ tsp ground cumin
- ½ tsp ground oregano
- ¼ tsp crushed red pepper flakes
- Pinch ground cloves
- ½ cup (120ml) stock or bone broth
- 1 bay leaf

Directions:

Start by grabbing a bowl and throwing in the chili, salt, cumin, oregano, red pepper flakes, and a pinch of cloves then stir well to combine.

Lay the pork out on a clean plate, remove the skin if applicable, then rub the spice mixture into the pork. Put into the fridge within 1-2 hours.

When you're ready to cook, pop the pork in the bottom of the slow cooker, add the bay leaf and the stock or broth, replace the lid and switch on. Cook on low for 8-10 hours (or overnight) until tender.

Remove the lid, lift the pork from the slow cooker, and place onto a cutting board then shred with two forks.

Serve and enjoy!

Nutrition:

Calories: 210

Carbs: 0g

Fat: 15g

Protein: 0g

354. RANCH PORK CHOPS

Preparation Time: 15 minutes

Cooking Time: 6 hours

Servings: 8

Ingredients:

- 3 lbs. pork chops
- 1 tsp garlic powder
- 1 oz ranch dressing mix
- 1 oz onion soup mix
- 22.5 oz cream of mushroom soup
- 1/2 tsp black pepper

Directions:

Spray slow cooker form inside with cooking spray. Put all listed items into the slow cooker, then mix well.

Cook within 6 hours on low. Serve and enjoy.

Nutrition:

Calories 591

Fat 44.6 g

Carbohydrates 5.4 g

Sugar 0.9 g

Protein 39.2 g

Cholesterol 146 mg

Fiber 0.3 g

Net carbs 5.1 g

355. DELICIOUS COCONUT PORK

Preparation Time: 15 minutes
Cooking Time: 8 hours
Servings: 6

Ingredients:
- 3 lbs. pork shoulder, boneless and cut into chunks
- 1/2 cup fresh cilantro, chopped
- 1 1/2 cups coconut water
- 1/4 cup fish sauce
- 2 tbsp olive oil
- 5 scallions, chopped

Directions:

Heat-up olive oil in a pan over medium heat. Brown the meat in hot oil. Transfer meat into the slow cooker.

Add the rest of the items into the slow cooker and mix well. Cook on low within 8 hours. Serve and enjoy.

Nutrition:

Calories 722
Fat 53.3 g
Carbohydrates 3.6 g
Sugar 2.3 g
Protein 54.1 g
Cholesterol 204 mg
Fiber 1 g
Net carbs 2.6 g

356. SPICY ADOBO PULLED PORK

Preparation Time: 15 minutes
Cooking Time: 8 hours
Servings: 4

Ingredients:
- 2 lbs. pork
- 1 tbsp ground cumin
- 1 tbsp garlic, minced
- 7 oz chipotle peppers in adobo sauce
- 1 can chicken broth

Directions:

Put all listed items into the slow cooker and stir well. Cook within 8 hours on low.

Shred the meat using a fork. Stir well and serve.

Nutrition:

Calories 391
Fat 9.9 g
Carbohydrates 10.1 g
Sugar 3.3 g
Protein 62.7 g
Cholesterol 166 mg
Fiber 5.9 g
Net carbs 4.2 g

357. TASTY PORK TACOS

Preparation Time: 15 minutes
Cooking Time: 8 hours
Servings: 8

Ingredients:
- 2 lbs. pork tenderloin
- 2 tsp cayenne pepper
- 24 oz salsa
- 3 tsp garlic powder
- 2 tbsp ground cumin
- 2 tbsp chili powder
- 1 1/2 tsp salt

Directions:

Place pork tenderloin into the slow cooker.

Mix all rest of the ingredients except salsa in a small bowl.

Rub spice mixture over pork tenderloin. Pour salsa on top of pork tenderloin.

Cook within 8 hours, low. Transfer the pork from the slow cooker, and shred using a fork.

Return shredded pork into the slow cooker and stir well with salsa. Serve and enjoy.

Nutrition:

Calories 202
Fat 4.9 g
Carbohydrates 8 g
Sugar 3.1 g
Protein 31.7 g
Cholesterol 83 mg
Fiber 2.4 g

358. STUFFED PEPPERS

Preparation Time: 10 minutes
Cooking Time: 8 hours
Servings: 6

Ingredients:
- 1 cup cauliflower rice
- 1 small red bell peppers
- 18-ounce minced pork, pasture-raised
- 1 teaspoon garlic powder
- 3/4 teaspoon salt
- 1 teaspoon red chili powder

- 1 cup shredded Monterey jack cheese and more for topping
- 2 tablespoons avocado oil
- 1 cup water

Directions:

Separate and discard the stem from each pepper and then scoop out the seeds.

Place the meat in a large bowl, add garlic, salt, and red chili powder, and stir until combined.

Then stir in cauliflower rice and oil until just combine and then stir in cheese.

Fill the blend into each pepper and place them in a 4-quart slow cooker.

Pour water into the bottom of the slow cooker, switch it on, and close it.

Cook peppers for 4 hours at a high heat setting or 8 hours at a low heating and top peppers with additional cheese in the last 10 minutes of cooking time. Serve straight away.

Nutrition:

Calories 270
Fat 18 g
Carbohydrates 4 g
Sugar 3 g
Protein 21 g
Fiber 2 g

359. ONION PORK CHOPS

Preparation Time: 15 minutes
Cooking Time: 6 hours
Servings: 6

Ingredients:

- 2 lbs. pork chops, boneless
- 1/4 tsp garlic powder
- 1 tbsp apple cider vinegar
- 2 tbsp Worcestershire sauce
- 1/3 cup butter, sliced
- 1 large onion, sliced
- 1/8 tsp red pepper flakes
- 1 tbsp olive oil
- 1/4 tsp pepper
- 1/4 tsp salt

Directions:

Heat-up the olive oil in a pan over medium-high heat. Brown pork chops in hot oil from both sides.

Add remaining ingredients except for onion and butter into the slow cooker and stir well.

Place brown pork chops into the slow cooker and top with butter and onion.

Cook within 6 hours, low. Serve and enjoy.

Nutrition:

Calories 611
Fat 50.2 g
Carbohydrates 3.5 g
Sugar 2.1 g
Protein 34.4 g
Cholesterol 157 mg
Fiber 0.6 g
Net carbs 2.9 g

360. CREAMY PORK CHOPS

Preparation Time: 15 minutes
Cooking Time: 4 hours
Servings: 4

Ingredients:

- 4 pork chops, boneless
- 1 cup chicken stock
- 1/2 cup sour cream
- 1 can onion soup

Directions:

Pour chicken broth into the slow cooker. Place pork chops into the slow cooker.

Cook within 3 1/2 hours, low. Once it is done, then open the slow cooker and drain juices from the slow cooker.

Mix the sour cream plus onion soup in a small bowl, and pour over pork chops.

Cook again within 30 minutes, low. Serve and enjoy.

Nutrition:

Calories 354
Fat 27.1 g
Carbohydrates 6.4 g
Sugar 2.3 g
Protein 21.3 g
Cholesterol 81 mg
Fiber 0.5 g

361. SCRUMPTIOUS BAY LEAF PORK ROAST SHOULDER

Preparation Time: 15 minutes
Cooking Time: 8 hours
Servings: 4

Ingredients:

- 3 pounds of whole pork shoulder
- 1 can of Italian diced tomatoes
- 1 diced sweet onion
- 3 chopped cloves of garlic
- 4 tbsp of lard

- 1 cup of water
- 1 bay leaf
- ¼ tsp of ground cloves
- Salt and pepper to taste

Directions:

Put all the items in the slow cooker. Cook for 8 hours on low.

Nutrition:

Carbs: 10 g
Protein: 33 g
Fat: 30 g
Calories: 421

362. DRESSED PORK LEG ROAST

Preparation Time: 15 minutes
Cooking Time: 8 hours
Servings: 14

Ingredients:

- 8 pounds pork leg
- 1 Tbsp butter
- 1 yellow onion, sliced
- 6 garlic cloves, peeled and minced
- 2 Tbsp ground cumin
- 2 Tbsp ground thyme
- 2 Tbsp ground chili
- 1 tsp salt
- 1 tsp fresh ground black pepper
- 1 cup hot water

Directions:

Butter the slow cooker. Slice crisscrosses along the top of the pork leg.

Arrange onion slices and minced garlic along the bottom of the slow cooker.

Place meat on top of vegetables.

In a small bowl, mix the herbs. Rub it all over the pork leg.

Add the water. Cover, cook on high for 8 hours.

Remove and transfer, cover with foil. Let it rest for 1 hour.

Shred the meat and serve.

Nutrition:

Calories: 143
Carbs: 0g
Fat: 3g
Protein: 28g

363. SERIOUSLY DELICIOUS LAMB ROAST

Preparation Time: 15 minutes
Cooking Time: 8 hours
Servings: 8

Ingredients:

- 12 medium radishes, scrubbed, washed, and cut in half
- Salt and pepper to taste
- 1 red onion, diced
- 2 garlic cloves, minced
- 1 lamb joint (approximately 4.5 pounds) at room temperature
- 2 tbsp olive oil
- 1 tsp dry oregano
- 1 tsp dry thyme
- 1 sprig of fresh rosemary
- 4 cups heated broth, your choice

Directions:

Place cut radishes along the bottom of the slow cooker. Season. Add onion and garlic.

Blend the herbs plus olive oil in a small bowl until it forms to paste.

Place the meat on top of the radishes. Knead the paste over the meat.

Heat the stock, pour it around the meat.

Cover, cook on low for 8 hours. Let it rest for 20 minutes. Slice and serve.

Nutrition:

Calories: 206
Carbs: 4g
Fat: 9g
Protein: 32g

364. KASHMIRI LAMB CURRY

Preparation Time: 40 minutes
Cooking Time: 7 hours
Servings: 6

Ingredients:

- ¼ cup unsweetened coconut meat, shredded
- 3 long green fresh chili peppers
- 4 dried red chili peppers
- 1 tsp. garam masala
- 1 tsp. cumin seeds
- 5 cloves of garlic, crushed
- 1-piece ginger root, peeled and grated
- 2-pounds lamb meat
- 2 large onions, sliced
- 3 tomatoes, chopped
- 6 tbsp. vegetable oil
- ½ ground turmeric

- 1 cup plain yogurt
- ¼ cup cilantro, chopped
- 1 cup water
- Pepper and salt to taste

Directions:

Take the chilies, garam masala, cumin seeds, garlic, ginger, tomatoes, and coconut in a blender and pulse until smooth. Set aside.

In a skillet, heat vegetable oil and sauté the onions and lamb meat for 3 minutes.

Transfer the meat mixture to the slow cooker. Pour in chili paste mixture on top of the lamb.

Add the turmeric, yogurt, cilantro, and water—season with pepper and salt.

Cook within 7 hours, low, until tender.

Nutrition:

Calories: 489

Carbohydrates: 3g

Protein: 25g

Fat: 40g

Sugars: 0g

Sodium: 166mg

Fiber: 2.5g

365. TASTY LAMB SHOULDERS

Preparation Time: 15 minutes

Cooking Time: 4 hours

Servings: 4

Ingredients:

- 2 lbs. lamb shoulder
- 1/4 cup beef broth
- 1/4 cup fresh mint
- 1/4 cup onion, chopped
- 1/4 lb. carrots
- 2 tbsp spice rub

Directions:

Pour beef broth into the slow cooker. Rub spice all over the lamb shoulder and place lamb shoulder into the slow cooker.

Add remaining ingredients into the slow cooker—Cook within 4 hours on high.

Shred the meat using a fork. Serve and enjoy.

Nutrition:

Calories 441

Fat 16.8 g

Carbohydrates 4 g

Sugar 1.7 g

Protein 64.5 g

Cholesterol 204 mg

Fiber 1.2 g

Net carbs 2.8 g

366. THYME LAMB CHOPS

Preparation Time: 15 minutes

Cooking Time: 6 hours

Servings: 2

Ingredients:

- 2 lamb shoulder chops, bone-in
- 1/4 cup fresh thyme
- 1 tsp garlic paste
- 1/2 cup red wine
- 1 cup beef broth
- Pepper and salt to taste

Directions:

Put all fixing into the slow cooker, and mix well. Cook within 6 hours, low setting. Serve and enjoy.

Nutrition:

Calories 257

Fat 10.1 g

Carbohydrates 6.4 g

Sugar 0.9 g

Protein 25.1 g

Cholesterol 75 mg

Fiber 2.3 g

367. GARLIC HERBED LAMB CHOPS

Preparation Time: 15 minutes

Cooking Time: 4 hours

Servings: 4

Ingredients:

- 8 lamb loin chops
- 2 garlic cloves, minced
- 1/8 tsp black pepper
- 1/2 tsp garlic powder
- 1/2 tsp dried thyme
- 1 tsp dried oregano
- 1 medium onion, sliced
- 1/4 tsp salt

Directions:

Mix oregano, garlic powder, thyme, pepper, and salt in a small bowl.

Rub herb mixture over the lamb chops.

Place lamb chops into the slow cooker—top lamb chops with garlic and sliced onion.

Cook within 4 hours, low. Serve and enjoy.

Nutrition:

Calories 656

Fat 52.1 g
Carbohydrates 3.7 g
Sugar 1.3 g
Protein 38.5 g
Cholesterol 160 mg
Fiber 0.9 g

368. BARBACOA LAMB

Preparation Time: 25 minutes
Cooking Time: 6 hours
Servings: 12

Ingredients:
- ¼ cup dried mustard
- 5 ½ lbs. leg of lamb - boneless
- 2 tbsp. of each:
- Smoked paprika
- Himalayan salt
- 1 tbsp. of each:
- Chipotle powder
- Dried oregano
- ground cumin
- 1 cup water

Directions:
Combine the paprika, oregano, chipotle powder, cumin, and salt.

Cover the roast with the dried mustard, and sprinkle with the prepared spices. Arrange the lamb in the slow cooker, cover it, and let it marinate in the refrigerator overnight.

In the morning, let the pot come to room temperature. Once you're ready to cook, just add the water to the slow cooker on the high heat setting—Cook for six hours.

When done, remove all except for one cup of the cooking juices, and shred the lamb.

Using the rest of the cooking juices, adjust the seasoning as you desire, and serve.

Nutrition:
Calories 492
Carbs 1.2 g
Fat 35.8 g
Protein 37.5 g

369. LAMB PROVENÇAL

Preparation Time: 15 minutes
Cooking Time: 8 hours
Servings: 4

Ingredients:
- 2 racks lamb, approximately 2 pounds
- 1 tbsp olive oil
- 2 tbsp fresh rosemary, chopped
- 1 tbsp fresh thyme, chopped
- 4 garlic cloves, minced
- 1 tsp dry oregano
- 1 lemon, the zest
- 1 tsp minced fresh ginger
- 1 cup (Good) red wine
- Salt and pepper to taste

Directions:
Preheat the slow cooker on low.

In a pan, heat 1 tbsp olive oil. Brown the meat for 2 minutes per side.

Mix remaining ingredients in a bowl.

Place the lamb in the slow cooker, pour the remaining seasoning over the meat.

Cover, cook on low for 8 hours.

Nutrition:
Calories: 140
Carbs: 3g
Fat: 5g
Protein: 21g

370. GREEK STYLE LAMB SHANKS

Preparation Time: 15 minutes
Cooking Time: 6 hours
Servings: 8

Ingredients:
- 3 tbsp butter
- 4 lamb shanks, approximately 1 pound each
- 2 tbsp olive oil
- 8-10 pearl onions
- 5 garlic cloves, minced
- 2 beef tomatoes, cubed
- ¼ cup of green olives
- 4 bay leaves
- 1 sprig of fresh rosemary
- 1 tsp dry thyme
- 1 tsp ground cumin
- 1 cup fresh spinach
- ¾ cup hot water
- ½ cup red wine, Merlot or Cabernet
- Salt and pepper to taste

Directions:
Liquify the butter in a pan, then cook the shanks on each side.

Remove, then add oil, onions, garlic. Cook for 3-4 minutes. Add tomatoes, olives, spices, then stir well. Put the liquids and return the meat. Boil for 1 minute.

Transfer everything to the slow cooker.

Cover, cook on medium-high for 6 hours.

Nutrition:

Calories: 250

Carbs: 3g

Fat: 16g

Protein: 22g

371. LAMB WITH MINT & GREEN BEANS

Preparation Time: 15 minutes

Cooking Time: 10 hours

Servings: 4

Ingredients:

- ½ tsp salt – Himalayan pink
- Freshly cracked black pepper
- 1 lamb leg – bone-in
- 2 tbsp. lard/ghee/tallow
- 4 garlic cloves
- 6 cup trimmed green beans
- ¼ freshly chopped mint/1-2 tbsp. dried mint

Directions:

Heat-up the slow cooker with a high setting.

Dry the lamb with some paper towels. Sprinkle with pepper and salt. Grease a Dutch oven or similar large pot with the ghee/lard.

Sear the lamb until golden brown and set aside.

Remove the peels from the garlic and mince—dice up the mint. Arrange the seared meat into the slow cooker and give it a shake of the garlic and mint.

Secure the lid and program the cooker on the low-heat function (10 hrs.) or the high-function (6 hrs.).

After about four hours, switch the lamb out of the cooker. Toss in the green beans and return the lamb into the pot.

Let the flavors mingle for about two more hours. The meat should be tender and the beans crispy. Serve and enjoy!

Nutrition:

Calories 525

Carbs 7.6 g

Protein 37.3 g

Fat 36.4 g

372. DELICIOUS BALSAMIC LAMB CHOPS

Preparation Time: 15 minutes

Cooking Time: 6 hours

Servings: 6

Ingredients:

- 3.4 lbs. lamb chops, trimmed off
- 1/2 tsp ground black pepper
- 2 tbsp rosemary
- 2 tbsp balsamic vinegar
- 4 garlic cloves, minced
- 1 large onion, sliced
- 1/2 tsp salt

Directions:

Put the onion to the bottom of the slow cooker.

Place lamb chops on top of onions, add rosemary, vinegar, garlic, pepper, and salt.

Cook within 6 hours on low. Serve and enjoy.

Nutrition:

Calories 496

Fat 19.1 g

Carbohydrates 3.9 g

Sugar 1.1 g

Protein 72.7 g

Cholesterol 231 mg

Fiber 1.1 g

373. SUCCULENT LAMB

Preparation Time: 20 minutes

Cooking Time: 8 hours

Servings: 6

Ingredients:

- ¼ cup olive oil
- 1 (2 lb.) leg of lamb
- 1 tbsp. Stevia
- 2 tbsp. whole grain mustard
- 4 thyme sprigs
- 6-7 mint leaves
- ¾ tsp of each:
- Dried rosemary
- Garlic
- Pepper & salt to taste

Directions:

Cut the string off of the lamb, then slice three slits over the top.

Cover the meat with the oil and the rub (mustard, pepper, salt, and Stevia). Put the rosemary plus garlic into the slits.

Prepare on the low setting for seven hours. Garnish with the mint and thyme—Cook one more hour. Place on a platter and serve.

Nutrition:

Calories 414

Carbs 0.3 g

Fat 35.2 g

Protein 26.7 g

374. TARRAGON LAMB & BEANS

Preparation Time: 15 minutes

Cooking Time: 9 hours

Servings: 12

Ingredients:
- 4 (1 ½ lb.) lamb shanks
- 1 can (19 Oz.) white beans/cannellini- for example
- 1 ½ cup peeled - diced carrot
- 2 thinly sliced garlic cloves
- 1 cup onion
- ¾ cup celery
- 2 tbsp dried tarragon
- ¼ tsp freshly cracked black pepper
- 2 tbsp dried tarragon
- 1 can (28 oz.) diced tomatoes - not drained
- Recommended: 7-quart slow cooker

Directions:

Discard all the fat from the lamb shanks. Pour the beans, cloves of garlic, chopped carrots, chopped celery, and onion into the cooker.

Put the shanks over the beans, and sprinkle with the salt, pepper, and tarragon. Empty the tomatoes over the lamb - including the juices—Cook, the lamb in the slow cooker on high for approximately one hour.

Reduce the temperature to the low setting and cook for nine hours or until the lamb is tender.

Remove, and set it aside. Empty the bean mixture through a colander over a bowl to reserve the liquid. Let the juices stand for five minutes and skim off the fat from the surface.

Return the bean mixture to the liquid in the slow cooker. Strip the lamb bones and throw the bones away. Serve with the bean mixture and enjoy.

Nutrition:

Calories 353

Carbs 12.9 g

Fat 16.3 g

Protein 50.3 g

375. APRICOT PULLED PORK

Preparation Time: 15 minutes

Cooking Time: 11 hours

Servings: 10

Ingredients:
- 3 pounds pork
- 1 cup barbecue sauce
- 6 ounces dried apricots
- 10 pounds apricot spread that does not contain any sugar
- 1 sweet onion

Directions:

Put the pork in the cooker. Add the barbecue, apricots, spread, and onions. Low cook for 11 hours.

Nutrition:

Calories 458

Fat 30 g

Protein 33 g

Carbs 15 g

376. PORK CHOPS WITH CUMIN BUTTER AND GARLIC

Preparation Time: 15 minutes

Cooking Time: 4 hours

Servings: 4

Ingredients:
- 3.5 pounds of pork sirloin chops with the bone
- ½ cup of salsa
- 3 tbsp of butter
- 5 tbsp of lime juice
- ½ tsp of ground cumin
- ¾ tsp of garlic powder
- ¾ tsp of salt
- ¾ tsp of black pepper

Directions:

Combine the spices and season the pork chops.

Melt the butter in a saucepan and brown the pork chops for 3 minutes on each side.

Put it inside the slow cooker and pour the salsa over the top.

Cook on high within 3-4 hours. Divide onto plates and serve.

Nutrition:

Calories: 364

Fat: 17 g

Carbs: 3 g

Fiber: 0 g

Protein: 51 g

377. NEW MEXICO CARNE ADOVADA

Preparation Time: 30 minutes

Cooking Time: 6 hours

Servings: 4

Ingredients:

- 2 tsp apple cider vinegar
- 1 tsp kosher salt
- 1 tsp ground coriander
- 1 tsp ground cumin
- 2 tsp dried Mexican oregano
- 6 garlic, sliced
- 1 onion, sliced
- 2 cups chicken stock
- 6-8 ounces dried chilies, rinsed
- 3 pounds pork shoulder, cubes

Directions:

Put all the items in a pot, except the pork. Simmer it within 30-60 minutes, low.

Remove, then cooldown it within a few minutes.

Puree the batter in batches using a blender.

Put now the pork meat in a baking dish, covering it with the sauce. Chill within 1 to 2 days to marinate, stirring frequently.

Cook it in a slow cooker within 4 to 6 hours, low. Serve warm.

Nutrition:

Calories 120.2
Fat 5.3g
Carb 11.3g
Protein 8.0g

378. SMOKY PORK WITH CABBAGE

Preparation Time: 10 minutes
Cooking Time: 8 hours
Servings: 6

Ingredients:

- lbs pastured pork roast
- 1/3 cup liquid smoke
- 1/2 cabbage head, chopped
- 1 cup water
- 1 tbsp kosher salt

Directions:

Rub pork with kosher salt and place into the slow cooker.

Pour liquid smoke over the pork. Add water.

Cover slow cooker with lid and cook on low for 7 hours.

Remove pork from the slow cooker and add cabbage to the bottom of the slow cooker.

Now place pork on top of the cabbage.

Cover again and cook for 1 hour more.

Shred pork with a fork and serves.

Nutrition:

Calories 484
Fat 21.5 g
Carbohydrates 3.5 g
Sugar 1.9 g
Protein 65.4 g
Cholesterol 195 mg

379. SIMPLE ROASTED PORK SHOULDER

Preparation Time: 10 minutes
Cooking Time: 9 hours
Servings: 8

Ingredients:

- lbs pork shoulder
- 1 tsp garlic powder
- 1/2 cup water
- 1/2 tsp black pepper
- 1/2 tsp sea salt

Directions:

Season pork with garlic powder, pepper, and salt and place in the slow cooker. Add water.

Cover slow cooker with lid and cook on high for 1 hour then turn heat to low and cook for 8 hours.

Remove meat from slow cooker and shred using a fork.

Serve and enjoy.

Nutrition:

Calories 664
Fat 48.5 g
Carbohydrates 0.3 g
Sugar 0.1 g
Protein 52.9 g
Cholesterol 204 mg

380. FLAVORS PORK CHOPS

Preparation Time: 10 minutes
Cooking Time: 4 hours
Servings: 4

Ingredients:

- Pork chops
- 2 garlic cloves, minced
- 1 cup chicken broth
- 1 tbsp poultry seasoning
- 1/4 cup olive oil
- Pepper and salt to taste

Directions:

In a bowl, whisk together olive oil, poultry seasoning, garlic, broth, pepper, and salt.

Pour olive oil mixture into the slow cooker then place pork chops into the slow cooker.

Cover slow cooker with lid and cook on high for 4 hours.

Serve and enjoy.

Nutrition:
Calories 386
Fat 32.9 g
Carbohydrates 2.9 g
Sugar 0.7 g
Protein 19.7 g

381. PORK LOIN WITH PEANUT SAUCE

Preparation Time: 10 minutes
Cooking Time: 8 hours
Servings: 8

Ingredients:
- 2 pounds pork tenderloin
- 2 tbsp olive oil
- 1 tsp salt
- 1 tsp black pepper
- 2 cups cabbage, shredded
- 1 cup chicken stock
- ½ cup peanut butter
- ¼ cup soy sauce
- 1 tbsp rice vinegar
- 1 tbsp crushed red pepper flakes
- 1 tbsp cayenne pepper sauce
- 2 cloves garlic crushed and minced
- ½ cup peanuts, chopped
- 1 tbsp fresh lemongrass, chopped

Directions:
Brush the tenderloin with olive oil and season it with salt and black pepper.

Arrange the tenderloin and cabbage in a slow cooker.

In a bowl, combine the chicken stock, peanut butter, soy sauce, rice vinegar, crushed red pepper flakes, cayenne pepper sauce, and garlic. Whisk them together and pour the sauce into the slow cooker. Stir gently to distribute the sauce.

Sprinkle in the peanuts and lemongrass.

Cover and cook on low for 8 hours.

Nutrition:
Calories 427.4,
Total Fat 25.5 g,
Saturated Fat 4.9 g,
Total Carbs 6.9 g,
Approx. Net Carbs: 5 g,
Dietary Fiber 2.3 g
Sugars 1.1 g,
Protein 40.4 g

382. CREAMY HERBED TENDERLOIN

Preparation Time: 10 minutes
Cooking Time: 6 hours
Servings: 8

Ingredients:
- 2 pounds pork tenderloin
- 2 tbsp olive oil
- 1 tsp salt
- 1 tsp black pepper
- 2 cloves garlic, crushed and minced
- 1 tbsp fresh tarragon, chopped
- 1 tbsp fresh oregano
- ½ cup fresh parsley, chopped
- 4 cups broccoli florets
- 1 cup onion, sliced
- 2 cups heavy cream, warmed
- 1 cup chicken stock

Directions:
Heat the olive oil in a skillet over medium-high heat.

Season the tenderloin with salt and black pepper.

Place the tenderloin in the skillet and brown it on all sides, approximately 5 minutes.

Remove the tenderloin from the heat and season it with garlic, tarragon, oregano, and parsley, using your hands to pat it into the surface of the meat as necessary.

Place the tenderloin in the slow cooker, along with the broccoli and onion.

Combine the heavy cream and chicken stock. Pour the liquid into the slow cooker.

Cover and cook on low for 6 hours, or until the cream has thickened and the pork has cooked through.

Nutrition:
Calories 484.4,
Total Fat 35.1 g,
Saturated Fat 16.7 g,
Total Carbs 5.8 g,
Approx. Net Carbs: 4 g,
Dietary Fiber 1.7 g
Sugars 0.2 g,
Protein 36.2 g

383. CLASSIC SAUSAGE AND PEPPERS

Preparation Time: 10 minutes
Cooking Time: 6 hours
Servings: 8

Ingredients:
- 2 pounds spicy Italian sausage links
- ¼ cup olive oil

- ½ cup dry red wine
- 4 cloves garlic, crushed and minced
- 2 cups green bell peppers, sliced thick
- 1 cup red bell peppers, sliced thick
- 1 cup onion, sliced thick
- 1 tsp salt
- 1 tsp black pepper
- 1 tbsp fresh thyme, chopped
- ½ cup fresh grated Parmesan cheese

Directions:

Heat the olive oil in a skillet over medium-high heat.

Add the sausage links to the skillet and cook until browned on all sides, approximately 5-7 minutes.

Add the red wine to the skillet and cook for 2-3 minutes, until the wine reduces, taking the time to scrape any browned bits off of the bottom of the skillet. Remove the skillet from the heat.

Add the green bell pepper, red bell pepper, onion, garlic, salt, black pepper, and thyme to the slow cooker. Toss to mix.

Add the sausages and any pan sauce.

Cover the slow cooker and cook on low for 6 hours.

Sprinkle with freshly grated Parmesan cheese before serving.

Nutrition:

Calories 393.8,
Total Fat 30.5 g,
Saturated Fat 14.7 g,
Total Carbs 6.5 g,
Approx. Net Carbs: 5 g,
Dietary Fiber 1.1 g
Sugars 2.7 g,
Protein 19.3 g

384. RIBS WITH A KICK

Preparation Time: 10 minutes
Cooking Time: 8 hours
Servings: 8

Ingredients:

- 2 ½ pounds pork spareribs
- ¼ cup apple cider vinegar
- ¼ cup Worcestershire sauce
- 2 tbsp tomato paste
- 1 tsp dark molasses
- 1 tbsp spicy mustard
- 1 tbsp prepared horseradish
- 1 tbsp smoked paprika
- 1 tsp chili powder
- 2 cloves garlic, crushed and minced

Directions:

In a saucepan, combine the apple cider vinegar, Worcestershire sauce, tomato paste, molasses, mustard, horseradish, paprika, chili powder, and garlic.

Mix well and bring the mixture to a boil over medium-high heat. Reduce the heat to low and let the sauce simmer for 15 minutes. Remove it from the heat and allow it to cool slightly.

Cut the ribs into smaller sections and place them in the slow cooker.

Pour the sauce over the ribs and toss to make sure the sauce coats the ribs evenly on all sides.

Cover and cook for 8 hours on low.

Preheat the broiler and line a baking sheet with aluminum foil.

Remove the ribs from the slow cooker and place them on the baking sheet. Place them under the broiler for 3-5 minutes before serving.

Nutrition:

Calories 534.8,
Total Fat 41.9 g,
Saturated Fat 15.6 g,
Total Carbs 2.6 g,
Approx. Net Carbs: 2 g,
Dietary Fiber 0.2 g
Sugars 1.9 g,
Protein 34.5 g

385. SALSA PORK CHOPS

Preparation Time: 10 minutes
Cooking Time: 3 hours
Servings: 8

Ingredients:

- 8 pork chops, bone-in
- 3 tbsp olive oil
- 1 tsp garlic powder
- 1/2 tsp ground cumin
- 1/4 cup fresh lime juice
- 1/2 cup salsa
- Pepper and salt to taste

Directions:

Add all ingredients into the cooking pot and stir well.

Cover slow cooker with lid.

Select slow cook mode and cook on HIGH for 3 hours.

Serve and enjoy.

Nutrition:

Calories 307
Fat 25.2 g
Carbohydrates 1.5 g

Sugar 0.6 g
Protein 18.3 g
Cholesterol 69 mg

386. CURRIED PORK CHOPS

Preparation Time: 10 minutes
Cooking Time: 6 hours
Servings: 8

Ingredients:
- 2 lbs pork chops
- 1 tbsp dried rosemary
- 1/4 cup olive oil
- 1 tbsp ground cumin
- 1 tbsp fennel seeds
- 1 tbsp fresh chives, chopped
- 1 tbsp curry powder
- 1 tbsp dried thyme
- 1 tsp salt

Directions:

In a small bowl, mix cumin, rosemary, 2 tbsp oil, fennel seeds, chives, curry powder, thyme, and salt.

Rub cumin mixture over pork chops.

Place pork chops into the cooking pot.

Pour remaining olive oil over pork chops.

Cover slow cooker with lid.

Select slow cook mode and cook on LOW for 6 hours.

Serve and enjoy.

Nutrition:
Calories 427
Fat 35 g
Carbohydrates 1.7 g
Sugar 0.1 g
Protein 25.9 g
Cholesterol 98 mg

387. POULTRY SEASONED PORK CHOPS

Preparation Time: 10 minutes
Cooking Time: 4 hours
Servings: 4

Ingredients:
- 4 pork chops
- 1 tbsp garlic powder
- 2 garlic cloves, minced
- 1 cup organic chicken broth
- 1 tsp dried basil
- 1 tsp dried oregano
- 1 tbsp poultry seasoning
- 1/4 cup olive oil
- Pepper and salt to taste

Directions:

In a large bowl, whisk together oil, basil, oregano, poultry seasoning, garlic powder, garlic, and broth.

Pour bowl mixture into the cooking pot then place pork chops into the cooking pot.

Cover slow cooker with lid.

Select slow cook mode and cook on HIGH for 4 hours.

Serve and enjoy.

Nutrition:
Calories 387
Fat 33 g
Carbohydrates 3.1 g
Sugar 0.8 g
Protein 19.8 g
Cholesterol 69 mg

388. NO STICK RIBS

Preparation Time: 10 minutes
Cooking Time: 8 hours
Servings: 8

Ingredients:
- 2 ½ pounds pork ribs
- ¼ cup olive oil
- 1 tsp salt
- 1 tsp black pepper
- 1 tsp chili powder
- 1 tsp coriander
- 1 cup chicken stock

Directions:

Brush the ribs with olive oil and season them with salt, black pepper, chili powder, and coriander.

Cut the ribs into smaller sections, if desired, and place them in the slow cooker.

Add the chicken stock.

Cover and cook on low for 8 hours.

Nutrition:
Calories 570.4,
Total Fat 47.2 g,
Saturated Fat 16.4 g,
Total Carbs 0.1 g,
Approx. Net Carbs: 0 g,
Dietary Fiber 0.0 g
Sugars 0.1 g,
Protein 34.5 g

389. MACADAMIA CRUSTED PORK STEAKS

Preparation Time: 10 minutes

Cooking Time: 6 hours

Servings: 4

Ingredients:
- 1-pound boneless pork steaks
- 1 tsp allspice
- ½ tsp nutmeg
- ½ tsp ground ginger
- ½ tsp cayenne powder
- ½ tsp thyme
- ¼ cup buttermilk
- ½ cup macadamia nuts, chopped
- ¼ cup unsweetened shredded coconut
- 2 tbsp coconut oil
- 1 tbsp jalapeño pepper, diced
- ½ cup chicken stock
- 1 tbsp lime juice
- 6 cups fresh spinach

Directions:

In a bowl, combine the allspice, nutmeg, ginger, cayenne powder, thyme, and buttermilk. Whisk together well.

Place the pork chops in the bowl and cover them with the buttermilk mixture. Allow them to saturate for 15 minutes.

In another bowl, combine the macadamia nuts and coconut.

Remove each pork chop and coat it on both sides with the crushed macadamia nuts and coconut.

Heat the coconut oil in a skillet over medium heat.

Add the pork chops and brown for approximately 2 minutes per side.

Place the spinach, jalapeño pepper, chicken stock, and lime juice in the slow cooker and stir gently to mix.

Add the pork steaks, cover, and cook on low for 5 ½ hours.

Nutrition:

Calories 361.6,

Total Fat 27.4 g,

Saturated Fat 12.4 g,

Total Carbs 5.8 g,

Approx. Net Carbs: 3 g,

Dietary Fiber 2.9 g

Sugars 2.1 g,

Protein 24.5 g

390. FETA MEATBALLS

Preparation Time: 10 minutes

Cooking Time: 6 hours

Servings: 8

Ingredients:
- 1 pound ground pork
- 1 pound ground beef
- 1 cup summer squash, shredded
- ½ cup celery, diced
- ½ cup onion, diced
- 1 cup feta cheese
- 2 eggs
- 1 tsp salt
- 1 tsp black pepper
- 1 tsp oregano
- 1 tsp thyme
- 1 tsp garlic powder
- 2 tbsp olive oil
- 1 cup chicken stock
- 1 cup tomatoes, chopped
- 1 tbsp capers
- ¼ cup fresh basil

Directions:

In a large bowl, combine the ground pork, ground beef, summer squash, celery, onion, feta cheese, and eggs. Mix well.

Season the mixture with salt, black pepper, oregano, thyme, and garlic powder.

Once the mixture has been seasoned, take large spoonful's of the mixture and form them into golf ball-sized meatballs.

Heat the olive oil in a skillet over medium heat.

Add the meatballs to the skillet and brown on all sides for approximately 5 minutes.

Transfer the meatballs from the skillet into a slow cooker.

In a blender, combine the chicken stock, tomatoes, capers, and basil. Blend until smooth and then pour the sauce into the slow cooker.

Cover and cook on low for 6 hours.

Nutrition:

Calories 454.8,

Total Fat 35.7 g,

Saturated Fat 14.3 g,

Total Carbs 3.6 g,

Approx. Net Carbs: 3 g,

Dietary Fiber 0.7 g

Sugars 0.5 g,

Protein 28.9 g

391. LEMON LAMB AND ASPARAGUS

Preparation Time: 10 minutes

Cooking Time: 6 hours

Servings: 6

Ingredients:
- 2 pounds lamb stew meat
- ¼ cup butter, melted
- 1 tsp salt
- 1 tsp black pepper
- 2 tsp marjoram
- 1 tsp caraway seed, ground
- 2 cloves garlic, crushed and minced
- 1 cup onion, chopped
- 4 cups asparagus spears, cut
- 1 cup chicken stock
- 1 cup lemon slices

Directions:

Pour the melted butter into a slow cooker.

Season the meat with salt, black pepper, marjoram, and caraway seed.

Add the stew meat to the slow cooker, along with the garlic, onion, and asparagus, and mix.

Pour the chicken stock into the slow cooker and cover the contents with lemon slices.

Cover and cook on low for 6 hours.

Nutrition:

Calories 306.5,

Total Fat 16.0 g,

Saturated Fat 7.9 g,

Total Carbs 8.4 g,

Approx. Net Carbs: 5 g,

Dietary Fiber 3.2 g

Sugars 0.2 g,

Protein 33.4 g

392. LAMB OF ITALY WITH BRUSSELS SPROUTS

Preparation Time: 10 minutes

Cooking Time: 8 hours

Servings: 6

Ingredients:
- 2 pounds lamb stew meat
- 1 tsp salt
- 1 tsp black pepper
- ¼ cup olive oil
- 1 cup onion, sliced
- 2 cups Brussels sprouts, halved
- 2 cups tomatoes, chopped
- 3 cloves garlic, crushed and minced
- ¼ cup fresh basil, chopped
- ¼ cup fresh parsley, chopped
- 1 tbsp fresh thyme
- ½ cup water
- ¼ cup butter, cubed

Directions:

Season the lamb meat with salt and black pepper.

Heat the olive oil in a skillet over medium heat. Add the lamb to the skillet and cook until browned.

Place the onions and Brussels sprouts in the slow cooker, followed by the lamb.

In a bowl, combine the tomatoes with the garlic, basil, parsley, and thyme. Toss to mix.

Add the tomato mixture to the slow cooker.

Pour in the water and top the contents with cubed butter.

Cover and cook on low for 8 hours.

Nutrition:

Calories 365.9,

Total Fat 23.0 g,

Saturated Fat 8.8 g,

Total Carbs 7.7 g,

Approx. Net Carbs: 5 g,

Dietary Fiber 2.3 g

Sugars 0.6,

Protein 32.4 g

393. ASIAN LAMB

Preparation Time: 10 minutes

Cooking Time: 4 hours

Servings: 6

Ingredients:
- 3 lbs lamb shoulder
- 1/4 cup rice wine vinegar
- 1 tbsp garlic, minced
- 1 tbsp olive oil
- 1/4 cup Stevia
- 1/4 cup hoisin sauce
- 1/2 cup soy sauce

Directions:

Add oil into the cooking pot and set slow cooker on sauté mode.

Add lamb shoulder into the cooking pot and sauté until brown from all the sides.

Mix remaining ingredients and pour over meat.

Cover slow cooker with lid.

Select slow cook mode and cook on HIGH for 2 hours.

Turn lamb, cover, and cook on HIGH for 2 hours more.

Serve and enjoy.

Nutrition:

Calories 508

Fat 19.3 g

Carbohydrates 12.7 g
Sugar 9.1 g
Protein 65.5 g
Cholesterol 204 mg

394. MOROCCAN LAMB

Preparation Time: 10 minutes
Cooking Time: 4 hours
Servings: 8

Ingredients:
- 2 lbs lamb chops
- 1 cup beef stock
- 1/2 cup dried apricots, chopped
- 1 cup yogurt
- 2 tbsp almond flour
- 14 oz can tomato, crushed
- 14 oz can chickpeas, rinsed & drained
- 1 carrot, chopped
- 1 onion, sliced
- 1 tsp Stevia
- 1 tsp turmeric
- 1 tsp cinnamon
- 1 tsp ground ginger
- 1 tsp ground coriander
- 1 tsp ground cumin
- 1 tsp salt

Directions:
In a bowl, mix stock and spices.
Add lamb chops and remaining ingredients into the cooking pot.
Pour stock mixture over lamb chops.
Cover slow cooker with lid.
Select slow cook mode and cook on HIGH for 4 hours.
Serve and enjoy.

Nutrition:
Calories 330
Fat 9.5 g
Carbohydrates 21.6 g
Sugar 6.1 g
Protein 37.5 g
Cholesterol 104 mg

395. MOROCCAN LAMB STEW

Preparation Time: 10 minutes
Cooking Time: 8 hours
Servings: 6

Ingredients:
- 2 lbs lamb shoulder, cut into chunks
- 2 tsp thyme
- 1/2 cup beef stock
- 14 oz can tomato, chopped
- 2 tbsp Stevia
- 2 garlic cloves, minced
- 1 onion, sliced
- 1 tbsp olive oil
- Pepper & Salt to taste

Directions:
Add all ingredients into the cooking pot and stir well.
Cover slow cooker with lid.
Select slow cook mode and cook on LOW for 8 hours.
Stir well and serve.

Nutrition:
Calories 348
Fat 13.5 g
Carbohydrates 11.4 g
Sugar 8.8 g
Protein 43.6 g
Cholesterol 136 mg

BEEF

396. SLOW COOKER BEEF ROAST

Preparation Time: 20 minutes

Cooking Time: 10 hours

Servings: 6

Ingredients:
- 2-pounds beef chuck roast, trimmed of excess fat
- 1 ½ tsp. salt
- ¾ tsp. black pepper
- 2 tbsp. fresh basil, chopped
- 4 cloves of garlic, minced
- 2 bay leaves
- 1 large yellow onion, chopped
- 2 cup beef stock

Directions:

Pat dries the beef roast with a paper towel and rub with salt, pepper, and chopped basil.

Take inside the slow cooker and spread the onion, garlic, and bay leaves.

Pour over the beef stock, then cook on low within 10 hours until tender.

Nutrition:

Calories: 234

Carbohydrates: 2.4g

Protein: 33.1g

Fat: 10.3g

Sugars: 0.9 g

Sodium: 758.2mg

Fiber: 0.5g

397. BEEF AND CABBAGE ROAST

Preparation Time: 15 minutes

Cooking Time: 8 hours

Servings: 10

Ingredients:
- 1 red onion, quartered
- 2 garlic cloves, minced
- 2-3 stocks celery, diced (approximately 1 cup)
- 4-6 dry pimento berries
- 2 bay leaves
- 5.5 pounds beef brisket (two pieces)

- 1 tsp chili powder
- 1 tsp ground cumin
- 2 cups broth, beef + 2 cups hot water
- Salt and pepper to taste
- 1 medium cabbage (approximately 2.2 pounds), cut in half, then quartered

Directions:

Add all ingredients, except cabbage, to the slow cooker in order of the list.

Cover, cook on low for 7 hours.

Uncover, add the cabbage on top of the stew. Re-cover, cook for 1 additional hour.

Nutrition:

Calories: 150

Carbs: 8g

Fat: 3g

Protein: 22g

398. COFFEE- BRAISED BRISKET

Preparation Time: 15 minutes

Cooking Time: 10 hours

Servings: 4

Ingredients:

- 1/2 tbsp of balsamic vinegar
- 4 cups of strong brewed coffee
- 1 large sliced onion
- 1/2 (3-pound) boneless beef brisket
- 1/2 tsp of salt
- 1/2 tsp of ground black pepper
- 1/2 tsp of garlic powder
- 1/2 tbsp of paprika
- 1/2 tbsp of ground coffee
- 1 tbsp of Stevia

Directions:

Mix Stevia, paprika, garlic powder, pepper, salt, and ground coffee.

Remove the fat from the brisket, put the batter all over its surface.

Put the meat in the Crock-Pot, then the onions. Mix in the vinegar plus coffee, then pour inside.

Cover and now cook on low heat for 10 hours or on high heat setting for 5 hours.

Serve the onion mixture with the meat.

Nutrition:

Calories 229

Proteins 32g

Carbs 8g

Fat 8g

399. BEEF SHOULDER IN BBQ SAUCE

Preparation Time: 15 minutes

Cooking Time: 10 hours

Servings: 12

Ingredients:

- 8 pounds beef shoulder, whole
- 1 tbsp butter
- 1 yellow onion, diced
- 1 garlic bulb, peeled and minced
- 4 tbsp red wine vinegar
- 2 tbsp Worcestershire sauce
- 4 tbsp Swerve (or a suitable substitute)
- 1 tbsp mustard
- 1 tsp salt
- 1 tsp fresh ground black pepper

Directions:

In a bowl, mix seasoning. Set aside.

Liquify the butter in a pan, add the meat. Brown on all sides. Transfer to slow cooker.

Fry the onion within 2-3 minutes in the same pan, then pour over the meat.

Pour in the seasoning. Cover, cook on low for 10 hours.

Remove, cover it with foil, then let it rest for 1 hour.

Turn the slow cooker on high, reduce the remaining liquid by half and serve with the shredded beef.

Nutrition:

Calories: 140

Carbs: 5g

Fat: 9g

Protein: 8g

400. HOMEMADE MEATBALLS AND SPAGHETTI SQUASH

Preparation Time: 15 minutes

Cooking Time: 8 hours

Servings: 8

Ingredients:

- 1 medium-sized spaghetti squash, washed, halved
- 1 Tbsp butter, to grease the slow cooker
- 2.2 pounds lean ground beef
- 2 garlic cloves
- 1 red onion, chopped
- ½ cup almond flour
- 2 tbsp of dry Parmesan cheese
- 1 egg, beaten
- 1 tsp ground cumin
- Salt and pepper to taste

- 4 cans diced Italian tomatoes
- 1 small can tomato paste, 28 ounces
- 1 cup hot water
- 1 red onion, chopped
- ¼ cup chopped parsley
- ½ tsp each, salt and sugar (optional)
- 1 bay leaf

Directions:

Grease the slow cooker, place both squash halves open side down in the slow cooker.

Mix meatball ingredients in a bowl—form approximately 20 small meatballs.

In a pan, heat the olive oil. Fry the meatballs within 2-3 minutes per side. Transfer to the slow cooker.

In the small bowl, add the tomatoes, tomato paste, oil, water, onion, and parsley, add ½ tsp each of salt and sugar. Mix well.

Pour the marinara sauce in the slow cooker around the squash halves.

Cover, cook on low for 8 hours.

Nutrition:

Calories: 235

Carbs: 12g

Fat: 14g

Protein: 15g

401. BACON CHEESEBURGER CASSEROLE

Preparation Time: 50 minutes

Cooking Time: 4 hours

Servings: 8

Ingredients:

- 2-pounds ground beef
- ½ onion, sliced thinly
- ½ tsp. salt
- ½ tsp. black pepper
- 1 15-ounce can cream of mushroom soup
- 1 15-ounce can cheddar cheese soup
- Pounds bacon, cooked and crumbled
- 2 cups cheddar cheese, grated

Directions:

Cook the ground beef plus the onions in a skillet over medium heat. Season with pepper and salt to taste.

Take the beef in the slow cooker and add the cream of mushroom soup and cheese soup.

Pour in the bacon and half of the cheddar cheese. Give a stir. Cook on low for 4 hours.

Put the remaining cheese on top an hour before it is done cooking.

Nutrition:

Calories: 322

Carbohydrates: 2g

Protein: 36g

Fat: 21g

Sugars: 0g

Sodium: 271mg

Fiber: 1.3g

402. BBQ BEEF BURRITOS

Preparation Time: 15 minutes

Cooking Time: 8 hours

Servings: 4

Ingredients:

- 2 lb. top sirloin steak
- ½ t. black pepper
- 1 tsp of each:
- Ground chipotle pepper – optional
- Cinnamon
- 2 tsp of each:
- Sea salt
- Garlic powder
- 4 minced garlic cloves
- ½ white onion
- 2 bay leaves
- 1 cup of each:
- Chicken broth
- BBQ sauce – your favorite

Assembly

Ingredients:

- 1 ½ cup coleslaw mix
- 8 low-carb wraps
- ½ c. mayonnaise

Directions:

Pat the steak dry using some paper towels. Slice using a sharp knife along the sides. Combine the seasonings and sprinkle on the meat.

Chop the onion, then the garlic, and put to the slow cooker. Pour in the broth. Add the steak and bay leaf. Secure the lid and cook eight hours on the low setting

When done, remove the steak and drain the juices. Arrange the beef, garlic, and onion back into the cooker and shred. Put in the barbecue sauce, then stir well.

Assemble the burritos using the beef fixings, a bit of slaw, and a dab of mayo.

Nutrition:

Calories 750

Carbs 14 g

Fat 48 g

Protein 58 g

403. BEEF RIBS

Preparation Time: 30 minutes
Cooking Time: 6 hours
Servings: 4

Ingredients:
- 3 lb. beef back ribs
- 1 tbsp. of each:
- Sesame oil
- Rice vinegar
- Hot sauce
- Garlic powder
- Kosher salt
- ½ tsp black pepper
- 1 tbsp. cauliflower starch/ cornstarch
- ¼ cup light soy sauce or 1/8 cup coconut aminos

Directions:

Cut and add the ribs to fit in the slow cooker. Whisk the rest of the ingredients together but omit the cornstarch for now. Put the mixture over the ribs, making sure the sauce covers all sides.

Use the low setting and cook for six hours. It will be fall off the bone tender.

Prepare the oven to 200°F. Transfer the prepared ribs to a baking pan, and cover.

Strain the liquid into a saucepan. Prepare on the high setting and whisk in the cornstarch with a little bit of cold water.

Continue cooking - whisking often - just until the sauce has thickened into a glaze - usually about five to ten minutes.

Brush the sauce glaze over the ribs and serve.

Nutrition:

Calories 342
Fat 27 g
Carbs 7 g
Protein 23 g

404. BRAISED OXTAILS

Preparation Time: 20 minutes
Cooking Time: 7 hours
Servings: 3

Ingredients:
- 2 cups beef broth
- 2 lbs. (bone-in) oxtails
- 1 tbsp. fish sauce
- 1/3 cup butter
- 2 tbsp. soy sauce
- 1 tsp of each:
- Minced garlic
- Onion powder
- Dried thyme
- 3 tbsp. tomato paste
- Pepper & salt to taste
- ½ tbsp guar gum
- ½ tbsp ground ginger

Directions:

On the stovetop, warm up the broth and combine it with the fish sauce, soy sauce, butter, and tomato paste. Pour into the cooker along with the meat and flavor with the spices.

Prepare for six to seven hours on the low setting. Remove the oxtail and set it aside on towels to drain.

Add the guar gum to the rest of the liquids and blend to thicken using an immersion blender.

Enjoy with your favorite side dish.

Nutrition:

Calories 433
Carbs 3.2 g
Fat 29.7 g
Protein 28.3 g

405. BRISKET & ONIONS

Preparation Time: 30 minutes
Cooking Time: 8 hours
Servings: 6

Ingredients:
- 1 ½ lb. red/yellow onions -2 larges
- 1 tbsp. olive oil
- 3 ½ lb. beef brisket
- 6 minced garlic cloves
- Coarse kosher salt
- Freshly cracked black pepper
- 1 tbsp. soy sauce
- 2 cups beef broth
- 2 tbsp. Worcestershire sauce – homemade

Directions:

Prepare a cast iron skillet with the oil (med heat). Slice the onions into half-moons and add them to the pan. Sauté about 20 minutes until they are lightly caramelized.

Pat the brisket dry and season with pepper and salt. Sear until it's crusty brown. Add to the cooker with the fat side up.

Add the garlic over the meat along with the lightly browned onions.

Prepare the broth (soy, Worcestershire, and broth). Pour it into the slow cooker. Secure the lid and prepare for six to eight hours on the low heat function.

Set the cooker to warm when done and let it rest for at least 20 minutes or place it in a warm oven in a baking dish. Slice and serve.

Nutrition:

Calories 127

Fat 61.3 g

Carbs 4.7 g

Protein 48 g

406. ITALIAN RAGU

Preparation Time: 15 minutes

Cooking Time: 8 hours

Servings: 2

Ingredients:

- ¼ of each - diced:
- Carrot
- Rib of celery
- Onion
- 1 minced garlic clove
- ½ lb. top-round lean beef
- 6 tbsp. (3 oz.) of each:
- Diced tomatoes
- Crushed tomatoes
- 2 ½ tbsp beef broth (+) ¼ c.
- 1 ¼ tbsp of each:
- Chopped fresh thyme
- Minced fresh rosemary
- 1 bay leaf
- Pepper & salt to taste

Directions:

Arrange the prepared celery, onion, garlic, and carrots into the slow cooker. Trim away the fat, and toss in the meat. Sprinkle with salt and pepper

Stir in the rest of the fixings. Prepare on the low setting for six to eight hours.

Enjoy any way you choose.

Nutrition:

Calories 224

Carbs 6 g

Protein 27 g

Fat 9 g

407. POT ROAST BEEF BRISKET

Preparation Time: 15 minutes

Cooking Time: 12 hours

Servings: 10

Ingredients:

- 6.6 pounds beef brisket, whole
- 2 tbsp olive oil
- 2 tbsp apple cider vinegar
- 1 tsp dry oregano
- 1 tsp dry thyme
- 1 tsp dried rosemary
- 2 tbsp paprika
- 1 tsp Cayenne pepper
- 1 tbsp salt
- 1 tsp fresh ground black pepper

Directions:

In a bowl, mix dry seasoning, add olive oil, apple cider vinegar.

Place the meat in the slow cooker, generously coat with seasoning mix.

Cover, cook on low for 12 hours.

Remove the brisket, place it on a pan. Sear it under the broiler for 2-4 minutes, observe it, so the meat doesn't burn.

Wrap it using a foil, then let it rest for 1 hour. Slice and serve.

Nutrition:

Calories: 280

Carbs: 4g

Fat: 20g

Protein: 20g

408. AMAZING SPICED BEEF EYE SLOW COOKED

Preparation Time: 15 minutes

Cooking Time: 8 hours

Servings: 4

Ingredients:

- 3 lb. lean ground beef eye roast
- 2 tbsp Worcestershire sauce
- 4 tbsp fresh lime juice
- 1 ½ cup onion, diced
- 1 cup red bell pepper, diced
- 3 garlic cloves, minced
- 3 serrano chilies, seeded, minced
- Salt and pepper to taste
- ½ cup beef broth, non-fat
- 1 cup canned diced tomatoes
- ½ tsp dried oregano

Directions:

Massage the beef roast with salt plus pepper and put it in the slow cooker. Whisk the rest of the ingredients together and pour over the beef.

Cook for 8 hours on LOW. Shred the beef using 2 forks.

Nutrition:
Calories: 247
Fats: 23 g
Carbs: 5 g
Fiber: 1 g
Protein: 40 g

409. BEEF STROGANOFF

Preparation Time: 10 minutes
Cooking Time: 8 hours
Servings: 2

Ingredients:
- 1/2 lb. beef stew meat
- 1/2 cup sour cream
- 2.5 oz mushrooms, sliced
- Oz mushroom soup
- 1 medium onion, chopped
- Pepper and salt to taste

Directions:
Add all ingredients except sour cream into the slow cooker and mix well.
Cover slow cooker with lid and cook on low for 8 hours.
Add sour cream and stir well.
Serve and enjoy.

Nutrition:
Calories 471
Fat 25.3 g
Carbohydrates 8.6 g
Sugar 3.1 g
Protein 48.9 g
Cholesterol 109 mg

410. CHILI LIME BEEF

Preparation Time: 10 minutes
Cooking Time: 6 hours
Servings: 4

Ingredients:
- 1 lb. beef chuck roast
- 1 tsp chili powder
- 2 cups lemon-lime soda
- 1 fresh lime juice
- 1 garlic clove, crushed
- 1/2 tsp salt

Directions:
Place beef chuck roast into the slow cooker.
Season roast with garlic, chili powder, and salt.
Pour lemon-lime soda over the roast.
Cover slow cooker with lid and cook on low for 6 hours.
Shred the meat using a fork.
Add lime juice over shredded roast and serve.

Nutrition:
Calories 355
Fat 16.8 g
Carbohydrates 14 g
Sugar 11.3 g
Protein 35.5 g
Cholesterol 120 mg

411. BEEF IN SAUCE

Preparation Time: 10 minutes
Cooking Time: 9 hours
Servings: 4

Ingredients:
- 1-pound beef stew meat, chopped
- 1 tsp g masala
- 1 cup of water
- 1 tbsp almond flour
- 1 tsp garlic powder
- 1 onion, diced

Directions:
Whisk flour with water until smooth and pour the liquid into the slow cooker.
Add g masala and beef stew meat.
After this, add onion and garlic powder.
Close the lid and cook the meat on low for 9 hours.
Serve the cooked beef with thick gravy from the slow cooker.

Nutrition:
Calories 231
Protein 35g
Carbohydrates 4.6g
Fat 7.1g
Fiber 0.7g
Cholesterol 101mg
Sodium 79mg
Potassium 507mg

412. BEEF WITH GREENS

Preparation Time: 15 minutes
Cooking Time: 8 hours
Servings: 3

Ingredients:
- 1 cup fresh spinach, chopped
- Oz. beef stew meat, cubed
- 1 cup Swiss chard, chopped
- 2 cups of water

- 1 tsp olive oil
- 1 tsp dried rosemary

Directions:

Heat olive oil in the skillet.

Add beef and roast it for 1 minute per side.

Then transfer the meat to the slow cooker.

Add Swiss chard, spinach, water, and rosemary.

Close the lid and cook the meal on Low for 8 hours.

Nutrition:

177 calories,

26.3g protein,

1.1g carbohydrates,

7g fat,

0.6g fiber,

76mg cholesterol,

95mg sodium,

449mg potassium

413. BEEF AND SCALLIONS BOWL

Preparation Time: 10 minutes

Cooking Time: 5 hours

Servings: 4

Ingredients:

- 1 tsp chili powder
- 2 oz. scallions, chopped
- 1-pound beef stew meat, cubed
- 1 cup corn kernels, frozen
- 1 cup of water
- 2 tbsp tomato paste
- 1 tsp minced garlic

Directions:

Mix water with tomato paste and pour the liquid into the slow cooker.

Add chili powder, beef, corn kernels, and minced garlic.

Close the lid and cook the meal on high for 5 hours.

When the meal is cooked, transfer the mixture to the bowls and top with scallions.

Nutrition:

258 calories,

36.4g protein,

0.4g carbohydrates,

7.7g fat,

2g fiber,

101mg cholesterol,

99mg sodium,

697mg potassium

414. BALSAMIC BEEF

Preparation Time: 15 minutes

Cooking Time: 9 hours

Servings: 4

Ingredients:

- 1 pound beef stew meat, cubed
- 1 tsp cayenne pepper
- 1 tbsp balsamic vinegar
- ½ cup of water
- 2 tbsp butter

Directions:

Toss the butter in the skillet and melt it.

Then add meat and roast it for 2 minutes per side on medium heat.

Transfer the meat with butter to the slow cooker.

Add balsamic vinegar, cayenne pepper, and water.

Close the lid and cook the meal on Low for 9 hours.

Nutrition:

266 calories,

34.5g protein,

0.4g carbohydrates,

12.9g fat,

0.1g fiber,

117mg cholesterol,

117mg sodium,

479mg potassium

415. BALSAMIC BEEF ROAST

Preparation Time: 15 minutes

Cooking Time: 4 hours

Servings: 10

Ingredients:

- 1 boneless (3 lb.) chuck roast
- 1 tbsp Kosher salt
- 1 tbsp Black ground pepper
- 1 tbsp Garlic powder
- 1/4 cup balsamic vinegar
- 1/2 cup chopped onion
- 2 cup water
- 1/4 tsp xanthan gum
- Fresh parsley

Directions:

Season the chuck roast with garlic powder, pepper, and salt over the whole surface.

Use a large skillet to sear the roast until browned.

Deglaze the base of the pot by applying balsamic vinegar.

Cook one minute and add to the slow cooker.

Whisk in the onion and add the water. Once it starts to boil, close the lid and continue cooking on low for three to four hours.

Take the meat out and place it in a large bowl. Break it up carefully into large chunks. Remove all fat.

Whisk the xanthan gum into the broth, and add it back to the slow cooker. Serve and enjoy!

Nutrition:

393 calories,

30g protein,

3g carbohydrates,

15.5g fat,

0.3g fiber,

91mg sodium,

416. ONION BEEF

Preparation Time: 10 minutes

Cooking Time: 5.5 hours

Servings: 14

Ingredients:

- 4-pounds beef sirloin, sliced
- 2 cups white onion, chopped
- 2 cups of water
- ½ cup butter
- 1 tsp ground black pepper
- 1 tsp salt
- 1 bay leaf

Directions:

Mix beef sirloin with salt and ground black pepper and transfer to the slow cooker.

Add butter, water, onion, and bay leaf.

Close the lid and cook the meat on High for 5.5 hours.

Nutrition:

306 calories,

39.6g protein,

1.7g carbohydrates,

14.7g fat,

0.4g fiber,

133mg cholesterol,

301mg sodium,

551mg potassium

417. CILANTRO BEEF

Preparation Time: 10 minutes

Cooking Time: 4.5 hours

Servings: 4

Ingredients:

- 1-pound beef loin, roughly chopped
- ¼ cup apple cider vinegar
- 1 tbsp dried cilantro
- ½ tsp dried basil
- 1 cup of water
- 1 tsp tomato paste

Directions:

Mix meat with tomato paste, dried cilantro, and basil.

Then transfer it to the slow cooker.

Add apple cider vinegar and water.

Cook the cilantro beef for 4.5 hours on High.

Nutrition:

211 calories,

30.4g protein,

0.4g carbohydrates,

9.5g fat,

0.1g fiber,

81mg cholesterol,

66mg sodium,

412mg potassium

418. BEEF AND ARTICHOKES BOWLS

Preparation Time: 10 minutes

Cooking Time: 7 hours

Servings: 2

Ingredients:

- Oz. beef sirloin, chopped
- ½ tsp cayenne pepper
- ½ tsp white pepper
- Artichoke hearts, chopped
- 1 cup of water
- 1 tsp salt

Directions:

Mix meat with white pepper and cayenne pepper. Transfer it to the slow cooker bowl.

Add salt, artichoke hearts, and water.

Close the lid and cook the meal on Low for 7 hours.

Nutrition:

313 calories,

36.5g protein,

4.6g carbohydrates,

5.9g fat,

17.8g fiber,

76mg cholesterol,

1527mg sodium,

1559mg potassium

419. MUSTARD BEEF

Preparation Time: 10 minutes

Cooking Time: 8 hours
Servings: 4

Ingredients:
- 1-pound beef sirloin, chopped
- 1 tbsp capers, drained
- 1 cup of water
- 2 tbsp mustard
- 1 tbsp coconut oil

Directions:
Mix meat with mustard and leave for 10 minutes to marinate.
Then melt the coconut oil in the skillet.
Add meat and roast it for 1 minute per side on high heat.
After this, transfer the meat to the slow cooker.
Add water and capers.
Cook the meal on Low for 8 hours.

Nutrition:
267 calories,
35.9g protein,
2.1g carbohydrates,
12.1g fat,
0.9g fiber,
101mg cholesterol,
140mg sodium,
496mg potassium

420. BEEF MASALA

Preparation Time: 15 minutes
Cooking Time: 9 hours
Servings: 6

Ingredients:
- 1-pound beef sirloin, sliced
- 1 tsp g masala
- 2 tbsp lemon juice
- 1 tsp ground paprika
- ½ cup of coconut milk
- 1 tsp dried mint

Directions:
In the bowl mix coconut milk with dried mint, ground paprika, lemon juice, and g masala.
Then add beef sirloin and mix the mixture. Leave it for at least 10 minutes to marinate.
Then transfer the mixture to the slow cooker.
Cook it on Low for 9 hours.

Nutrition:
283 calories,
35.3g protein,
2.2g carbohydrates,
14.4g fat,
0.9g fiber,
101mg cholesterol,
82mg sodium,
560mg potassium

421. BEEF SAUTÉ WITH ENDIVES

Preparation Time: 10 minutes
Cooking Time: 8 hours
Servings: 4

Ingredients:
- 1-pound beef sirloin, chopped
- oz. endives, roughly chopped
- 1 tsp peppercorns
- 1 carrot, diced
- 1 onion, sliced
- 1 cup of water
- ½ cup tomato juice

Directions:
Mix beef with onion, carrot, and peppercorns.
Place the mixture in the slow cooker.
Add water and tomato juice.
Then close the lid and cook it on High for 5 hours.
After this, add endives and cook the meal for 3 hours on Low.

Nutrition:
238 calories,
35.4g protein,
6.4g carbohydrates,
7.2g fat,
1.9g fiber,
101mg cholesterol,
175mg sodium,
689mg potassium

422. SWEET BEEF

Preparation Time: 10 minutes
Cooking Time: 5 hours
Servings: 4

Ingredients:
- 1-pound beef roast, sliced
- 1 tbsp Stevia
- 2 tbsp lemon juice
- 1 tsp dried oregano
- 1 cup of water

Directions:
Mix water with Stevia, lemon juice, and dried oregano.

Then pour the liquid into the slow cooker.

Add beef roast and close the lid.

Cook the meal on High for 5 hours.

Nutrition:

227 calories,

34.5g protein,

3.8g carbohydrates,

7.2g fat,

0.2g fiber,

101mg cholesterol,

78mg sodium,

483mg potassium

423.THYME BEEF

Preparation Time: 15 minutes

Cooking Time: 5 hours

Servings: 2

Ingredients:

- Oz. beef sirloin, chopped
- 1 tbsp dried thyme
- 1 tbsp olive oil
- ½ cup of water
- 1 tsp salt

Directions:

Preheat the skillet well.

Then mix beef with dried thyme and olive oil.

Put the meat in the hot skillet and roast for 2 minutes per side on high heat.

Then transfer the meat to the slow cooker.

Add salt and water.

Cook the meal on High for 5 hours.

Nutrition:

274 calories,

34.5g protein

, 0.9g carbohydrates,

14.2g fat,

0.5g fiber

, 101mg cholesterol,

1240mg sodium,

469mg potassium

424.HOT BEEF

Preparation Time: 15 minutes

Cooking Time: 8 hours

Servings: 4

Ingredients:

- 1-pound beef sirloin, chopped
- 2 tbsp hot sauce
- 1 tbsp olive oil
- ½ cup of water

Directions:

In the shallow bowl mix hot sauce with olive oil.

Then mix beef sirloin with hot sauce mixture and leave for 10 minutes to marinate.

Put the marinated beef in the slow cooker.

Add water and close the lid.

Cook the meal on Low for 8 hours.

Nutrition:

241 calories,

34.4g protein,

0.1g carbohydrates,

10.6g fat,

0g fiber,

101mg cholesterol,

266mg sodium,

467mg potassium

425.BEEF CHOPS WITH SPROUTS

Preparation Time: 10 minutes

Cooking Time: 7 hours

Servings: 5

Ingredients:

- 1-pound beef loin
- ½ cup bean sprouts
- 1 cup of water
- 1 tbsp tomato paste
- 1 tsp chili powder
- 1 tsp salt

Directions:

Cut the beef loin into 5 beef chops and sprinkle the beef chops with chili powder and salt.

Then place them in the slow cooker.

Add water and tomato paste. Cook the meat on low for 7 hours.

Then transfer the cooked beef chops to the plates, sprinkle with tomato gravy from the slow cooker, and top with bean sprouts.

Nutrition:

175 calories, 2

5.2g protein,

1.6g carbohydrates,

7.8g fat,

0.3g fiber,

64mg cholesterol,

526mg sodium,

386mg potassium.

426. BEEF RAGOUT WITH BEANS

Preparation Time: 10 minutes
Cooking Time: 5 hours
Servings: 5

Ingredients:
- 1 tbsp tomato paste
- 1 cup mug beans, canned
- 1 carrot, grated
- 1-pound beef stew meat, chopped
- 1 tsp ground black pepper
- 2 cups of water

Directions:
Pour water into the slow cooker.
Add meat, ground black pepper, and carrot.
Cook the mixture on High for 4 hours.
Then add tomato paste and mug beans. Stir the meal and cook it on high for 1 hour more.

Nutrition:
321 calories,
37.7g protein,
28g carbohydrates,
6.2g fat,
7.3g fiber,
81mg cholesterol,
81mg sodium,
959mg potassium

427. BRAISED BEEF

Preparation Time: 8 minutes
Cooking Time: 9 hours
Servings: 2

Ingredients:
- Oz. beef tenderloin, chopped
- 1 garlic clove, peeled
- 1 tsp peppercorn
- 1 tsp salt
- 1 tbsp dried basil
- 2 cups of water

Directions:
Put all ingredients from the list above in the slow cooker.
Gently stir the mixture and close the lid.
Cook the beef on low for 9 hours.

Nutrition:
239 calories,
33.1g protein,
1.2g carbohydrates,
10.4g fat,
0.3g fiber,
104mg cholesterol,
1238mg sodium,
431mg potassium.

428. COCONUT BEEF

Preparation Time: 10 minutes
Cooking Time: 8 hours
Servings: 5

Ingredients:
- 1 cup baby spinach, chopped
- 1 cup of coconut milk
- 1-pound beef tenderloin, chopped
- 1 tsp avocado oil
- 1 tsp dried rosemary
- 1 tsp garlic powder

Directions:
Roast meat in the avocado oil for 1 minute per side on high heat.
Ten transfer the meat in the slow cooker.
Add garlic powder, dried rosemary, coconut milk, and baby spinach.
Close the lid and cook the meal on Low for 8 hours.

Nutrition:
303 calories,
27.6g protein,
3.5g carbohydrates,
19.9g fat,
1.4g fiber,
83mg cholesterol,
66mg sodium,
495mg potassium

429. BLUE BEEF DIP

Preparation Time: 10 minutes
Cooking Time: 10 hours
Servings: 6

Ingredients:
- ½ cup heavy cream
- 1 onion, diced
- 1 tsp cream cheese
- ½ cup Blue Cheese
- 1 tsp garlic powder
- oz. dried beef, chopped
- ½ cup of water

Directions:
Put all ingredients in the slow cooker.
Gently stir the ingredients and close the lid.

Cook the dip on Low for 10 hours.
Nutrition:
123 calories,
8.6g protein,
2.5g carbohydrates,
8.2g fat,
0.4g fiber,
41mg cholesterol,
78mg sodium,
126mg potassium

430. BEEF ROAST
Preparation Time: 10 minutes
Cooking Time: 6 hours
Servings: 5
Ingredients:
- 1-pound beef chuck roast
- 1 tbsp ketchup
- 1 tbsp mayonnaise
- 1 tsp chili powder
- 1 tsp olive oil
- 1 tsp lemon juice
- ½ cup of water

Directions:
In the bowl mix ketchup, mayonnaise, chili powder, olive oil, and lemon juice.
Then sprinkle the beef chuck roast with ketchup mixture.
Pour the water into the slow cooker.
Add beef chuck roast and close the lid.
Cook the meat on High for 6 hours.
Nutrition:
354 calories,
23.9g protein,
1.8g carbohydrates,
27.3g fat,
0.2g fiber,
94mg cholesterol,
119mg sodium,
230mg potassium

431. LUNCH BEEF
Preparation Time: 10 minutes
Cooking Time: 8 hours
Servings: 2
Ingredients:
- ½ white onion, sliced
- 1 tsp Stevia
- 1 tsp chili powder
- 1 tsp hot sauce
- ½ cup okra, chopped
- 1 cup of water
- oz. beef loin, chopped

Directions:
Mix the beef loin with hot sauce, chili powder, and Stevia.
Transfer the meat to the slow cooker.
Add water, okra, and onion.
Cook the meal on Low for 8 hours.
Nutrition:
179 calories,
19.3g protein,
7.8g carbohydrates,
7.4g fat,
1.8g fiber,
53mg cholesterol,
520mg sodium,
146mg potassium.

432. BRAISED BEEF STRIPS
Preparation Time: 10 minutes
Cooking Time: 5 hours
Servings: 4
Ingredients:
- ½ cup mushroom, sliced
- 1 onion, sliced
- 1 cup of water
- 1 tbsp coconut oil
- 1 tsp salt
- 1 tsp white pepper
- Oz. beef loin, cut into strips

Directions:
Melt the coconut oil in the skillet.
Add mushrooms and roast them for 5 minutes on medium heat.
Then transfer the mushrooms to the slow cooker.
Add all remaining ingredients and close the lid.
Cook the meal on High for 5 hours
Nutrition:
173 calories,
19.6g protein,
3.2g carbohydrates,
9.4g fat,
0.8g fiber,
50mg cholesterol,
624mg sodium,

316mg potassium

433. BEEF DIP

Preparation Time: 10 minutes
Cooking Time: 10 hours
Servings: 6

Ingredients:
- ½ cup heavy cream
- 1 onion, diced
- 1 tsp cream cheese
- ½ cup Cheddar cheese, shredded
- 1 tsp garlic powder
- oz. dried beef, chopped
- ½ cup of water

Directions:
Put all ingredients in the slow cooker.
Gently stir the ingredients and close the lid.
Cook the dip on Low for 10 hours.

Nutrition:
118 calories,
8.6g protein,
2.5g carbohydrates,
8.2g fat,
0.4g fiber,
41mg cholesterol,
78mg sodium,
126mg potassium

434. BEEF & FENNEL

Preparation Time: 15 minutes
Cooking Time: 7 hours
Servings: 4

Ingredients:
- 1 red bell pepper, sliced
- 4 fennels
- 1/2 tsp salt
- 1/4 tsp red pepper flakes
- 3 garlic cloves, minced
- 1 tsp grated ginger
- 3 tbsp sweetener
- 1 cup beef broth
- 2/3 cup liquid amigos
- 2 lbs. flank steak, chunks
- 1 tsp sesame seeds, optional

Directions:
Set the slow cooker on low, put the steak, salt, pepper, garlic, sweetener, beef broth, and coconut aminos.
Cook within 5 to 6 hours. Clean the fennels and cut the layers in slices.
Mix the steak, then put in the red pepper plus the fennel. Cook within 1 hour, then toss the batter.
Serve with sesame seeds and a drop of olive oil.

Nutrition:
Calories 428
Fat 19g
Carbs 4g
Protein 54g

435. CAPERS FETA BEEF

Preparation Time: 10 minutes
Cooking Time: 6 hours
Servings: 6

Ingredients:
- 2 lbs beef stew meat, cut into half-inch pieces
- 1/4 cup capers
- 4 artichoke hearts
- 30 oz can tomato, diced
- 1/2 cup feta cheese, crumbled
- 1/4 tsp pepper
- 12 tsp salt

Directions:
Make sure to use the tender parts of the artichokes.
Add all ingredients into the cooking pot and stir well.
Cover the slow cooker with lid and cook on HIGH for 6 hours.
Serve and enjoy.

Nutrition:
Calories 528
Fat 13.7 g
Carbohydrates 28g
Sugar 5.3 g
Protein 49.1 g
Cholesterol 146 mg

436. BEEF AND SAUERKRAUT BOWL

Preparation Time: 10 minutes
Cooking Time: 5 hours
Servings: 4

Ingredients:
- 1 cup sauerkraut
- 1-pound corned beef, chopped
- ¼ cup apple cider vinegar
- 1 cup of water

Directions:
Pour water and apple cider vinegar into the slow cooker.

Add corned beef and cook it on High for 5 hours.

Then chop the meat roughly and put it in the serving bowls.

Top the meat with sauerkraut.

Nutrition:
202 calories,
15.5g protein,
1.7g carbohydrates,
14.2g fat,
1g fiber,
71mg cholesterol,
1240mg sodium,
236mg potassium

437. EASY MEATBALL SLOW COOKER

Preparation Time: 15 minutes
Cooking Time: 2 hours
Servings: 3

Ingredients:
For the meatballs:
- 1 tbsp tomato paste
- 1 cup bone broth
- Sea salt and pepper to taste
- 1/2 tsp paprika
- 1/2 tbsp cumin
- 1 lb. ground beef
- A small handful of fresh parsley, diced

For the cauliflower:
- Sea salt and Pepper to taste
- 2 tbsp butter or ghee
- 1/2 large head cauliflower, florets

Directions:
Mix the meat, pepper, salt, paprika, and cumin in a bowl.

Form meatballs, then put them inside the slow cooker.

Mix the paste and the broth in a bowl and pour over the meatballs. Cook on high, 2 hours.

Steam the cauliflower florets until well cooked.

Remove the water, then put salt, butter, plus pepper.

Blend the batter using an immersion blender until smooth.

Mash the cauliflower onto a serving plate, top with meatballs, and enough amount of sauce on top. Garnish with parsley and enjoy.

Nutrition:
Calories: 413
Protein: 46.7g
Fat: 17.4g

Carbs: 2.5g

438. BEEF & BROCCOLI

Preparation Time: 15 minutes
Cooking Time: 7 hours
Servings: 4

Ingredients:
- 1 red bell pepper, sliced
- 1 broccoli, florets
- 1/2 tsp salt
- 1/4 tsp red pepper flakes
- 3 garlic cloves, minced
- 1 tsp grated ginger
- 3 tbsp sweetener
- 1 cup beef broth
- 2/3 cup liquid amigos
- 2 lbs. flank steak, chunks
- 1 tsp sesame seeds, optional

Directions:
Set the slow cooker on low, put the steak, salt, pepper, garlic, sweetener, beef broth, and coconut aminos.

Cook within 5 to 6 hours.

Mix the steak, then put in the red pepper plus the broccoli. Cook within 1 hour, then toss the batter.

Serve with sesame seeds.

Nutrition:
Calories 430
Fat 19g
Carbs 4g
Protein 54g

439. CHILI COLORADO

Preparation Time: 15 minutes
Cooking Time: 10 hours
Servings: 12

Ingredients:
- 2.5 pounds beef
- 3 cloves garlic
- 27 ounces green chilies, canned
- 1 tsp salt
- 0.5 tsp chili powder
- 1 onion
- 43.5 ounces tomatoes, canned
- 1 tsp ground cumin
- 1 tsp pepper

Directions:
Put the meat in the cooker. Add the garlic and onion.

Add the tomatoes and chilies. Add the seasonings.

Low cook for 10 hours. Serve.

Nutrition:
Calories 164
Fat 3 g
Protein 20 g
Carbs 10 g

440. MISSISSIPPI ROAST

Preparation Time: 15 minutes
Cooking Time: 8 hours
Servings: 6

Ingredients:
- 2 pounds roast beef
- 1 pack dressing mix, ranch
- 0.5 cups butter, salted
- 3 tbsp olive oil
- 1 yellow onion
- 1 cup au jus
- 6 peperoncini

Directions:
Sear the roast. Cover with chopped onion. Pour in au jus.
Sprinkle ranch mix. Evenly disperse the butter.
Evenly place pepperoncini. Low cook for 8 hours.

Nutrition:
Calories 608
Fat 49 g
Protein 30 g
Carbs 8 g

441. PEPPERS & ONION STEAK

Preparation Time: 15 minutes
Cooking Time: 8 hours
Servings: 8

Ingredients:
- Cubed steaks (28 oz.)
- 1 3/4 t. adobo seasoning/garlic salt
- 1 can (8 oz.) tomato sauce
- 1 cup water
- 1/2 med. onion
- 1 small red pepper
- 1/3 cup green pitted olives (+) 2 tbsp. brine
- Black pepper to taste

Directions:
Slice the peppers and onions into 1/4-inch strips.
Sprinkle the steaks with the pepper and garlic salt as needed and place them in the cooker.
Fold in the peppers and onion along with the water, sauce, and olives (with the liquid/brine from the jar).
Close the lid. Cook using the low-temperature setting for eight hours.

Nutrition:
Calories 154
Fat 5.5 g
Protein 23.5 g
Carbs 4 g

442. BEEF CHIMICHANGAS

Preparation Time: 15 minutes
Cooking Time: 12 hours
Servings: 16

Ingredients:
- 3 pounds beef, boneless
- 10 ounces green chilies and tomatoes, canned
- 3 ounces garlic
- 3 tbsp seasoning, taco
- 3 garlic cloves
- 16 flour tortillas
- Toppings:
- Refried beans
- Sour cream
- Guacamole
- Lettuce
- Cheese
- Salsa

Directions:
Prepare the meat. Add it to the cooker after applying seasoning. Add chilies and tomatoes. Toss in garlic.
Low cook for 12 hours. Shred the beef. Once removed, add it and all desired toppings to tortillas. Fry folded tortillas. Serve.

Nutrition:
Calories 249
Fat 18 g
Protein 14 g
Carbs 3 g

443. ARTICHOKE PEPPER BEEF

Preparation Time: 10 minutes
Cooking Time: 6 hours
Servings: 6

Ingredients:
- 2 lbs stew beef, cut into 1-inch cubes
- 12 oz artichoke hearts, drained
- 1 onion, diced

- 2 cups marinara sauce
- 1 tsp dried basil
- 1 tsp dried oregano
- 12 oz roasted red peppers, drained and sliced

Directions:

Add all ingredients into the cooking pot and stir well.
Cover slow cooker with lid.
Select slow cook mode and cook on LOW for 6 hours.
Stir well and serve.

Nutrition:

Calories 343
Fat 11.6 g
Carbohydrates 22.8 g
Sugar 11.2 g
Protein 37.3 g
Cholesterol 2 mg

444. ITALIAN BEEF ROAST

Preparation Time: 10 minutes
Cooking Time: 6 hours
Servings: 6

Ingredients:

- 2 lbs chuck roast, boneless
- 2 tbsp balsamic vinegar
- 2 tsp herb de Provence
- 1/3 cup sun-dried tomatoes, chopped
- 8 garlic cloves, chopped
- 1/4 cup fresh parsley, chopped
- 1/4 cup olives, chopped
- 1/2 cup chicken stock

Directions:

Add all ingredients into the cooking pot and stir well.
Cover the slow cooker with lid.
Select slow cook mode and cook on LOW for 6 hours.
Remove meat from pot and shred using a fork.
Serve and enjoy.

Nutrition:

Calories 349
Fat 13.5 g
Carbohydrates 2.3 g
Sugar 0.4 g
Protein 51.1 g
Cholesterol 153 mg

445. OLIVE FETA BEEF

Preparation Time: 10 minutes
Cooking Time: 6 hours
Servings: 6

Ingredients:

- 2 lbs beef stew meat, cut into half-inch pieces
- 1 cup olives, pitted, and cut in half
- 30 oz can tomato, diced
- 1/2 cup feta cheese, crumbled
- 1/4 tsp pepper
- 12 tsp salt

Directions:

Add all ingredients into the cooking pot and stir well.
Cover the slow cooker with lid.
Select slow cook mode and cook on HIGH for 6 hours.
Serve and enjoy.

Nutrition:

Calories 370
Fat 14.5 g
Carbohydrates 9.2 g
Sugar 5.3 g
Protein 49.1 g
Cholesterol 146 mg

446. OLIVE ARTICHOKES BEEF

Preparation Time: 10 minutes
Cooking Time: 7 hours
Servings: 6

Ingredients:

- 2 lbs stew beef, cut into 1-inch cubes
- 1 tsp dried oregano
- 1/2 cup olives, pitted and chopped
- 14 oz can tomato, diced
- 15 oz can tomato sauce
- 32 oz chicken stock
- 1 bay leaf
- 1/2 tsp ground cumin
- 1 tsp dried basil
- 1 tsp dried parsley
- 3 garlic cloves, chopped
- 1 onion, diced
- 14 oz can artichoke hearts, drained and halved
- 1 tbsp olive oil

Directions:

Add the meat into the cooking pot then mix the remaining ingredients and pour over the meat.
Cover slow cooker with lid.
Select slow cook mode and cook on LOW for 7 hours.
Stir well and serve.

Nutrition:

Calories 322
Fat 13.2 g

Carbohydrates 14.2 g
Sugar 7.1 g
Protein 36.8 g
Cholesterol 0 mg

447. SRIRACHA BEEF
Preparation Time: 10 minutes
Cooking Time: 4 hours
Servings: 6

Ingredients:
- 2 lbs beef chuck, sliced
- 1 tbsp sriracha sauce
- 1/3 cup parsley, chopped
- 2 tsp garlic powder
- 1 cup beef broth
- 1/2 medium onion, sliced
- 2 cups bell pepper, chopped
- 1 tsp black pepper
- 2 tsp salt

Directions:
Add the meat into the cooking pot then mix the remaining ingredients and pour over the meat.
Cover slow cooker with lid.
Select slow cook mode and cook on HIGH for 4 hours.
Stir well and serve.

Nutrition:
Calories 310
Fat 9.8 g
Carbohydrates 5.5 g
Sugar 3.1 g
Protein 47.5 g
Cholesterol 135 mg

448. GARLIC TOMATOES CHUCK ROAST
Preparation Time: 10 minutes
Cooking Time: 10 hours
Servings: 6

Ingredients:
- 2 lbs beef chuck roast
- 1/2 cup beef broth
- 1/4 cup sun-dried tomatoes, chopped
- 25 garlic cloves, peeled
- 1/4 cup olives, sliced
- 1 tsp dried Italian seasoning, crushed
- 2 tbsp balsamic vinegar

Directions:

Add the meat into the cooking pot then mix the remaining ingredients except for couscous and pour over the meat.
Cover slow cooker with lid.
Select slow cook mode and cook on LOW for 8 hours.
Remove meat from pot and shred using a fork.
Return shredded meat to the pot and stir well.

Nutrition:
Calories 582
Fat 43.1 g
Carbohydrates 5 g
Sugar 0.5 g
Protein 40.8 g
Cholesterol 156 mg

449. STUFFED BELL PEPPERS
Preparation Time: 10 minutes
Cooking Time: 4 hours
Servings: 4

Ingredients:
- 6 large eggs
- 4 oz green chilies, chopped
- 4 oz jack cheese, shredded
- 1/2 lb ground breakfast sausage
- 4 bell pepper, cut top, and clean
- 1/8 tsp black pepper
- 1/4 tsp salt

Directions:
Brown sausage in a pan over medium heat. Drain excess grease.
Pour 1/2 cup water into the cooking pot.
In a bowl, whisk eggs until smooth. Stir green chilies, cheese, black pepper, and salt in eggs.
Spoon egg mixture and brown sausage into each bell pepper.
Place stuffed bell pepper in the cooking pot.
Cover slow cooker with lid.
Select slow cook mode and cook on LOW for 4 hours.
Serve and enjoy.

Nutrition:
Calories 445
Fat 23.4 g
Carbohydrates 30.4 g
Sugar 18.2 g
Protein 29.7 g
Cholesterol 348 mg

450. BUTTER BEEF

Preparation Time: 10 minutes

Cooking Time: 8 hours

Servings: 8

Ingredients:
- 3 lbs beef stew meat, cubed
- 1/2 cup butter
- 1 oz dry onion soup mix

Directions:

Place beef into the cooking pot and sprinkle with onion soup mix.

Add butter over the beef.

Cover slow cooker with lid.

Select slow cook mode and cook on LOW for 8 hours.

Stir well and serve.

Nutrition:

Calories 428,

Fat 22.1g,

Carbohydrates 2.3g,

Sugar 0.2g,

Protein 52g,

Cholesterol 183mg

DESSERTS

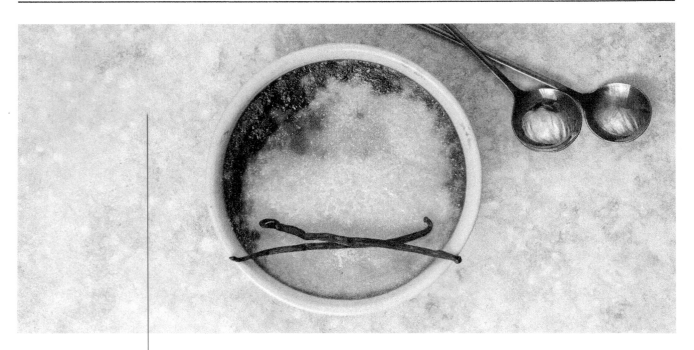

451. HOT FUDGE CAKE

Preparation Time: 25 minutes
Cooking Time: 3 hours
Servings: 10

Ingredients:
- 1¼ cup Sukrin Gold, divided
- 1 cup almond flour
- ¼ cup plus 3 tbsp. unsweetened cocoa powder, divided
- 2 tsp baking powder
- ½ tsp. salt
- ½ cup heavy cream
- 2 Tbsp melted butter
- ½ tsp. vanilla extract
- 1¾ cups boiling water

Directions:
Mix ¾ cup Sukrin Gold, almond flour, cocoa, baking powder, and salt. Stir in heavy cream, butter, and vanilla. Put it inside the slow cooker.

Mix ½ cup Sukrin Gold and ¼ cup cocoa, then sprinkle over the mixture in the slow cooker. Pour in boiling water. Do not stir.

Cook 2-3 hours, high. Serve.

Nutrition:
Calories 252
Fat 13 g
Sodium 177 mg
Carbs 28 g
Sugar 25 g
Protein 3 g

452. FUDGY SECRET BROWNIES

Preparation Time: 10 minutes
Cooking Time: 2 hours
Servings: 8

Ingredients:
- 4 oz. unsweetened chocolate
- ¾ cup of coconut oil
- ¾ cup frozen diced okra, partially thawed
- 3 large eggs
- 36 stevia packets
- 1 tsp pure vanilla extract
- ¼ tsp. mineral salt
- ¾ cup coconut flour
- ½-¾ cup coarsely chopped walnuts or pecans, optional

Directions:
Melt chocolate and coconut oil in a small saucepan. Put okra and eggs in a blender. Blend until smooth.

Measure all other ingredients in the mixing bowl.

Pour melted chocolate and okra over the dry ingredients and stir with a fork just until mixed.

Pour into the greased slow cooker—cover and cook on high for 1½-2 hours.

Nutrition:

Calories 421
Fat 38 g
Sodium 113 mg
Carbs 15 g
Sugar 1 g
Protein 8 g

453. BLACK AND BLUE COBBLER

Preparation Time: 20 minutes
Cooking Time: 2 hours
Servings: 6

Ingredients:
- 1 cup almond flour
- 36 packets stevia, divided
- 1 tsp baking powder
- ¼ tsp salt
- ¼ tsp ground cinnamon
- ¼ tsp ground nutmeg
- 2 eggs, beaten
- 2 tbsp. whole milk
- 2 tbsp. coconut oil, melted
- 2 cups fresh or frozen blackberries
- ¾ cup of water
- 1 tsp. grated orange peel

Directions:

Combine almond flour, 18 packets of stevia, baking powder, salt, cinnamon, and nutmeg.

Combine eggs, milk, and oil. Stir into dry fixing. Put it inside the greased slow cooker.

Mix the berries, water, orange peel, and remaining 18 packets of stevia in a saucepan. Bring to boil. Remove from heat and pour over batter. Cook on 2-2½ hours, high. Let it cool within 30 minutes. Serve.

Nutrition:
Calories 224
Fat 16 g
Sodium 174 mg
Carbs 21 g
Sugar 8 g
Protein 7 g

454. BAKED CUSTARD

Preparation Time: 15 minutes
Cooking Time: 3 hours
Servings: 6

Ingredients:
- 2 cups whole milk
- 3 eggs, slightly beaten
- 2½ tsp., plus ¼ tsp., erythritol, divided
- 1 tsp. vanilla extract
- ¼ tsp. cinnamon

Directions:

Heat milk in a small uncovered saucepan until a skin forms on top. Remove from heat and let cool slightly.

Mix the eggs, 2½ tbsp erythritol, and vanilla in a large bowl. Slowly stir cooled milk into the egg-erythritol mixture.

Pour into a greased 1-qt baking dish which will fit into your slow cooker, or into a baking insert designed for your slow cooker.

Mix cinnamon and 1/2 tsp reserved erythritol in a small bowl. Sprinkle over custard mixture.

Cover baking dish or insert with foil—set the container on a metal rack or trivet in the slow cooker. Pour warm water around the dish to a depth of 1 inch.

Cover cooker. Cook on High 2-3 hours, or until custard is set. Serve warm from baking dish or insert.

Nutrition:
Calories 254
Fat 3 g
Sodium 6 g
Carbs 52 g
Sugar 11 g
Protein 4 g

455. MAPLE POT DE CRÈME

Preparation Time: 15 minutes
Cooking Time: 3 hours
Servings: 6

Ingredients:
- 2 egg yolks
- 2 eggs
- 1 cup heavy cream
- ½ cup whole milk
- ½ cup plus 1 tbsp. Sukrin Gold
- Pinch salt
- 1 tsp. vanilla extract
- ¼ tsp. ground nutmeg
- Whipped cream, for garnish, optional

Directions:

1. Whisk the egg yolks plus eggs in a bowl until light and frothy.
2. Add cream, milk, 1 tbsp Sukrin Gold, salt, vanilla, and nutmeg. Mix well.
3. Pour mixture into a baking dish and set it in a slow cooker. Carefully pour water around the baking dish until the water comes halfway up the sides.

4. Cover cooker. Cook on high for 2-3 hours, until Pot de Crème is set but still a little bit jiggly in the middle.
5. Wearing oven mitts to protect your knuckles, carefully remove the hot dish from the cooker. Set on a wire rack to cool to room temperature.
6. Chill within 2 hours before you serve. Garnish with whipped cream if you wish.

Nutrition:

Calories 102

Fat 18 g

Sodium 46 g

Carbs 12 g

Sugar 2 g

Protein 5 g

456. SLOW-COOKER PUMPKIN PIE PUDDING

Preparation Time: 7 minutes

Cooking Time: 7 hours

Servings: 6

Ingredients:

- 15-oz. can solid pack pumpkin
- 12-oz. can evaporate milk
- ¼ cup plus 2 tbsp. erythritol
- ½ cup keto-friendly baking mix
- 2 eggs, beaten
- 2 tbsp. melted butter
- 1 tbsp. pumpkin pie spice
- 2 tsp. vanilla extract

Directions:

1. Mix all ingredients. Pour into the greased slow cooker.
2. Cook within 6-7 hours, high. Serve.

Nutrition:

Calories 168

Fat 15 g

Sodium 91 g

Carbs 22 g

Sugar 3 g

Protein 9 g

457. TASTY APPLE AND CRANBERRY DESSERT

Preparation Time: 15 minutes

Cooking Time: 3 hours

Servings: 4

Ingredients:

- 4 medium-sized sliced apples
- 1 cup of frozen or fresh cranberries
- 1 tsp of vanilla
- 8 tbsp of light brown packed sugar
- 2 tsp of ground cinnamon, divided
- 1 packet of super moist yellow cake mix, 15 ounces
- 8 tbsp of melted butter
- Whipped cream

Directions:

1. Grease the slow cooker. Add 1 tsp of cinnamon, Stevia, apples, and cranberries to the slow cooker and combine them.
2. Mix the rest of 1 tsp of cinnamon with the dry cake mix in a bowl.
3. Spread the mixture onto the fruits and drizzle the melted butter over the top. Cook within 3 hours, on high. Serve it with whipped cream.

Nutrition:

Calories: 230

Fat: 12 g

Protein: 30 g

Carbohydrates: 4.5 g

458. CARAMEL PECAN PUDDING

Preparation Time: 15 minutes

Cooking Time: 3 hours

Servings: 4

Ingredients:

- 1 ½ cups of Bisquick mix
- 16 tbsp of Stevia, divided
- 8 tbsp of unsweetened baking cocoa
- 8 tbsp of milk
- 12 tbsp of caramel topping, divided
- 1 2/3 cups of hot water
- ½ cup of chopped pecans

Directions:

Mix the Bisquick mix, 8 tbsp of Stevia, cocoa, milk, and 6 tbsp of caramel in a large bowl.

Pour the mixture into a slow cooker. Add the hot water.

Top with the remaining sugar then cooks on low within 3 hours.

Divide into bowls, spread the remaining caramel over the top, sprinkle with pecans, and serve.

Nutrition:

Carbohydrates: 19 g

Calories: 544

Fat: 5.6 g

Protein: 3.4 g

459. MOUTH-WATERING CHOCOLATE CAKE

Preparation Time: 15 minutes

Cooking Time: 3.5 hours

Servings: 4

Ingredients:

- 1 ½ cups of almond flour
- ¾ cup of granulated sugar or a sweetener of your preference
- 2/3 cup of cocoa powder
- ¼ cup of whey protein powder
- 2 tsp of baking powder
- ¼ tsp of salt
- ½ cup of melted butter
- 4 large eggs
- ¾ cup of unsweetened almond milk
- 1 tsp of vanilla extract
- Whipped cream

Directions:

Mix the dry fixing in a large bowl.

Put the wet fixing to it one at a time, stirring as you go along. Whisk together thoroughly.

Grease the slow cooker and add the cake mixture—cover and cook for 3.5 hours on low.

Divide into bowls and serve with whipped cream.

Nutrition:

Calories: 260

Fat: 14 g

Protein: 8 g

Carbohydrates: 15 g

460. FABULOUS PEANUT VANILLA CHOCOLATE CAKE

Preparation Time: 15 minutes

Cooking Time: 4 hours

Servings: 4

Ingredients:

- 3/4 cup of melted natural peanut butter
- 4 large eggs
- 2 cups of almond flour
- ½ a cup of water
- ¼ cup of unflavored whey protein powder
- ½ cup of melted butter
- 2 ounces of melted dark chocolate, sugar-free
- ¾ cup of your preferred sweetener
- ¼ cup of coconut flour
- 1 tsp of vanilla extract
- 1 tbsp of baking powder
- ¼ tsp of salt
- 1 tsp of vanilla extract

Directions:

Deglaze the inside of the slow cooker using butter.

Combine all the ingredients in a large bowl and whisk together thoroughly.

Spoon 2/3 of the batter onto the base of the slow cooker. Add half of the melted chocolate.

Add the remainder of the batter. Put the remaining chocolate on top.

Cover and cook for 4 hours. Divide onto plates and serve.

Nutrition:

Calories: 335

Carbohydrates: 11.5 g

Fat: 27 g

Fiber: 5.2 g

Protein: 8 g

461. POPPY SEED BUTTER CAKE

Preparation Time: 15 minutes

Cooking Time: 3 hours

Servings: 4

Ingredients:

- 4 large eggs
- The zest and juice of 4 lemons
- ½ cup of melted butter
- 2 cups of almond flour
- 3 tbsp of poppy seeds
- 2 tbsp of baking powder
- 1 tbsp of vanilla extract
- 1 tsp of salt
- ½ cup of vanilla protein powder
- 3 tbsp of vanilla protein powder
- ½ cup of xylitol

Directions:

Mix all the items except the eggs in a bowl.

Add the eggs one by one and whisk together thoroughly.

Grease the slow cooker with butter. Pour the batter into the slow cooker.

Cover and cook for 3 hours. Divide onto plates and serve.

Nutrition:

Calories: 143

Carbohydrates: 9 g

Fat: 10 g

Fiber: 1 g

Protein: 6 g

462. LEMON CAKE

Preparation Time: 15 minutes

Cooking Time: 3 hours

Servings: 8

Ingredients:
- 1 ½ cup ground almonds
- ½ cup coconut flakes
- 6 Tbsp sweetener like Swerve (Erythritol, or a suitable substitute)
- 2 tsp baking powder
- Pinch of salt
- ½ cup softened coconut oil
- ½ cup cooking cream
- 2 Tbsp lemon juice
- Zest from two lemons
- 2 eggs
- Topping:
- 3 tbsp Swerve (or a suitable substitute)
- ½ cup boiling water
- 2 tbsp lemon juice
- 2 tbsp softened coconut oil

Directions:

In a bowl, combine the almonds, coconut, sweetener, baking powder. Whisk until combined.

In a separate bowl, blend coconut oil, cream, juice, and eggs.

Add the egg mixture to the dry fixing, mix.

Line the slow cooker with aluminum foil, pour in the batter.

In a bowl, mix the topping. Pour it over the cake batter.

Cover it with paper towels to absorb the water.

Cover, cook on high for 3 hours. Serve warm.

Nutrition:

Calories: 142

Carbs: 0g

Fat: 8g

Protein: 0g

463. RASPBERRY & COCONUT CAKE

Preparation Time: 15 minutes

Cooking Time: 3 hours

Servings: 10

Ingredients:
- 2 cups ground almonds
- 1 cup shredded coconut
- ¾ cup sweetener, Swerve (or a suitable substitute)
- 2 tsp baking soda
- ¼ tsp salt
- 4 large eggs
- ½ cup melted coconut oil
- ¾ cup of coconut milk
- 1 cup raspberries, fresh or frozen
- ½ cup sugarless dark chocolate chips

Directions:

Butter the slow cooker.

In a bowl, mix the dry ingredients.

Beat in the eggs, melted coconut oil, and coconut milk.

Mix in the raspberries plus chocolate chips.

Combine the cocoa, almonds, and salt in a bowl.

Pour the batter into the buttered slow cooker.

Cover the cooker with a paper towel to absorb the water.

Cover, cook on low for 3 hours. Let the cake cool in the pot.

Nutrition:

Calories: 201

Carbs: 24g

Fat: 10g

Protein: 0g

464. CHOCOLATE CHEESECAKE

Preparation Time: 15 minutes

Cooking Time: 2.5 hours

Servings: 8

Ingredients:
- 3 cups cream cheese
- Pinch of salt
- 3 eggs
- 1 cup powder sweetener of your choice, Swerve (or a suitable substitute)
- 1 tsp vanilla extract
- ½ cup sugarless dark chocolate chips

Directions:

Whisk the cream cheese, sweetener, and salt in a bowl.

Add the eggs one at a time. Combine thoroughly.

Spread the cheesecake in a cake pan, which fits in the slow cooker you are using.

Dissolved the chocolate chips in a small pot and pour over the batter. Using a knife, swirl the chocolate through the batter.

Put 2 cups of water inside the slow cooker and set the cake pan inside. Cover it with a paper towel to absorb the water, then cook on high for 2.5 hours. Remove from the slow cooker and let it cool in the pan for 1 hour. Refrigerate.

Nutrition:

Calories: 330

Carbs: 34g

Fat: 19g

Protein: 6g

465. CRÈME BRULE

Preparation Time: 15 minutes

Cooking Time: 2 hours

Servings: 6

Ingredients:
- 5 large egg yolks
- 6 tbsp sweetener, Erythritol
- 2 cups double cream
- 1 Bourbon vanilla pod, scraped
- Pinch of salt

Directions:

In a bowl, beat the eggs and sweetener together.

Add the cream and vanilla. Whisk together.

Put it in one big dish.

Set it in the slow cooker and pour hot water around- so the water reaches halfway up the dish.

Cover, cook on high for 2 hours.

Take the dishes out, let them cool. Refrigerate for 6-8 hours.

Nutrition:

Calories: 120

Carbs: 18g

Fat: 4g

Protein: 3g

466. PEANUT BUTTER & CHOCOLATE CAKE

Preparation Time: 15 minutes

Cooking Time: 4 hours

Servings: 12

Ingredients:
- 1 tbsp butter for greasing the slow cooker
- 2 cups almond flour
- ¾ cup sweetener of your choice
- ¼ cup coconut flakes
- ¼ cup whey protein powder
- 1 tsp baking powder
- ¼ tsp salt
- ¾ cup peanut butter, melted
- 4 large eggs
- 1 tsp vanilla extract
- ½ cup of water
- 3 tbsp sugarless dark chocolate, melted

Directions:

Grease the slow cooker well.

In a bowl, mix the dry ingredients. Stir in the wet ingredients one at a time.

Spread about 2/3 of the batter in the slow cooker, add half the chocolate. Swirl with a fork. Top up with the remaining batter and chocolate. Swirl again.

Cook on low for 4 hours. Switch off. Let it sit covered for 30 minutes.

Nutrition:

Calories: 270

Carbs: 39g

Fat: 11g

Protein: 5g

467. KETO COCONUT HOT CHOCOLATE

Preparation Time: 15 minutes

Cooking Time: 4 hours

Servings: 8

Ingredients:
- 5 cups full-fat coconut milk
- 2 cups heavy cream
- 1 tsp vanilla extract
- 1/3 cup cocoa powder
- 3 ounces dark chocolate, roughly chopped
- ½ tsp cinnamon
- Few drops of stevia to taste

Directions:

Add the coconut milk, cream, vanilla extract, cocoa powder, chocolate, cinnamon, and stevia to the slow cooker and stir to combine.

Cook for 4 hours, high, whisking every 45 minutes.

Taste the hot chocolate and if you prefer more sweetness, add a few more drops of stevia.

Nutrition:

Calories: 135

Carbs: 5g

Fat: 11g

Protein: 5g

468. AMBROSIA

Preparation Time: 15 minutes

Cooking Time: 3 hours

Servings: 10

Ingredients:
- 1 cup unsweetened shredded coconut
- ¾ cup slivered almonds
- 3 ounces dark chocolate (high cocoa percentage), roughly chopped
- 1/3 cup pumpkin seeds
- 2 ounces salted butter
- 1 tsp cinnamon
- 2 cups heavy cream

- 2 cups full-fat Greek yogurt
- 1 cup fresh berries - strawberries and raspberries are best

Directions:

Place the shredded coconut, slivered almonds, dark chocolate, pumpkin seeds, butter, and cinnamon into the slow cooker.

Cook for 3 hours, high, stirring every 45 minutes to combine the chocolate and butter as it melts.

Remove the mixture from the slow cooker, place in a bowl, and leave to cool.

In a large bowl, whip the cream until softly whipped.

Stir the yogurt through the cream.

Slice the strawberries into pieces, then put it in the cream mixture, along with the other berries you are using, fold through.

Sprinkle the cooled coconut mixture over the cream mixture.

Nutrition:

Calories: 57

Carbs: 11g

Fat: 1g

Protein: 1g

469. DARK CHOCOLATE AND PEPPERMINT POTS

Preparation Time: 15 minutes

Cooking Time: 2 hours

Servings: 6

Ingredients:

- 2 ½ cups heavy cream
- 3 ounces dark chocolate, melted in the microwave
- 4 egg yolks, lightly beaten with a fork
- Few drops of stevia
- Few drops of peppermint essence to taste

Directions:

Mix the beaten egg yolks, cream, stevia, melted chocolate, and peppermint essence in a medium-sized bowl.

Prepare the pots by greasing 6 ramekins with butter.

Pour the chocolate mixture into the pots evenly.

Put the pots inside the slow cooker and put hot water below halfway up.

Cook for 2 hours, high. Take the pots out of the slow cooker and leave to cool and set.

Serve with a fresh mint leaf and whipped cream.

Nutrition:

Calories: 125

Carbs: 15g

Fat: 6g

Protein: 1g

470. CREAMY VANILLA CUSTARD

Preparation Time: 15 minutes

Cooking Time: 3 hours

Servings: 8

Ingredients:

- 3 cups full-fat cream
- 4 egg yolks, lightly beaten
- 2 tsp vanilla extract
- Few drops of stevia

Directions:

Mix the cream, egg yolks, vanilla extract, and stevia in a medium-sized bowl.

Pour the mixture into a heat-proof dish. Place the dish into the slow cooker.

Put hot water into the pot, around the dish, halfway up. Set the temperature to high.

Cook for 3 hours. Serve hot or cold!

Nutrition:

Calories: 206

Carbs: 30g

Fat: 7g

Protein: 6g

471. COCONUT, CHOCOLATE, ALMOND TRUFFLE BAKE

Preparation Time: 15 minutes

Cooking Time: 4 hours

Servings: 8

Ingredients:

- 3 ounces butter, melted
- 3 ounces dark chocolate, melted
- 1 cup ground almonds
- 1 cup desiccated coconut
- 3 tbsp unsweetened cocoa powder
- 2 tsp vanilla extract
- 1 cup heavy cream
- A few extra squares of dark chocolate, grated
- ¼ cup toasted almonds, chopped

Directions:

In a large bowl, mix the melted butter, chocolate, ground almonds, coconut, cocoa powder, and vanilla extract.

Roll the mixture into balls. Grease a heat-proof dish.

Place the balls into the dish—Cook for 4 hours, low setting.

Leave the truffle dish to cool until warm. Mix the cream until soft peak.

Spread the cream over the truffle dish and sprinkle the grated chocolate and chopped toasted almonds over the top. Serve immediately!

Nutrition:

Calories: 115

Carbs: 8g

Fat: 10g

Protein: 2g

472. PEANUT BUTTER, CHOCOLATE, AND PECAN CUPCAKES

Preparation Time: 15 minutes

Cooking Time: 4 hours

Servings: 14

Ingredients:

- 14 paper cupcake cases
- 1 cup smooth peanut butter
- 2 ounces butter
- 2 tsp vanilla extract
- 5 ounces dark chocolate
- 2 tbsp coconut oil
- 2 eggs, lightly beaten
- 1 cup ground almonds
- 1 tsp baking powder
- 1 tsp cinnamon
- 10 pecan nuts, toasted and finely chopped

Directions:

Dissolve the dark chocolate plus coconut oil in the microwave, stir to combine, and set aside.

Place the peanut butter and butter into a medium-sized bowl, microwave for 30 seconds at a time until the butter has just melted.

Mix the peanut butter plus butter until combined and smooth.

Stir the vanilla extract into the peanut butter mixture.

Mix the ground almonds, eggs, baking powder, and cinnamon in a small bowl.

Pour the melted chocolate and coconut oil evenly into the 14 paper cases.

Spoon half of the almond/egg mixture evenly into the cases, on top of the chocolate, and press down slightly.

Spoon the peanut butter mixture into the cases, on top of the almond/egg mixture.

Spoon the remaining almond/egg mixture into the cases.

Put the pecans on top of each cupcake.

Put the filled cases into the slow cooker—Cook for 4 hours, high setting.

Nutrition:

Calories: 145

Carbs: 20g

Fat: 3g

Protein: 4g

473. VANILLA AND STRAWBERRY CHEESECAKE

Preparation Time: 15 minutes

Cooking Time: 6 hours

Servings: 8

Ingredients:

Base:

- 2 ounces butter, melted
- 1 cup ground hazelnuts
- ½ cup desiccated coconut
- 2 tsp vanilla extract
- 1 tsp cinnamon

Filling:

- 2 cups cream cheese
- 2 eggs, lightly beaten
- 1 cup sour cream
- 2 tsp vanilla extract
- 8 large strawberries, chopped

Directions:

Mix the melted butter, hazelnuts, coconut, vanilla, and cinnamon in a medium-sized bowl.

Press the base into a greased heat-proof dish.

Mix the cream cheese, eggs, sour cream, and vanilla extract, beat with electric egg beaters in a large bowl until thick and combined.

Fold the strawberries through the cream cheese mixture.

Put the cream cheese batter into the dish, on top of the base, spread out until smooth.

Put it in the slow cooker and put hot water around the dish until halfway up.

Cook for 6 hours, low setting until just set but slightly wobbly.

Chill before serving.

Nutrition:

Calories: 156

Carbs: 4g

Fat: 7g

Protein: 15g

474. COFFEE CREAMS WITH TOASTED SEED CRUMBLE TOPPING

Preparation Time: 15 minutes

Cooking Time: 4 hours

Servings: 6

Ingredients:

- 2 cups heavy cream

- 3 egg yolks, lightly beaten
- 1 tsp vanilla extract
- 3 tbsp strong espresso coffee (or 3tsp instant coffee dissolved in 3tbsp boiling water)
- ½ cup mixed seeds – sesame seeds, pumpkin seeds, chia seeds, sunflower seeds,
- 1 tsp cinnamon
- 1 tbsp coconut oil

Directions:

Heat-up the coconut oil in a small frypan until melted.

Add the mixed seeds, cinnamon, and a pinch of salt, toss in the oil, and heat until toasted and golden, place into a small bowl, and set aside.

Mix the cream, egg yolks, vanilla, and coffee in a medium-sized bowl.

Pour the cream/coffee mixture into the ramekins.

Place the ramekins into the slow cooker. Put hot water inside until halfway.

Cook on low setting for 4 hours.

Remove, then leave to cool slightly on the bench.

Sprinkle the seed mixture over the top of each custard before serving.

Nutrition:

Calories: 35

Carbs: 4g

Fat: 2g

Protein: 1g

475. LEMON CHEESECAKE

Preparation Time: 15 minutes

Cooking Time: 6 hours

Servings: 10

Ingredients:

- 2 ounces butter, melted
- 1 cup pecans, finely ground in the food processor
- 1 tsp cinnamon
- 2 cups cream cheese
- 1 cup sour cream
- 2 eggs, lightly beaten
- 1 lemon
- Few drops of stevia
- 1 cup heavy cream

Directions:

Mix the melted butter, ground pecans, and cinnamon until it forms a wet, sand-like texture.

Press the butter/pecan mixture into a greased, heat-proof dish and set aside.

Place the cream cheese, eggs, sour cream, stevia, zest, and juice of one lemon into a large bowl, beat with electric egg beaters until combined and smooth.

Put the cream cheese batter into the dish, on top of the base.

Place the dish inside the slow cooker, then put warm water halfway up.

Cook within 6 hours, low setting.

Set the cheesecake on the bench to cool and set.

Whip the cream until soft peak, and spread over the cheesecake before serving.

Nutrition:

Calories: 271

Carbs: 33g

Fat: 15g

Protein: 2g

476. APPLE, AVOCADO, AND MANGO BOWLS

Preparation Time: 10 minutes

Cooking Time: 2 hours

Servings: 2

Ingredients:

- 1 cup avocado, peeled, pitted, and cubed
- 1 cup mango, peeled and cubed
- 1 apple, cored and cubed
- 1 tbsp Stevia
- 1 cup heavy cream
- 1 tbsp lemon juice

Directions:

In your slow cooker, combine the avocado with the mango and the other ingredients, toss gently, put the lid on and cook on Low for 2 hours.

Divide the mix into bowls and serve.

Nutrition:

Calories 60,

Fat 1g,

Fiber 2g,

Carbs 20g,

Protein 1g.

477. RICOTTA CREAM

Preparation Time: 2 hours and 10 minutes

Cooking Time: 1 hour

Servings: 10

Ingredients:

- ½ cup hot coffee
- 2 Cups ricotta cheese
- And ½ tsp gelatin
- 1 tsp vanilla extract

- 1 tsp espresso powder
- 1 tsp. Stevia
- 1 cup whipping cream

Directions:

In a bowl, mix coffee with gelatin, stir well and leave aside until coffee is cold.

In your slow cooker, mix espresso, Stevia, vanilla extract, and ricotta and stir.

Add coffee mix and whipping cream, cover, cook on Low for 1 hour.

Divide into dessert bowls and keep in the fridge for 2 hours before serving.

Nutrition:

Calories 200,

Fat 13g,

Fiber 0g,

Carbs 5g,

Protein 7g.

478. TOMATO JAM

Preparation Time: 10 minutes

Cooking Time: 3 hours

Servings: 2

Ingredients:

- ½ pound tomatoes, chopped
- 1 green apple, grated
- 1 tbsp red wine vinegar
- 1 tbsp Stevia

Directions:

In your slow cooker, mix the tomatoes with the apple with the other ingredients, put the lid on, and cook on Low for 3 hours.

Whisk the jam well, blend a bit using an immersion blender, divide into bowls and serve cold.

Nutrition:

Calories 70,

Fat 1g,

Fiber 1g,

Carbs 18g,

Protein 1g.

479. GREEN TEA PUDDING

Preparation Time: 10 minutes

Cooking Time: 1 hour

Servings: 2

Ingredients:

- ½ cup coconut milk
- 1 and ½ cup avocado, pitted and peeled
- 1 ½ tbsp green tea powder
- 1 tsp lime zest, grated
- 1 tbsp Stevia

Directions:

In your slow cooker, mix coconut milk with avocado, tea powder, lime zest, and Stevia, stir, cover, and cook on Low for 1 hour.

Divide into cups and serve cold.

Nutrition

Calories 107,

Fat 5g,

Fiber 3g,

Carbs 6g,

Protein 8g.

480. COCONUT JAM

Preparation Time: 10 minutes

Cooking Time: 3 hours

Servings: 2

Ingredients:

- ½ cup coconut flesh, shredded
- 1 cup coconut cream
- ½ cup heavy cream
- 1 ¼ cup Stevia
- 1 tbsp lemon juice

Directions:

In your slow cooker, mix the coconut cream with the lemon juice, add other ingredients, whisk, put the lid on and cook on Low for 2 hours.

Whisk well, divide into bowls and serve cold.

Nutrition:

Calories 50,

Fat 1g,

Fiber 1g,

Carbs 10g,

Protein 2g.

481. BANANA BREAD

Preparation Time: 10 minutes

Cooking Time: 3 hours

Servings: 6

Ingredients:

- ¾ cup Stevia
- 1/3 cup butter, soft
- 1 tsp vanilla extract
- 1 egg
- Bananas, mashed
- 1 tsp baking powder
- 1 and ½ cups flour

- ½ tsp baking soda
- 1/3 cup milk
- 1 and ½ tsp cream of tartar
- Cooking spray

Directions:

In a bowl, combine milk with cream of tartar and stir well.

Add Stevia, butter, egg, vanilla, and bananas and stir everything.

In another bowl, mix flour with salt, baking powder, and soda.

Combine the 2 mixtures and stir them well.

Grease your slow cooker with cooking spray, add bread batter, cover, and cook on High for 3 hours.

Leave the bread to cool down, slice, and serve it.

Nutrition:

Calories 300,

Fat 3g,

Fiber 4g,

Carbs 28g,

Protein 5g.

482. BREAD AND BERRIES PUDDING

Preparation Time: 10 minutes

Cooking Time: 3 hours

Servings: 8

Ingredients:

- 3 cups white bread, cubed
- 1 cup blackberries
- 1 tbsp butter, melted
- 1 tbsp Stevia or other Keto-approved sugar
- 1 cup almond milk
- ¼ cup heavy cream
- 4 eggs whisked
- 1 tbsp lemon zest, grated
- ¼ tsp vanilla extract

Directions:

In your slow cooker, mix the bread with the berries, butter, and the other ingredients, toss gently, put the lid on, and cook on Low for 3 hours.

Divide pudding between dessert plates and serve.

Nutrition:

Calories 354,

Fat 12g,

Fiber 4g,

Carbs 20g,

Protein 11g.

483. CANDIED LEMON

Preparation Time: 20 minutes

Cooking Time: 4 hours

Servings: 4

Ingredients:

- 5 lemons, peeled and cut into medium segments
- 2 ¼ cups Stevia or other Keto-approved Stevia, divided
- 5 cups water, divided

Directions:

In your slow cooker,

mix lemons with Stevia and water,

cover, cook on Low for 4 hours,

transfer them to bowls and serve cold.

Nutrition:

Calories 62,

Fat 3g,

Fiber 5g,

Carbs 3g,

Protein 4g.

484. TAPIOCA AND CHIA PUDDING

Preparation Time: 10 minutes

Cooking Time: 3 hours

Servings: 2

Ingredients:

- 1 cup almond milk
- ¼ cup tapioca pearls
- 2 tbsp chia seeds
- 2 eggs whisked
- ½ tsp vanilla extract
- 1 tbsp Stevia
- ½ tbsp lemon zest, grated

Directions:

In your slow cooker, mix the tapioca pearls with the milk, put the lid on, and cook on Low for 3 hours.

Divide the pudding into bowls and serve cold.

Nutrition

Calories 180,

Fat 3g,

Fiber 4g,

Carbs 12g,

Protein 4g.

485. CHOCOLATE AND LIQUOR CREAM

Preparation Time: 10 minutes

Cooking Time: 2 hours

Servings: 4

Ingredients:
- 1 cup crème Fraiche
- 5 Ounces dark chocolate, cut into chunks
- 1 tsp. liquor
- 1 tsp. Stevia

Directions:

In your slow cooker,

Mix crème Fraiche with chocolate, liquor, and Stevia,

Stir, cover,

Cook on Low for 2 hours,

Divide into bowls and serve cold

Nutrition:

Calories 200,

Fat 12g,

Fiber 4g,

Carbs 6g,

Protein 3g.

486. DATES AND RICE PUDDING

Preparation Time: 10 minutes

Cooking Time: 3 hours

Servings: 2

Ingredients:
- 1 cup dates, chopped
- ½ cup white rice
- 1 cup almond milk
- 1 tbsp Stevia
- 1 tsp almond extract

Directions:

In your slow cooker, mix the rice with the milk and the other ingredients, whisk, put the lid on and cook on Low for 3 hours.

Divide the pudding into bowls and serve.

Nutrition:

Calories 152,

Fat 5g,

Fiber 2g,

Carb 6g,

Protein 3g.

487. BUTTERNUT SQUASH SWEET MIX

Preparation Time: 10 minutes

Cooking Time: 3 hours

Serving: 8

Ingredients:
- 2 lbs. butternut squash, steamed, peeled, and mashed
- 2 Eggs
- 1 cup milk
- ¾ cup Stevia
- 1 tsp cinnamon powder
- ½ tsp ginger powder
- ¼ tsp cloves, ground
- 1 tbsp cornstarch
- Whipped cream for serving

Directions:

In a bowl, mix squash with Stevia, milk, eggs, cinnamon, cornstarch, ginger, cloves, and cloves and stir very well.

Pour this into your slow cooker, cover, cook on Low for 2 hours, divide into cups and serve with whipped cream on top.

Nutrition:

Calories 152,

Fat 3g,

Fiber 4g,

Carbs 16g,

Protein 4g.

488. ALMONDS, WALNUTS, AND MANGO BOWLS

Preparation Time: 10 minutes

Cooking Time: 2 hours

Servings: 2

Ingredients:
- 1 cup walnuts, chopped
- 1 tbsp almonds, chopped
- 1 cup mango, peeled and roughly cubed
- 1 cup heavy cream
- ½ tsp vanilla extract
- 1 tsp almond extract
- 1 tbsp Stevia

Directions:

In your slow cooker, mix the nuts with the mango, cream, and the other ingredients, toss, put the lid on and cook on High for 2 hours.

Divide the mix into bowls and serve.

Nutrition:

Calories 220,

Fat 4g,

Fiber 2g,

Carbs 4g,

Protein 6g.

489. TAPIOCA PUDDING

Preparation Time: 10 minutes

Cooking Time: 1 hour

Servings: 6

Ingredients:

- 1 and ¼ cups milk
- 1/3 cup tapioca pearls, rinsed
- ½ cup water
- ½ cup Stevia
- Zest of ½ lemon

Directions:

In your slow cooker,

Mix tapioca with milk, Stevia, water, and lemon zest,

Stir, cover,

Cook on Low for 1 hour, divide into cups and serve warm.

Nutrition:

Calories 200,

Fat 4g,

Fiber 2g,

Carbs 37g,

Protein 3g.

490.BERRIES SALAD

Preparation Time: 10 minutes

Cooking Time: 1 hour

Servings: 2

Ingredients:

- ½ tbsp Stevia
- 1 tbsp lime juice
- 1 tbsp lime zest, grated
- 1 cup blueberries
- ½ cup cranberries
- 1 cup blackberries
- 1 cup strawberries
- ½ cup heavy cream

Directions:

In your slow cooker, mix the berries with the Stevia and the other ingredients, toss, put the lid on and cook on High for 1 hour.

Divide the mix into bowls and serve.

Nutrition:

Calories 262,

Fat 7g,

Fiber 2g,

Carbs 5g,

Protein 8g.

491.FRESH CREAM MIX

Preparation Time: 1 hour

Cooking Time: 1 hour

Servings: 6

Ingredients:

- 2 cups fresh cream
- 1 tsp cinnamon powder
- Egg yolks
- Tbsp Stevia or other Keto-approved sugar
- Zest of 1 orange, grated
- A pinch of nutmeg for serving
- ½ tbsp Stevia
- 2 cups water

Directions:

In a bowl, mix cream, cinnamon, and orange zest and stir.

In another bowl, mix the egg yolks with Stevia and whisk well.

Add this over the cream, stir, strain, and divide into ramekins.

Put ramekins in your slow cooker, add 2 cups water to the slow cooker, cover, cook on Low for 1 hour, leave cream aside to cool down, and serve.

Nutrition:

Calories 200,

Fat 4g,

Fiber 5g,

Carbs 15g,

Protein 5g.

492.PEARS AND APPLES BOWLS

Preparation Time: 10 minutes

Cooking Time: 2 hours

Servings: 2

Ingredients:

- 1 tsp vanilla extract
- 2 Pears, cored and cut into wedges
- 2 Apples, cored and cut into wedges
- 1 tbsp walnuts, chopped
- 1 Tbsp Stevia
- ½ cup coconut cream

Directions:

In your slow cooker, mix the pears with the apples, nuts, and the other ingredients, toss, put the lid on, and cook on Low for 2 hours.

Divide the mix into bowls and serve cold.

Nutrition

Calories 120,

Fat 2,

Fiber 2,

Carbs 4,

Protein 3

493.MACADAMIA FUDGE TRUFFLES

Preparation Time: 15 minutes

Cooking Time: 4 hours

Servings: 25

Ingredients:

- 1 cup roasted macadamia nuts, finely chopped
- ½ cup ground almonds
- 2 ounces butter, melted
- 5 ounces dark chocolate, melted
- 1 tsp vanilla extract
- 1 egg, lightly beaten

Directions:

Place the macadamia nuts, almonds, melted butter, melted chocolate, vanilla, and egg into a large bowl, stir until combined.

Grease the bottom of the slow cooker by rubbing it with butter. Place the mixture into the slow cooker and press down.

Set to cook low setting within 4 hours.

Allow the batter to cool until just warm. Take a tsp, scoop the mixture out, and roll into balls.

Refrigerate to harden slightly. Store the truffle balls in the fridge.

Nutrition:

Calories: 150

Carbs: 19g

Fat: 6g

Protein: 6g

494. CHOCOLATE COVERED BACON CUPCAKES

Preparation Time: 15 minutes

Cooking Time: 3 hours

Servings: 10

Ingredients:

- 10 paper cupcake cases
- 5 slices streaky bacon, cut into small pieces, fried in a pan until crispy
- 5 ounces dark chocolate, melted
- 1 cup ground hazelnuts
- 1 tsp baking powder
- 2 eggs, lightly beaten
- ½ cup full-fat Greek yogurt
- 1 tsp vanilla extract

Directions:

Mix the fried bacon pieces and melted chocolate in a bowl, set aside.

Mix the ground hazelnuts, baking powder, eggs, yogurt, vanilla, and a pinch of salt in a medium-sized bowl.

Spoon the hazelnut mixture into the cupcake cases.

Spoon the chocolate and bacon mixture on top of the hazelnut mixture.

Place the cupcake cases into the slow cooker. Cook for 3 hours, high setting.

Remove the cupcakes from the pot and leave them to cool on the bench before storing the serving. Serve with whipped cream!

Nutrition:

Calories: 185

Carbs: 27g

Fat: 8g

Protein: 4g

495. CHOCOLATE & BERRY LAYERED JARS

Preparation Time: 15 minutes

Cooking Time: 6 hours

Servings: 6

Ingredients:

- 5 ounces dark chocolate, melted
- ½ cup mixed berries, (fresh) - any berries you like
- 3/4 cup toasted macadamia nuts, chopped
- 7 ounces cream cheese
- ½ cup heavy cream
- 1 tsp vanilla extract

Directions:

Whisk the cream cheese, cream, and vanilla extract in a medium-sized bowl.

Scoop a small amount of melted chocolate, put it into each jar or ramekin.

Place a few berries on top of the chocolate.

Sprinkle some toasted macadamias onto the berries. Scoop the cream cheese mixture into the ramekin.

Place another layer of chocolate, berries, and macadamia nuts on top of the cream cheese mixture.

Put the jars inside the slow cooker and put the hot water until it reaches halfway up.

Set to low, then cook for 6 hours.

Remove the jars and leave them to cool and set them on the bench for about 2 hours before serving.

Nutrition:

Calories: 150

Carbs: 25g

Fat: 15g

Protein: 3g

496. CHOCO-PEANUT CAKE

Preparation Time: 15 minutes

Cooking Time: 2 hours

Servings: 10

Ingredients:

- 15.25 oz. devil's food cake mix

- 1 cup of water
- 1/2 cup salted butter, melted
- 3 eggs
- 8 oz. pkg. mini-Reese's peanut butter cups
- For the topping
- 1 cup creamy peanut butter
- 3 tbsp. powdered sugar
- Ten bite-size Reese's peanut butter cups

Directions:

Mix the cake mixture, ice, butter, and eggs in a large bowl until smooth. Some lumps are all right, that's all right. Cut the cups of the mini peanut butter.

Cleaner non-stick spray on the slow cooker. Add the butter slowly and spread over an even layer.

Cover and cook on high during the cooking time for 2 hours without opening the lid.

Melt the peanut butter over medium heat in a pan. Stir until melted and smooth; observe as it burns hard. To smooth, add the powdered sugar and whisk.

Pour over the butter of the sweetened peanut in the cake, then serve.

Nutrition:

Calories: 607

Carbohydrates: 42g

Protein: 13g

Fat: 39g

Saturated Fat: 13g

497. SLOW COOKER APPLE PUDDING CAKE

Preparation Time: 15 minutes

Cooking Time: 2 hours

Servings: 10

Ingredients:

- 1 cup almond flour
- 2/3 plus 1/4 Stevia, divided
- 3 tsp baking powder
- 1 tsp salt
- 1/2 cup butter cold
- 1 cup milk
- 4 apples, diced
- 1 1& /2 cups orange juice
- 1/2 cup Stevia
- 2 tbsp butter melted
- 1 tsp cinnamon

Directions:

Mix the flour, 2/3 cup Stevia, baking powder, and salt. Slice the butter until you have coarse crumbs in the mixture.

Remove the milk from the crumbs until moistened.

Grease a 4 or 5 qt slow cooker's bottom and sides. Spoon the batter into the slow cooker's bottom and spread evenly. Place the diced apples evenly over the mixture.

Whisk together the orange juice, Stevia, butter, remaining Stevia, and cinnamon in a medium-sized pan. Garnish the apples.

Place the slow cooker opening with a clean kitchen towel, place the lid on, it prevents condensation from reaching the slow cooker from the cover.

Place the slow cooker on top and cook until apples are tender for 2 to 3 hours. Serve hot.

Nutrition:

Calories 431

Fat 9g

Saturated Fat 3g

Carbohydrates 38.9g

Fiber 1g

Sugar 44g

Protein 5g

498. SLOW COOKER BROWNIE COOKIES

Preparation Time: 15 minutes

Cooking Time: 2 hours

Servings: 10

Ingredients:

- One box brownie mix
- 1 eggs
- 1/4 c butter melted
- 1/2 c mini chocolate chips
- 1/2 c chopped walnuts optional
- 8 slices cookie dough slices

Directions:

Combine your brownie mixture with butter, eggs, chocolate chips, and nuts.

Sprinkle with non-stick spray the inside of your slow cooker. Place eight slices of ready-made cookie dough or pile tbsp of it on the bottom.

In your slow cooker, pour brownie mixture on top and smooth out evenly. Put on the lid and cook on top for 2 hours.

To get both textures in your meal, scoop from the middle out to the edge for each serving. If desired, serve warm for best results, top with ice cream.

Nutrition:

Calories 452

Fat 18g

Saturated Fat 6g

Carbohydrates 39g

Protein 4g

499. SLOW COOKER CHOCOLATE CARAMEL MONKEY BREAD

Preparation Time: 15 minutes
Cooking Time: 1 hour & 30 minutes
Servings: 6

Ingredients:
- 1/2 tbsp sugar
- 1/4 tsp ground cinnamon
- 15 oz buttermilk biscuits
- 20 milk chocolate-covered caramels
- Caramel sauce for topping (optional)
- Chocolate sauce for topping (optional)

Directions:

Mix sugar and cinnamon and set aside. Fill a parchment paper slow cooker, cover up to the bottom.

Wrap 1 buttermilk biscuit dough around one chocolate candy to cover the candy completely, pinching the seam closed.

Place the biscuit-wrapped candy in the slow cooker bottom, start in the middle of the slow cooker and work your way to the sides.

Continue to wrap candy and put it in the slow cooker, leaving roughly 1/2 inch between each. Repeat these steps with sweets wrapped in the second layer of biscuit.

Sprinkle the remaining cinnamon-sugar mixture on top when using all the dough and confectionery.

Cover the slow cooker and cook for 1 1/2 hours on the lower side. Once cooked, remove the lid and let cool slightly.

Use the edges of the parchment paper to lift the monkey bread out of the slow cooker. Allow cooling for at least 10-15 minutes.

Cut off any excess parchment paper around the edge when ready to serve. In a shallow bread or bowl, put monkey bread and drizzle with chocolate and caramel sauces.

Nutrition:

Calories: 337
Fat: 16g
Saturated Fat: 4g
Carbohydrates: 44g
Fiber: 1g
Sugars: 12g
Protein: 5g

500. SLOW COOKER COFFEE CAKE

Preparation Time: 15 minutes
Cooking Time: 2 hours & 30 minutes
Servings: 12

Ingredients:
- 2 1/2 cups of almond flour
- 1 & 1/2 cups of Stevia
- 2/3 cup vegetable oil
- 1 1/3 cups almond milk
- Two tsp baking powder
- 1/2 tsp baking soda
- One tsp ground cinnamon
- One tsp white vinegar
- One tsp salt
- Two eggs
- 1/2 cup chopped nuts optional

Directions:

In a large bowl, whisk in flour, Stevia, and salt. Remove the oil until it is crumbly mixed.

In the flour mixture, combine the baking powder, baking soda, and cinnamon with a wooden spoon or spatula. In a measuring cup, place milk, oil, eggs, and vinegar and whisk until the eggs are pounded, then add to the flour mixture and stir until mixed.

Spray a non-stick cooking spray 5-7Qt slow cooker or line with a slow cooker liner. Pour into the slow cooker with the batter.

Sprinkle the cake batter's nuts over the end. Put a paper towel over the slow cooker insert and place the lid on top of it.

Cook within 1 hour and 30 minutes, high s or 2 hours, and 30 minutes.

Serve warm directly from the slow cooker or store for up to 3 days in an airtight container.

Nutrition:

Calories: 411
Carbohydrates: 39.2g
Protein: 6g
Fat: 19g
Saturated Fat: 3g
Fiber: 2g
Sugars: 33g

501. SLOW COOKER APPLE PEAR CRISP

Preparation Time: 15 minutes
Cooking Time: 4 hours
Servings: 8

Ingredients:
- Four apples, peeled and cut into 1/2-inch slices
- 3 Bosc pears, peeled and cut into 1/2-inch slices
- 1/3 cup light Stevia
- One tbsp almond flour
- One tbsp lemon juice

- 1/2 tsp ground cinnamon
- 1/4 tsp kosher salt
- Pinch of ground nutmeg

For the Topping:
- 3/4 cup almond flour
- 3/4 cup old fashioned oats
- 1/2 cup chopped pecans
- 1/3 cup light Stevia
- 1/2 tsp ground cinnamon
- 1/2 tsp kosher salt
- Eight tbsp unsalted butter, cut into cubes

Directions:

Combine flour, oats, pecans, Stevia, cinnamon, and salt to make the topping. Press the butter into the dry fixing until it looks like coarse crumbs; set aside.

Coat lightly with a non-stick spray inside a 4-qt slow cooker: put apples and pears in the slow cooker. Add Stevia, flour, juice of lemon, cinnamon, salt, and nutmeg. Sprinkle with reserved topping, gently pressing the crumbs into the butter using your fingertips.

Layer the slow cooker with a clean dishtowel. Cover and cook for 2-3 hours at low heat or 90 minutes at high temperature, remove the dishtowel, and continue to cook, uncovered until the top is browned and apples are tender for about 1 hour. Serve cold.

Nutrition:
Calories: 267
Carbohydrates: 27g
Protein: 3g
Fat: 17g
Saturated Fat: 7g
Fiber: 4g
Sugars: 16g.

502. KEY LIME DUMP CAKE RECIPE

Preparation Time: 15 minutes
Cooking Time: 2 hours
Servings: 8

Ingredients:
- 15.25 oz. Betty Crocker French Vanilla Cake Mix box
- 44 oz. Key Lime Pie Filling
- 8 tbsp. or 1/2 cup butter melted

Directions:

Spray inside the Crock-Pot with a non-stick cooking spray. Empty key lime pie cans filling in the Crock-Pot bottom and then spread evenly.

Mix the dry vanilla cake mix with the dissolved butter in a bowl.

Pour the crumble cake/butter mixture over the slow cooker, spread evenly, and cover the slow cooker with the lid.

Cook for 2 hours at high or 4 hours at low. serve with ice cream or whip cream.

Nutrition:
Calories: 280
Carbohydrates: 41g
Protein: 2g
Fat: 4g
Saturated Fat: 2g
Sugars: 41g

503. SLOW COOKER CHERRY DUMP CAKE RECIPE

Preparation Time: 15 minutes
Cooking Time: 2 hours
Servings: 8

Ingredients:
- 12.25 oz. Betty Crocker Devil's Food Cake Mix
- 32 oz. Cherry Pie Filling
- 1/2 cup butter melted

Directions:

Spray with a non-stick cooking spray inside the slow cooker.

Empty cherry pie filling cans into slow cooker's bottom, then evenly spread out.

Combine dry cake mix with butter in a medium bowl.

Pour the crumble cake/butter mixture over the slow cooker plus cherries, scatter

evenly, and cover the slow cooker with a lid.

Cook for 2 hours at high, or 4 hours at low. Use an ice cream or whip cream to serve.

Nutrition:
Calories 566
Fat 17g
Saturated Fat 11g
Carbohydrates 52g
Fiber 1g
Sugar 37g
Protein 3g

504. SLOW COOKER PUMPKIN SPICE CAKE RECIPE

Preparation Time: 15 minutes
Cooking Time: 2 hours
Servings: 8

Ingredients:
- 15.25 oz. Betty Crocker Spice Cake Mix
- 15 oz. Libby's Pure Pumpkin
- ½ cup Applesauce

- 3 eggs
- 1 tsp. Pumpkin Pie Spice

Directions:

Whisk all the fixing with a mixer for 1 minute. Spray with a nonstick cooking spray inside the slow cooker.

Pour over and cover the mixture into the slow cooker.

Cook for 1.5 - 2 hours or until finished. Serve.

Nutrition:

Calories: 344

Fat: 30.38g

Carbohydrate: 10.03g

Fiber: 5.61g

Protein: 8.26g

505. SLOW COOKER BLUEBERRY DUMP CAKE RECIPE

Preparation Time: 15 minutes

Cooking Time: 2 hours

Servings: 8

Ingredients:

- 15.25 oz. Betty Crocker Lemon Cake Mix
- 42 oz. Blueberry Pie Filling
- 1/2 cup butter melted

Directions:

Spray with non-stick cooking spray the slow cooker. Put blueberry pie filling evenly into the bottom of the slow cooker.

In a mixing bowl, combine dry lemon cake mix with melted butter and stir until crumbly. Break some big chunks into the crumbles of a small spoon.

Pour the crumble cake/butter mixture over the blueberry mixture into the slow cooker, spread evenly, and cover with a lid the slow cooker.

Cook at high for 2 hours, and at low for 4 hours. Serve.

Nutrition:

Calories: 344

Fat: 30.38g

Carbohydrate: 10.03g

Fiber: 5.61g

Protein: 8.26g

506. SLOW COOKER STRAWBERRY DUMP CAKE RECIPE

Preparation Time: 15 minutes

Cooking Time: 2 hours

Servings: 8

Ingredients:

- 15.25 oz. Betty Crocker Strawberry Cake Mix
- 42 oz. Strawberry Pie Filling
- 1/2 cup butter melted

Directions:

Spray with a non-stick cooking spray inside the slow cooker.

Put the Strawberry Pie Filling into the slow cooker's bottom and spread evenly.

Combine strawberry dry cake mix with the butter in a mixing bowl.

Pour the cake/butter crumbled mixture into slow cooker over strawberries and spread evenly, covering the slow cooker with a lid.

Cook for 2 hours at high, or 4 hours at low. Serve.

Nutrition:

Calories: 344

Fat: 30.38g

Carbohydrate: 10.03g

Fiber: 5.61g

Protein: 8.26g

507. SUGAR-FREE CHOCOLATE MOLTEN LAVA CAKE

Preparation Time: 15 minutes

Cooking Time: 3 hours

Servings: 3

Ingredients:

- 1/2 cup hot water
- 1-ounce chocolate chips, sugar-free
- 1/4 tsp vanilla liquid stevia
- 1/4 tsp vanilla extract
- 1 egg yolk
- 1 whole egg
- 2 tbsp butter melted, cooled
- 1/4 tsp baking powder
- 1/8 tsp salt
- 3 ¾ tsp cocoa powder, unsweetened
- 2 tbsp almond flour
- 6 tbsp Swerve sweetener divided

Directions:

Grease the slow cooker, mix the flour, baking powder, 2 tbsp cocoa powder, almond flour, and 4 tbsp of Swerve in a bowl.

In a separate bowl, stir in eggs with melted butter, liquid stevia, vanilla extract, egg yolks, and eggs.

Mix the wet fixing to the dry ones and combine to incorporate fully. Pour the mixture into the slow cooker.

Top the mixture with chocolate chips.

Mix the remaining swerve with cocoa powder and hot water in a separate bowl, and pour this mixture over chocolate chips.

Cook on low within 3 hours. Once done, let cool and then serve.

Nutrition:
Calories 157
Fat 13g
Carbs 10.5g
Protein 3.9g

508. BLUEBERRY LEMON CUSTARD CAKE

Preparation Time: 15 minutes
Cooking Time: 3 hours
Servings: 3

Ingredients:
- 2 tbsp fresh blueberries
- 1/2 cup light cream
- 1/8 tsp salt
- 2 tbsp Swerve sweetener
- 1/4 tsp lemon liquid stevia
- 1 1/3 tbsp lemon juice
- 1/2 tsp lemon zest
- 2 tbsp coconut flour
- 1 ½ egg separated

Directions:
Put egg whites into a stand mixture and whip to achieve stiff peaks consistency.

Set the egg whites aside, whisk the yolks and the other ingredients apart from the blueberries.

Mix the egg whites into the batter to thoroughly combine, and then grease the slow cooker.

Put the batter into it, then top with the blueberries—Cook within 3 hours, low.

Let cool when not covered for 1 hour, then keep it chilled for at least 2 hours or overnight.

Serve the cake topped with unsweetened cream if you like.

Nutrition:
Calories 140
Fat 9.2g
Carbs 7.3g
Protein 3.9g

509. SLOW-COOKED PUMPKIN CUSTARD

Preparation Time: 15 minutes
Cooking Time: 2 hours & 45 minutes
Servings: 3

Ingredients:
- 2 large eggs
- 2 tbsp butter or coconut oil
- Dash sea salt
- 1/2 tsp pumpkin pie spice
- 1/4 cup superfine almond flour
- 1/2 tsp vanilla extract
- 1/2 cup pumpkin puree
- 1/4 cup granulated stevia

Directions:
Grease a slow cooker with butter or coconut oil and set it aside. With a mixer, break the eggs into a mixing bowl, and blend until incorporated and thickened.

Gently beat in the stevia, then add in vanilla extract and pumpkin puree. Then blend in pumpkin pie spice, salt, and almond flour.

Once almost incorporated, stream in coconut oil, ghee, and melted butter. Mix until smooth, then move the mixture into a slow cooker.

Put a paper towel over the slow cooker to help absorb condensed moisture and prevent it from dripping on your pumpkin custard. Then cover with a lid.

Now cook on low for 2 hours to 2 hours 45 minutes, and check the content after two hours elapse.

Serve the custard with whipped cream sweetened with a little stevia and a sprinkle of nutmeg if you like.

Nutrition:
Calories 147
Fat 12g
Carbs 4g
Protein 5g

510. ALMOND FLOUR MOCHA FUDGE CAKE

Preparation Time: 15 minutes
Cooking Time: 4 hours
Servings: 3

Ingredients:
- 1/8 tsp Celtic sea salt
- 1/3 tsp vanilla or chocolate extract
- 3 tbsp hot coffee
- 1/3 tsp baking soda
- 6 tbsp blanched almond flour
- 3 tbsp sour cream
- 3/4 oz. unsweetened chocolate, melted
- 1 egg
- 1 tbsp butter or coconut oil
- 6 tbsp Swerve

Directions:
Grease the slow cooker with oil. Then beat coconut oil and natural sweetener in a bowl until fully incorporated.

Beat in eggs, cream and chocolate. In a bowl, sift baking soda and almond flour and add in the chocolate mixture.

Then beat in coffee, salt, and vanilla until well incorporated. Once done, pour the batter into the cooking pot of the slow cooker.

Cook on low for 2 to 4 hours or until a toothpick inserted in the cake comes out clean.

Nutrition:

Calories 200

Carbs 5.8

Protein 6g

Fat 18g

511. PEARS AND CINNAMON CHEESECAKE SAUCE

Preparation Time: 15 minutes

Cooking Time: 6 hours

Servings: 1

Ingredients:

- ¾ lb. cream cheese
- ½ cup heavy cream
- 1 ½ ounces butter
- 4 pears
- 1 tbsp cinnamon
- 1 tsp vanilla extract
- Few drops of stevia

Directions:

Clean the pears.

Place the cream cheese, cream, butter, pears, cinnamon, vanilla, and stevia into the slow cooker.

Place the lid onto the pot and set the temperature to low.

Cook for 6 hours, stirring every 30 minutes to combine the butter and chocolate as it melts. Serve, or store in a fridge.

Nutrition:

Calories: 148

Carbs: 18g

Fat: 13g

Protein: 3g

512. SLOW COOKER BREAD PUDDING

Preparation Time: 15 minutes

Cooking Time: 5 hours

Servings: 4

Ingredients:

- 1 tbsp raisin
- 1/2 tsp cinnamon
- 1 1/2 tsp vanilla extract
- 1/4 cup swerve
- 1 egg white
- 1 whole egg
- 1 1/2 cups almond milk
- 4 slices of pumpkin bread

Directions:

Slice the pumpkin bread into pieces. Then mix all the rest of the fixing in the slow cooker.

Cook within 4 to 5 hours, then serve.

Nutrition:

Calories 182

Fat 2g

Carbs 11g

Protein 8g

513. TIRAMISU BREAD PUDDING

Preparation Time: 15 minutes

Cooking Time: 2 hours

Servings: 4

Ingredients:

- 3/4 tsp unsweetened cocoa
- 1/3 tsp vanilla extract
- 2 tbsp mascarpone cheese
- Cooking spray
- 3 1/4 cups Keto bread
- 1 large egg, lightly beaten
- 6.4 ounces of almond milk, divided
- 3/4 tbsp Kahlua (coffee-flavored liqueur)
- 1 3/4 tsp instant espresso granules
- 2 tbsp Stevia
- 1.6-ounce water

Directions:

Mix the water, Stevia, plus instant espresso granules in a saucepan.

Boil while occasionally stirring for 1 minute, remove, then mix in the Kahlua liqueur.

Whisk the eggs, then the almond milk in a large bowl. Mix in the espresso mixture into it.

Put the Keto friendly bread into a greased casserole. Cook it inside the slow cooker within 2 hours, low.

Mix vanilla, mascarpone cheese plus the remaining almond milk in a bowl.

Garnish with cocoa and serve.

Nutrition:

Calories 199

Fat 9g

Protein 6.7g

Carbs 9g

514. SLOW COOKER SUGAR-FREE DAIRY-FREE FUDGE

Preparation Time: 15 minutes

Cooking Time: 2 hours

Servings: 3

Ingredients:
- A dash of salt
- Dash of pure vanilla extract
- ½ tbsp coconut milk
- 4 tbsp sugar-free chocolate chips
- 1/4 tsp vanilla liquid stevia

Directions:

Mix in coconut milk, stevia, vanilla, chocolate chips plus salt in a slow cooker.

Cook within 2 hours, then let it sit within 30 minutes.

Mix in within 5 minutes. Put the butter in a casserole dish with parchment paper.

Chill, then serve.

Nutrition:

Calories 65

Fat 5g

Carbs 2g

Protein 1g

515. POPPY SEED-LEMON BREAD

Preparation Time: 15 minutes

Cooking Time: 2 hours

Servings: 3

Ingredients:
- 1/2 cups almond flour
- 1/4 tbsp baking powder
- 1 tbsp poppy seeds
- 1 egg
- 1/4 cup Stevia
- 1/8 tsp salt
- 2 tbsp vegetable oil
- 3 tbsp tofu (puree)
- 1/4 cup almond milk
- 3/4 cup plain Greek-style yogurt
- 1/4 cup lemon juice
- 3/4 tsp shredded lemon peel
- 1/4 tsp vanilla

Directions:

Grease the slow cooker using a non-stick cooking spray.

Mix the poppy seeds, flour, salt, and baking powder in a bowl, then put it aside.

Mix the tofu puree, Stevia, oil, milk, yogurt, lemon juice, lemon peel, and vanilla in a medium bowl.

Put the batter into the flour batter, then mix.

Transfer it to the slow cooker, then cook on high for 1 and 30 minutes to 2 hours, or until set.

Leave for 10-15 minutes to cool., then serve.

Nutrition:

Calories 295.6

Fat 24.3g

Carbs 17.9g

Protein 6.0g

516. NUTMEG-INFUSED PUMPKIN BREAD

Preparation Time: 15 minutes

Cooking Time: 3 hours

Servings: 4

Ingredients:
- 0.5 oz. unsalted pecan pieces, toasted
- 1/4 tbsp pure vanilla extract
- 1 tbsp safflower oil
- 1 egg white
- 2 tbsp plain Greek yogurt
- 1/4 cup cooked and puréed pumpkin
- 1/8 tsp sea salt
- Dash ground allspice
- 1/4 tsp ground nutmeg
- Dash tsp baking soda
- 1/2 tsp baking powder
- 2 tbsp Stevia
- 7 tbsp almond flour
- 2 tbsp dried apple cranberries, unsweetened
- 3 tbsp 100% apple juice, plain
- Olive oil cooking spray

Directions:

Lightly grease a non-stick loaf pan with cooking spray. Set aside.

Mix cranberries and apple juice in a small saucepan, heat the mixture on high to boil.

Remove, then let cool for around 10 minutes.

Then mix nutmeg, baking soda, allspice, baking powder, salt, stevia, and flour in a large bowl. Set aside.

Now mix vanilla, oil, egg whites, yogurt, pumpkin, and the cranberry mixture in a medium bowl.

To the flour mixture, add the pecans and cranberry-pumpkin mixture and stir to incorporate fully.

Spoon the batter into the pan, and use a rubber spatula or the back of a spoon to smooth the top.

Arrange a rack inside a slow cooker to elevate the pan, and then put the pan on top.

Cook within 3 hours, high.

Cool it down within 10 minutes, before slicing, then serve.

Nutrition:

Calories 159

Carbs 21g

Fat 65g

Protein 4g

517. SLOW COOKER BAKED APPLES RECIPE

Preparation Time: 15 minutes

Cooking Time: 4 hours

Servings: 6

Ingredients:

- Five medium Gala apples
- ½ cup Quaker Old Fashioned Oats
- ½ cup Stevia
- 3 tsp. Cinnamon
- 1 tsp. Allspice
- 1/4 cup butter

Directions:

Pour 1/4 cup of water at the slow cooker's edge.

Use a sharp knife to carefully core apples.

Mix the oats, cinnamon, Stevia, and allspice. Fill a single apple with a mixture of oats, Stevia, and spice.

Use a butter pat to top each apple. Set in slow cooker carefully and put the lid on slow cooker.

Cook for 3-4 hours or until finished.

Nutrition:

Calories: 121

Fat 3g

Carbohydrates 48g

Fiber 5g

Sugar 36g

Protein 1g

518. SALTY-SWEET ALMOND BUTTER AND CHOCOLATE

Preparation Time: 15 minutes

Cooking Time: 4 hours

Servings: 1

Ingredients:

- 1 cup almond butter
- 2 ounces salted butter
- 1-ounce dark chocolate
- ½ tsp sea salt
- Few drops of stevia

Directions:

Place the almond butter, butter, dark chocolate, sea salt, and stevia in the slow cooker.

Cook for 4 hours, high, stirring every 30 minutes to combine the butter and chocolate as they melt. Serve or store in a fridge.

Nutrition:

Calories: 200

Carbs: 21g

Fat: 7g

Protein: 15g

519. COCONUT SQUARES WITH BLUEBERRY GLAZE

Preparation Time: 15 minutes

Cooking Time: 3 hours

Servings: 20

Ingredients:

- 2 cups desiccated coconut
- 1-ounce butter, melted
- 3 ounces cream cheese
- 1 egg, lightly beaten
- ½ tsp baking powder
- 2 tsp vanilla extract
- 1 cup of frozen berries

Directions:

Beat the coconut, butter, cream cheese, egg, baking powder, and vanilla extract, using a wooden spoon in a bowl until combined and smooth.

Grease a heat-proof dish with butter. Spread the coconut mixture into the dish.

Defrost the blueberries in the microwave until they resemble a thick sauce. Spread the blueberries over the coconut mixture.

Put the dish into the slow cooker, then put hot water until it reaches halfway up the dish.

Cook for 3 hours, high. Remove the dish from the pot and leave it to cool on the bench before slicing into small squares.

Nutrition:

Calories: 115

Carbs: 20g

Fat: 3g

Protein: 3g

520. CHOCOLATE AND BLACKBERRY CHEESECAKE SAUCE

Preparation Time: 15 minutes

Cooking Time: 6 hours

Servings: 1

Ingredients:

- ¾ lb. cream cheese
- ½ cup heavy cream
- 1 ½ ounces butter
- 3 ounces dark chocolate
- ½ cup fresh blackberries, chopped
- 1 tsp vanilla extract
- Few drops of stevia

Directions:

Place the cream cheese, cream, butter, dark chocolate, blackberries, vanilla, and stevia into the slow cooker.

Place the lid onto the pot and set the temperature to low.

Cook for 6 hours, stirring every 30 minutes to combine the butter and chocolate as it melts. Serve, or store in a fridge.

Nutrition:

Calories: 200

Carbs: 18g

Fat: 13g

Protein: 3g

521. BERRY & COCONUT CAKE

Preparation Time: 15 minutes

Cooking Time: 2 hours

Servings: 8

Ingredients:

- 1 tbsp butter for greasing the crock
- 1 cup almond flour
- ¾ cup sweetener of your choice
- 1 tsp baking soda
- ¼ tsp salt
- 1 large egg, beaten with a fork
- ¼ cup coconut flour
- ¼ cup of coconut milk
- 2 tbsp coconut oil
- 4 cups fresh or frozen blueberries and raspberries

Directions:

Butter the slow cooker well.

In a bowl, whisk the egg, coconut milk, and oil together.

Mix the dry ingredients. Slowly stir in the wet ingredients. Do not over mix.

Pour the batter into the slow cooker, spread evenly.

Spread the berries on top.

Cover, cook on high for 2 hours. Cool in the crock for 1-2 hours.

Nutrition:

Calories: 263

Carbs: 9g

Fat: 22g

Protein: 5g

522. COCOA PUDDING CAKE

Preparation Time: 15 minutes

Cooking Time: 3 hours

Servings: 10

Ingredients:

- 1 tbsp butter for greasing the slow cooker
- 1 ½ cups ground almonds
- ¾ cup sweetener, Swerve (or a suitable substitute)
- ¾ cup cocoa powder
- ¼ cup whey protein
- 2 tsp baking powder
- ¼ tsp salt
- 4 large eggs
- ½ cup butter, melted
- ¾ cup full-fat cream
- 1 tsp vanilla extract

Directions:

Butter the slow cooker thoroughly.

Whisk the dry fixing in a bowl.

Stir in the melted butter, eggs, cream, and vanilla. Mix well.

Pour the batter into the slow cooker and spread evenly.

Cook within 2½ to 3 hours, low. If preferred – more like pudding, cook cake shorter; more dry cake, cook longer.

Cool in the slow cooker for 30 minutes. Cut and serve.

Nutrition:

Calories: 250

Carbs: 29g

Fat: 5g

Protein: 22g

523. WONDERFUL RASPBERRY ALMOND CAKE

Preparation Time: 15 minutes

Cooking Time: 3 hours

Servings: 4

Ingredients:

- 1 cup of fresh raspberries
- 1/3 cup of dark chocolate chips, sugar-free
- 2 cups of almond flour
- 1 tsp of coconut extract
- ¾ cup of almond milk
- 4 large eggs
- 2 tsp of baking soda
- ¼ tsp of salt
- 1 cup of Swerve
- ½ cup of melted coconut oil
- 1 cup of shredded coconut unsweetened
- ¼ cup of powdered egg whites

Directions:

Grease the slow cooker with butter. Mix all the fixing in a bowl.

Pour the batter inside, then cook within 3 hours on low.

Nutrition:

Calories: 362

Carbohydrates: 12.8 g

Fat: 26 g

Protein: 8 g

524. SCRUMPTIOUS CHOCOLATE COCOA CAKE

Preparation Time: 15 minutes

Cooking Time: 4 hours

Servings: 4

Ingredients:

- 1 ½ cups of ground almonds
- ½ cup of coconut flakes
- 6 tbsp of your preferred sweetener
- 2 tsp of baking powder
- A pinch of salt
- ½ cup of coconut oil
- ½ cup of cooking cream
- 2 tbsp of lemon juice
- The zest from 2 lemons
- 2 large eggs
- Espresso and whipped cream for serving
- Toppings:
- 3 tbsp of sweetener
- ½ a cup of boiling water
- 2 tbsp of lemon juice
- 2 tbsp of coconut oil

Directions:

Combine the baking powder, sweetener, coconut, and almonds in a large bowl. Whisk together thoroughly.

In another bowl, combine the eggs, juice, coconut oil, and whisk together thoroughly.

Combine the wet and the dry ingredients and whisk together thoroughly.

Put the aluminum foil inside the bottom of the slow cooker. Pour the batter into the slow cooker.

Mix all the topping fixing in a small bowl, and pour on top of the cake batter.

Cover the slow cooker with paper towels to absorb condensation, then cook within 3 hours on high.

Divide into bowls and serve with espresso and whipped cream.

Nutrition:

Carbs: 5g

Protein: 7g

Fat: 24g

Calories: 310.

525. CHOCOLATE AND STRAWBERRIES CUPCAKES

Preparation Time: 15 minutes

Cooking Time: 3 hours

Servings: 10

Ingredients:

- 10 paper cupcake cases
- 2 cups of strawberries cut into small pieces
- 5 ounces dark chocolate, melted
- 1 cup ground pecan nuts
- 1 tsp baking powder
- 2 eggs, lightly beaten
- ½ cup strawberry flavoured Greek yogurt

Directions:

Mix the strawberry pieces and melted chocolate in a bowl, set aside.

Mix the ground pecan nuts, baking powder, eggs, yogurt, and a pinch of salt in a medium-sized bowl.

Spoon the pecan mixture into the cupcake cases. Spoon the chocolate and strawberry mixture on top of the pecan mixture.

Place the cupcake cases into the slow cooker. Cook for 3 hours, high setting.

Remove the cupcakes from the pot and leave them to cool on the bench before storing the serving. Serve with vanilla ice-cream!

Nutrition:

Calories: 165

Carbs: 27g

Fat: 8g

Protein: 4g

CONCLUSION

Whether you have met your weight loss goals, your life changes, or you simply want to eat whatever you want again, here's the best way to come off the keto diet.

First, you need to prepare yourself mentally. You cannot just suddenly start consuming carbs again, for it will shock your system. Have an idea of what you want to allow back into your consumption slowly. Be familiar with portion sizes and stick to that amount of carbs for the first few times you eat post-keto. Start with non-processed carbs like whole grain, beans, and fruits. Start slow and see how your body responds before resolving to add carbs one meal at a time.

The things to watch out for when coming off keto are weight gain, bloating, more energy, and feeling hungry. The weight gain is nothing to freak out over; perhaps, you might not even gain any. It all depends on your diet, how your body processes carbs, and, of course, water weight. The length of your keto diet is a significant factor in how much weight you have lost, which is caused by the reduction of carbs. The bloating will occur because of the reintroduction of fibrous foods and your body getting used to digesting them again. The bloating van lasts for a few days to a few weeks. You will feel like you have more energy because carbs break down into glucose, which is the body's primary source of fuel. You may also notice better brain function and the ability to work out more.

Now, all you have to do is start with the keto meal plan for the coming week. The quicker you start with the diet plan, the faster you can see the results. Do not just sit and try to figure out the perfect day for starting with the diet. This way, you can never start with the diet plan. If you are waiting for the perfect day, then it is today. As soon as you start with twenty-one days keto meal plan, try your best not to deflect. It is not that tough. Cutting out carbs suddenly might seem to be a bit tough at the beginning. However, once you see the diet plan results after three weeks, you will be amazed. There is nothing too complex about the ketogenic diet.

Just take your grocery bag and go out shopping for all the items that you will need. You can create a shopping list according to the diet meal plan for each week. It will make your task a lot easier. The keto diet has shown positive results after the age of fifties. The recipes that I have included in this book, apart from the keto meal plan recipes, are very easy. You can gather the ingredients from your local grocery store. So, what are you waiting for? Start preparing healthy meals and lead a healthy life!

INDEX

Almond & Strawberry Oatmeal 36
Almond Banana Bread 35
Almond Flour Mocha Fudge Cake 178
Almond Lemon Blueberry Muffins 26
Almonds, Walnuts, and Mango Bowls 171
Amazing Sour Cream Chicken 103
Amazing Spiced Beef Eye SLOW COOKED 147
Ambrosia 165
Apple, Avocado, and Mango Bowls 168
Apricot Pulled Pork 135
Artichoke Pepper Beef 156
Arugula Cheese Herb Frittata 30
Asian Chicken 114
Asian Lamb 141
Asian-Inspired Ginger Tuna Steaks 94
Asparagus with Lemon 70
Avocado Pesto Kelp Noodles 69
Bacon and Cauliflower Soup 48
Bacon Cheddar Broccoli Salad 67
Bacon Cheeseburger Casserole 145
Bacon-Mushroom Breakfast 32
Bacon-Wrapped Cauliflower 77
Baked Custard 161
Balsamic Beef ROAST 149
Balsamic Beef 149
Balsamic Chicken Thighs 108
Balsamic Chicken 112
Banana & Blueberry Oats 38
Banana Bread 169
Barbacoa Lamb 132
BBQ Beef Burritos 145
BBQ Shrimp 98
Beautiful BBQ Ribs 124
Beef & Broccoli 155
Beef & Pumpkin Stew 54
Beef and Artichokes Bowls 150
Beef and Cabbage Roast 143
Beef and Sauerkraut Bowl 154
Beef and Scallions Bowl 149
Beef Barley Vegetable Soup 51
Beef Chimichangas 156
Beef Chops with Sprouts 152
Beef dijon 45
Beef Dip 154
Beef in Sauce 148
Beef Masala 151

Beef Ragout with Beans 152
Beef Ribs 146
Beef Roast 153
Beef Sauté with Endives 151
Beef Shoulder in BBQ Sauce 144
Beef Stew 46
Beef Stroganoff 148
Beef with Greens 148
Beef 143
Berries Salad 172
Berry & Coconut Cake 181
Black and Blue Cobbler 161
Blueberry Lemon Custard Cake 178
Blueberry Pancake 22
Boiled Lobster Tails 94
Braised Beef Strips 154
Braised Beef 153
Braised Cabbage 66
Braised Oxtails 146
Braised Squid with Tomatoes and Fennel 88
Bread and Berries Pudding 170
Breakfast Casserole 32
Breakfast Sausage Casserole 23
Breakfast 16
Brisket & Onions 146
Broccoli and Cheese Stuffed Squash 19
Broccoli Cheddar Soup 59
Broccoli Gratin with Parmesan and Cheese 21
Brussels Sprout Dip 66
Butter Beef 159
Butter Chicken 117
Butterfly Tilapia 81
Butternut Squash Soup 59
Butternut Squash Sweet Mix 171
Cabbage Steaks 76
Cabbage, Kielbasa, and Onion Soup 59
Cajun Corn Shrimp Chowder 98
Candied Lemon 170
Capers Salmon 100
Caramel Pecan Pudding 162
Caribbean Shrimp 96
Carrots and Zucchini Oatmeal 38
Catfish Creole 95
Cauliflower & Ham Cauliflower Stew 56
Cauliflower and Ham Casserole 29
Cauliflower Bolognese on Zucchini Noodles 71
Cauliflower Casserole with Goat Cheese 25
Cauliflower Casserole 77

Cauliflower Rice   77
Cauliflower Slow Breakfast Casserole   31
Cheddar & Bacon Casserole   37
Cheddar Cauliflower   37
Cheddar Sausage Cauliflower   36
Cheese and Sausage Breakfast   24
Cheese Broccoli Bouillabaisse   53
Cheesy Adobo Chicken   107
Cheesy Beer Dip Salsa   66
Cheesy Cauliflower Garlic Bread   72
Cheesy Cauliflower Gratin   73
Cheesy Garlic Brussels Sprouts   22
Cheesy Tater Tot Casserole   38
Cheesy Zucchini-Asparagus Frittata 64
Cherry Tomatoes Thyme Asparagus Frittata   16
Chicken & Kale Soup   46
Chicken & Tortilla Soup   55
Chicken and Vegetables   119
Chicken Chile Verde   55
Chicken Chili Soup   47
Chicken Cordon Bleu Soup   57
Chicken Gyros   119
Chicken in Salsa Verde   121
Chicken Kale Soup   61
Chicken Lo Mein   108
Chicken Orzo   114
Chicken Thigh & Breast Low Carb Soup   53
Chicken with Bacon Gravy   106
Chili Colorado   155
CHILI GROUND DUCK   121
Chili Lime Beef   148
Chili Pulled Pork   128
Chili Shrimps   91
Chinese 5-Spice Pork Ribs   126
Chinese Broccoli   75
Chinese Oyster Soup   62
Chipotle Barbecue Chicken   104
Chocolate & Berry Layered Jars   173
Chocolate and Blackberry Cheesecake Sauce   181
Chocolate and Liquor Cream   170
Chocolate and strawberries Cupcakes   183
Chocolate Cheesecake   164
Chocolate Covered Bacon Cupcakes   173
Chocolate Peanut Butter Breakfast Bars   30
Choco-peanut Cake   173
Cider-braised Chicken   117
Cilantro Beef   150

Clam Chowder   90
Classic Sausage and Peppers   137
Cocoa Pudding Cake   182
Coconut Beef   153
Coconut Cilantro Curry Shrimp   86
Coconut Cilantro Shrimp Curry   105
Coconut Fish Curry   97
Coconut Jam   169
Coconut Quinoa Mix   37
Coconut Raisins Oatmeal   39
Coconut Squares with Blueberry Glaze   181
Coconut, Chocolate, Almond Truffle Bake   166
COD AND VEGETABLES   83
Cod and Zoodles Stew   89
Cod with Fennel and Tomatoes   96
Coffee- Braised Brisket   144
Coffee Creams with Toasted Seed Crumble Topping   167
COLOMBIAN Chicken   104
Cracked-Out Keto Slaw   68
Cranberry Apple Oats   39
Cream Cheese Banana Breakfast   37
Cream of Zucchini Soup   60
Creamy Chicken Curry   116
Creamy Chicken Penne   113
Creamy Crab Zucchini Casserole   90
Creamy Curried Shrimp   100
Creamy Curry Sauce Noodle Bowl   69
Creamy Harvest Pumpkin Bisque   41
Creamy Herbed Tenderloin   137
Creamy Italian Chicken   119
Creamy Keto Mash   73
Creamy Pork Chops   130
Creamy Ricotta Spaghetti Squash   73
Creamy Shrimp Chowder   95
Creamy Smoked Salmon Soup   47
Creamy Vanilla Custard   166
Crème Brule   165
Slow cooker Benedict Casserole   20
Slow cooker Cream Cheese French Toast   21
Slow cooker Pork Stew with Tapioca   51
Slow cooker Sugar-Free Dairy-Free Fudge   179
Slow cooker Turkish Breakfast Eggs 25
Slow cooker Apple Pudding Cake   174
Slow cooker Baked Apples Recipe   180
Slow cooker Beef Roast   143
Slow cooker Blueberry Dump Cake Recipe   177
Slow cooker Brownie Cookies   174

Slow cooker Butter Masala Chicken 106
Slow cooker Cherry Dump Cake Recipe   176
Slow cooker Chocolate Caramel Monkey Bread 175
Slow cooker Crab Legs   94
Slow cooker Creamy Salsa Chicken 119
Slow cooker Pumpkin Coconut Breakfast Bars   34
Slow cooker Pumpkin Spice Cake Recipe   176
Slow cooker Ranch Chicken   105
Slow cooker Strawberry Dump Cake Recipe 177
Slow cooker Swordfish Steaks   92
Crustless Slow cooker Spinach Quiche   20
Curried Pork Chops   138
Curry Cauliflower 77
Dairy-Free Chili Chicken Soup   49
Dark Chocolate and Peppermint Pots   166
Dates and Rice Pudding   171
Delectable Spearmint Liver and Lamb Heart Soup   44
Delicious Bacon Cheese Cauliflower Soup   52
Delicious Balsamic Lamb Chops   134
Delicious BBQ Chicken   111
Delicious Beef Meatball and Sour Cream Soup   56
Delicious Chicken Soup with Lemongrass   51
Delicious Chickpea Chicken   118
Delicious Coconut Pork   129
Delicious Kernel Corn Taco Soup   50
Delicious Lasagna Consommé   53
Delicious Shrimp Fajitas   98
Delicious Southwest Chicken   109
Delicious Thyme Sausage Squash   18
Delightful Balsamic Oregano Chicken   104
Delightful Chicken-Chorizo Spicy Soup   44
Desserts 160
Dressed Pork Leg Roast   131
Duck in sauce   121
Easy Chicken Noodles   110
Easy Cilantro Lime Salmon 100
Easy Creamed Spinach   74
Easy Lemon Dill Salmon   102
Easy Meatball Slow cooker   155
Easy Mexican Chicken   112
Easy Salsa Chicken   110
Egg & Mushroom Breakfast   33
Egg and Cheese Casserole with Chayote Squash   28
Egg Cake with Peppers, Kale, and Cheddar 28
Egg Casserole with Italian Cheeses, Sun-Dried Tomatoes, and Herbs   27
Egg, Spinach, and Ham Breakfast Casserole 33

Eggplant Gratin   78
Eggplant Parmesan   71
Elbows Casserole 65
Ethiopian Doro Watt Chicken   109
Etouffee 82
Fabulous Peanut Vanilla Chocolate Cake   163
Fantastic Lemon Thyme Chicken   103
Fennel Scented Fish Stew 91
Feta Cheese and Kale Breakfast Casserole   29
Feta Meatballs   140
Fish & Shellfish   81
Fish and Tomatoes   88
Fish Curry   84
Flavorful Chicken Casserole   114
Flavors Peanut Butter Chicken   109
Flavors Pork Chops   136
Fresh Cream Mix 172
Fudgy Secret Brownies   160
Garlic Artichoke 79
Garlic Butter Chicken with Cream Cheese   106
Garlic Butter Keto Spinach 19
Garlic Cauliflower Steaks   78
Garlic Dill Chicken Thighs 108
Garlic Herb Roasted Pepper Chicken   115
Garlic Herbed Lamb Chops   132
Garlic Olive Chicken   118
Garlic Ranch Mushrooms 74
Garlic Shrimp   87
Garlic Tomato, Zucchini, and Yellow Squash 72
Garlic Tomatoes Chuck Roast   158
Garlicky Shrimp   101
Garlic-Parmesan Asparagus Slow cooker   18
Ginger Pumpkin Soup   58
GINGERY CHICKEN   122
Gluten-Free Zucchini Bread   71
Gorgeous Coconut Turmeric Pork Curry   124
Greek Eggs Breakfast Casserole   25
Greek Lemon Chicken   110
Greek Style Lamb Shanks 133
Green Chili Pork 125
Green Tea Pudding   169
Halibut Vinaigrette   93
Healthy Lime Salmon   99
Healthy Low Carb Walnut Zucchini Bread   16
Healthy Veggie Omelet   26
Heart and Tuna Stuffed Mushroom 82
Hearty Chicken Soup with Veggie Noodles   43
Hearty White Fish Stew   95

heddar Jalapeno Breakfast Sausages 30
Herb Chicken Breasts 112
Herb Flounder Fillet 101
Herb Lemon Cod 97
Homemade Meatballs and Spaghetti Squash 144
Homemade Vegetable Stock 67
Hot Beef 152
Hot Crab Dip 89
Hot Fudge Cake 160
Hot Shrimp 102
Italian Beef Roast 157
Italian Ragu 147
Kale and Cheese Omelet 27
KALE QUICHE 80
Kale, Mushrooms, And Caramelized Onions 27
Kalua Pork 124
Kashmiri Lamb Curry 131
Keto Coconut Hot Chocolate 165
Keto Slow cooker Tasty Onions 20
Keto Slow cooker Turkey Stuffed Peppers 21
Keto Egg Muffin 24
Keto Sausage & Egg Casserole 32
Keto Soup with Miso 34
Keto Spinach-Feta Quiche 64
Ketogenic Chicken Tikka Masala 107
Key Lime Dump Cake Recipe 176
Lamb and Eggplant Stew 48
Lamb and Rosemary Stew 47
Lamb of Italy with Brussels Sprouts 141
Lamb Provençal 133
Lamb with Mint & Green Beans 134
Lazy Man's Seafood Stew 93
Lean Beef & Mixed Veggies Soup 55
Lemon Cake 164
Lemon Cheesecake 168
Lemon Dill Halibut 86
Lemon Halibut 101
Lemon Herb Chicken 116
Lemon Lamb and Asparagus 140
Lemon Pepper Tilapia 88
Lemongrass coco-chicken 107
Lemongrass Coconut Pulled Pork 127
Lime Pork Chops 128
Lobster Bisque 90
Louisiana Shrimp 98
Lovely Lentil Sausage Soup 44
Low Carbohydrate Slow cooker Soup 49
Low-Carb Cauliflower Breakfast Casserole 17

Lunch Beef 154
Luscious Carrot Beef Stew with Cauliflower 52
Macadamia Crusted Pork Steaks 139
Macadamia Fudge Truffles 172
Mahi-Mahi Taco Wraps 83
Maple Pot de Crème 161
Mashed Cauliflower 76
Mashed Garlic Cauliflower 65
Melt-In-Your-Mouth Beef Stew 42
Mexican Chicken Soup 58
Mexican Chorizo Enchilada Soup 43
Mexican Corn and Shrimp Soup 60
Mexican Style Breakfast Casserole 26
Minestrone Ground Beef Soup 56
Mississippi Roast 156
Mississippi Roast 156
Moist & Juicy Chicken Breast 113
Moist and Spicy Pulled Chicken Breast 120
Moroccan Eggplant Mash 79
Moroccan Lamb Stew 142
Moroccan Lamb 141
Mouth-Watering Chocolate Cake 163
Mouth-Watering Minced Pork Zucchini Lasagna 123
Mushroom Risotto 69
Mushroom Stew 76
Mushrooms, Cauliflower, and Zucchini Toast 24
Mustard Beef 150
Mustard Mushroom Chicken 112
New Mexico Carne Adovada 135
No Stick Ribs 139
Nutmeg-Infused Pumpkin Bread 180
Olive Artichokes Beef 157
Olive Feta Beef 157
Onion Beef 150
Onion Broccoli Cream Cheese Quiche 17
Onion Pork Chops 130
Onion White Fish Fillet 101
Orange Chicken 111
Overnight Eggs Benedict Casserole 34
Paprika Pork Tenderloin 126
Parmesan Chicken Rice 111
Parmesan Mushrooms 65
Parmesan Zucchini and Tomato Gratin 72
Parmesan Zucchini Paprika & Ricotta Frittata 31
Peanut Butter & Chocolate Cake 165
Peanut Butter Oatmeal 39

Peanut Butter, Chocolate, And Pecan Cupcakes 167
Pear and Maple Oatmeal 36
Pears and Apples Bowls 172
Pepper Jalapeno Low Carb Soup 54
Persian Omelet Slow cooker 19
Pesto Chicken 117
Pesto Scrambled Eggs 27
Pizza Casserole 120
Poached Salmon in Court-Bouillon Recipe 88
Poached Salmon 83
Poppy Seed Butter Cake 163
Poppy Seed-Lemon Bread 179
Pork & Lamb 123
Pork Carnitas 127
Pork Chops with Cumin Butter and Garlic 135
Pork Loin Roast with Onion Gravy 127
Pork Loin with Peanut Sauce 136
Pork Ramen 62
Pork Stew with Oyster Mushrooms 126
Pot Roast Beef Brisket 147
Pot Roast Soup 48
Poultry Seasoned Pork Chops 139
Poultry 103
Pumpkin Soup 58
Queso Chicken Tacos 111
Rabbit Stew 46
Ranch Pork Chops 128
Raspberry & Coconut Cake 164
Ribs with a Kick 138
Ricotta Cream 168
Rosemary Turkey Breast 118
Rustic Buttered Mussels 94
Sage Cauliflower Casserole 35
Salmon and Asparagus 102
Salmon Lemon and Dill 89
Salmon Poached in White Wine and Lemon 87
Salmon with Creamy Lemon Sauce 85
Salmon with Lemon-Caper Sauce 85
Salsa Pork Chops 138
Salty-Sweet Almond Butter and Chocolate 180
Sausage and Kale Strata 28
Sausage and Peppers 22
Sausage-Stuffed Eggplants 29
Sautéed Bell Peppers 79
Savory Creamy Breakfast Casserole 17
Scrambled Eggs with Smoked Salmon 18
Scrumptious Bay Leaf Pork Roast Shoulder 130

Scrumptious Chocolate Cocoa Cake 182
Seafood Stir-Fry Soup 61
Seriously Delicious Lamb Roast 131
Shrimp Fajita Soup 62
Shrimp in Marinara Sauce 87
Shrimp Pasta 99
Shrimp Scampi with Spaghetti Squash 92
Shrimp Scampi 84
Shrimp Tacos 84
Simple Chicken & Mushrooms 115
Simple Chicken Chili 120
Simple Roasted Pork Shoulder 136
Slow Cook Turkey Breast 115
Slow Cooker Apple Pear Crisp 175
Slow Cooker Bread Pudding 179
Slow Cooker Cheeseburger Soup 50
Slow Cooker Coffee Cake 175
Slow Cooker Pork Loin 125
Slow Cooker Spaghetti Squash 75
SLOW TERIYAKI CHICKEN 106
Slow-Cooked Pumpkin Custard 178
Slow-Cooked Summer Vegetables 72
Slow-Cooked Tilapia 89
Slow-Cooked Yellow Squash Zucchini 65
Slow-Cooker Pumpkin Pie Pudding 162
Smoky Pork with Cabbage 136
Soups 41
Southern Paleo Slow cooker Chili 49
Soy-Ginger Steamed Pompano 90
Spaghetti Squash Carbonara 74
Spicy Adobo Pulled Pork 129
Spicy Barbecue Shrimp 86
Spicy Chili Chicken 117
SPICY HEALTHY CHICKEN 122
Spicy Shredded Chicken Lettuce Wraps 105
Spicy Shrimp Fra Diavolo 91
Spicy Shrimp 99
Spinach Artichoke Casserole 70
SPINACH PORTOBELLO 80
SPINACH Soup 58
Sriracha Beef 158
Stuffed Bell Peppers 158
Stuffed Breakfast Peppers 23
Stuffed Eggplant 67
Stuffed peppers 129
Succulent Lamb 134
Sugar-Free Chocolate Molten Lava Cake 177
Summery Bell Pepper + Eggplant Salad 75

Sumptuous Ham and Lentil Consommé 50
Superb Chicken, Bacon, Garlic Thyme Soup 43
Sweet and Sour Shrimp 93
Sweet Beef 151
Taco Chicken 116
Tantalizing Chicken Breast with Artichoke Stuffing 104
Tapioca and Chia Pudding 170
Tapioca Pudding 171
Tarragon Lamb & Beans 134
Tasty Apple and Cranberry Dessert 162
Tasty Chicken Fajita Pasta 113
Tasty Corned Beef and Heavy Cream Soup 45
Tasty Cuban Mojo Pork 124
Tasty Lamb Shoulders 132
Tasty Pork Tacos 129
Tasty Shrimp Curry 99
Tasty Tomato Soup with Parmesan and Basil 52
Thai Curried Pork 125
Thai Shrimp Rice 96
Thyme Beef 152
Thyme Lamb Chops 132
Tiramisu Bread Pudding 179
Tomato Jam 169
Tomato Soup 60
Toscana Soup 45
Tuna and Olive-Orange Tapenade 81
Tuna and White Beans 92
Tuscan Fish Soup 61
Tuscan Zucchini Stew 42
Twice Baked Spaghetti Squash 68
Vanilla and Strawberry Cheesecake 167
Vanilla Pumpkin Bread 35
Vegan Bibimbap 69
Vegan Cream of Mushroom Soup 62
Vegetable Korma 67
Vegetable Stew 56
Vegetables 64
Veggie Soup with Minty Balls 57
Veggie-Noodle Soup 63
Vietnamese Braised Catfish 91
White Fish Fillet with Tomatoes 97
Whole Roasted Chicken 120
Wonderful Raspberry Almond Cake 182
Yummy Cauliflower Crust Breakfast Pizza 30
Zesty White Chicken Chili 41
Zoodles with Cauliflower-Tomato Sauce 74
Zucchini and Yellow Squash 70

Zucchini Gratin 78
Zucchini Lasagna 71
Zucchini Pasta 68
Zucchini Pasta 75
Zucchini Sausage Breakfast "Bake" 29

Printed in Great Britain
by Amazon